HOLY SPIRIT
FOR REAL

Barbara Taylor Sanders

A wholly owned subsidiary of TBN

Holy Spirit For Real

Trilogy Christian Publishers A Wholly Owned Subsidiary of Trinity Broadcasting Network

2442 Michelle Drive Tustin, CA 92780

Rights Department, 2442 Michelle Drive, Tustin, CA 92780.

Trilogy Christian Publishing/TBN and colophon are trademarks of Trinity Broadcasting Network.

Photo Gallery by davidmunozart.com

Michael Compton, art design creation for "O Glory to the Lamb" sheet music and book cover for "The Laborers are Few."

For information about special discounts for bulk purchases, please contact Trilogy Christian Publishing.

Trilogy Disclaimer: The views and content expressed in this book are those of the author and may not necessarily reflect the views and doctrine of Trilogy Christian Publishing or the Trinity Broadcasting Network.

Manufactured in the United States of America

10 9 8 7 6 5 4 3 2 1

Library of Congress Cataloging-in-Publication Data is available.

ISBN: 978-1-68556-955-6 | E-ISBN: 978-1-68556-956-3

Dedicated to

Sid Roth

Thank you for proving to the world

that the Holy Spirit is *for real*

through the Living Messiah, our precious

Lord Jesus Christ.

Other books by
Barbara Taylor Sanders

The Laborers Are Few (non-fiction)

Hidden (historical fiction)

Bloodline Secrets (contemporary fiction)

Puttin' On the Dog & Gettin' Bit (humor)

FOREWORD

I don't believe that God is supernatural. I think it's perfectly normal for Him to raise the dead, heal the sick, perform extraordinary miracles, and talk to people about their future. As we follow in His footsteps and walk in the power of His love, speaking in the authority of His name, we get to become super-ordinary. We draw attention to the majesty of God, the astonishing grace and truth of Jesus, and the bubbling joy of the ever-enthusiastic and powerful Holy Spirit. It's not required that we draw attention to manifestations.

A testimony is birthed when we allow the truth of God to be established in our experience of the Lord in life situations. The test of faith produces a story of His goodness and faithfulness to man. Everything the Father does is marvelous. Everyone marveled at Jesus in the Gospels! A testimony like a testament is the evidence of a witness, a proven demonstration of intent by someone. When God moves, men marvel.

I love the testimonies in Barbara's latest book, *The Holy Spirit For Real*. It's the account of how ordinary people are learning to be led by an extraordinary God. He is the phenomenon, and we think He is marvelous. As we learn to love the life of Jesus within, He creates opportunities in the normal routines of life for the Kingdom to rise up within us and affect the world around us. The fullness of Jesus gathers up our ordinariness and combines both in a demonstration of the sheer power of His goodness. People taste and see that God is good.

It's wonderful to be ourselves in the Lord. It's marvelous when He is Himself in us. All of us need to gather our own testimonies about the fullness and abundance of all that God is in Himself. We must have testimonies of His nature and His name. My personal accounts of the Lord's love, joy, peace, gentleness, and kindness have touched tens of thousands. My testimonies in the power of Jesus' name to change lives by extraordinary means have opened up many people to the intentional majesty of God.

Testimonies open the doors of our hearts. They enlighten us about the immensity of all that God is for us. They provide us with an assurance that God will be the same for us. It is this essential evidence of what God is truly like that launches our own desire to know Him for ourselves.

I hope these testimonies open your heart. I hope they make you think. I hope they create a stirring in your spirit. I hope they lead you to seek His goodness. I hope you really want to marvel at Him. I hope you want to be super-ordinary. I hope…

—**Graham Cooke**
brilliantperspectives.com

INTRODUCTION

I don't know about you, but I need all the help I can get. You'll surely agree that life is not easy. In fact, most of us have experienced trials and tribulations that are beyond description. Thankfully, our Lord Jesus provides a Helper for anyone in need. As a recipient of this supernatural endowment, I am eternally grateful for a constant companion who walks with me, talks with me, and never leaves my side. Oh, what a wonder this Helper is to me!

This book is not a theological study on the controversial and often misunderstood subject of the Holy Spirit. Rather, it is an inspirational glimpse into the vast possibilities of having a personal Friend who provides comfort, instruction, wisdom, and an entrance into the heart of God.

My life has been far from ordinary. When I was completely lost, Jesus rescued me and turned my life upside down. It's been an extraordinary journey because when I got out of the driver's seat, Jesus took control of my life. I'd still be driving around in meaningless circles if He hadn't expanded my horizon by taking the wheel. The Lord re-routed me, and it's not been a smooth ride by any means. Without my Friend and Guide, I'd merely exist without purpose and be without vision to see the light at the end of the tunnel. My hope is eternal life with Jesus. He has proven Himself strong and mighty over and over throughout my forty-year year partnership with the Holy Spirit.

My personal and public experiences with God are unusual and

worth sharing with fellow Christians who need a boost or with believers who still aren't convinced that the Holy Spirit is *for real*.

Barbara Taylor Sanders, B.A.
Author/Advocate/Artist

Wise Women Council
Uniting HEARTS, Helping HANDS, Igniting HOPE

www.wisewomencouncil.org

Cape Coral, Florida
February 2023

JOHN 16:7–15 (TLB)

But the fact of the matter is that it is best for you that I go away, for if I don't, the Comforter won't come. If I do, he will—for I will send him to you.

"And when he has come he will convince the world of its sin, and of the availability of God's goodness, and of deliverance from judgment. The world's sin is unbelief in me; there is righteousness available because I go to the Father and you shall see me no more; there is deliverance from judgment because the prince of this world has already been judged.

"Oh, there is so much more I want to tell you, but you can't understand it now. When the Holy Spirit, who is truth, comes, he shall guide you into all truth, for he will not be presenting his own ideas, but will be passing on to you what he has heard. He will tell you about the future. He shall praise me and bring me great honor by showing you my glory. All the Father's glory is mine; this is what I mean when I say that he will show you my glory."

"Our help comes from Adonai,
The maker of Heaven and Earth."

Psalm 124:8 (CJB)

TABLE OF CONTENTS

Table of Contents

Table of Contents

You are holding significant stories from my life, a journey I am sharing to reveal the love of my precious redeemer, Christ Jesus, and the miraculous power of the Holy Spirit. It's been amazing, so I hope you'll keep reading.

Every memoir I have ever enjoyed reading includes photographs from the author, as well.

A life story becomes more intimate, being able to envision the person writing. Since I am not a well-known minister, celebrity, or sports figure, you probably don't know me. My two novels are in publication, though.

I grew up with a camera in my hand; therefore, I possess very few pictures of me. So, please indulge me on our picture journey together.

My goal in sharing my incredible testimonies is to help you accept Jesus as your Savior and embrace the astounding power of the Holy Spirit.

The details of each story are true; however, I have changed some names to protect the privacy of those who would wish to remain anonymous.

This remarkable excursion spans fifty years, and I am thankful for every memory stored within my heart forever.

A few years ago, I led a lady's Bible study at our church. Each week the Holy Spirit brought to my remembrance testimonies proving the power of the Holy Spirit at work. My Aunt Bonnie marveled, "I've known her all my life, and I've never heard these stories!" She made me think that I should record them for posterity's sake.

Barbara Taylor Sanders
Cape Coral, FL

THE KEY
TO A PURPOSEFUL LIFE

"I will place on his shoulder the key to the house of David; what he opens no one can shut, and what he shuts no one can open."

Isaiah 22:22 (NIV)

CHAPTER ONE

Central Park West, Broadway Shows, and A Holy Ghost Servant

Those seemingly insignificant experiences in early adulthood often have a lasting influence on ideas, feelings, and values. My perspective on life was certainly affected by eight days spent in high style while visiting New York City in 1969.

It's been humbling to consider the praying Christians who crossed my path when I was completely oblivious to God's plan and purpose for my life. When I arrive in heaven, I intend to warmly embrace a dear, petite black woman named Lu, who undoubtedly prayed for my soul when I was among the young and reckless.

One infamous summer night, my college buddy Diane Marable and I planned to fly on American Airlines, "student standby," from Detroit to New York City. On a tight budget with very little spending money, we nonetheless planned to have fun. If an airline had available seats, the cost was only $16.00 for a standby ticket. Diane had a summer job with Automobile Association of America, "AAA," so, with her employee discount, she booked us in an inexpensive hotel near 42nd Street and Times Square.

We were oblivious to the dangers of staying in such an unsavory area of Manhattan near a red-light district. Subway tokens were 10 cents to travel to clubs in the Village to dance every night away. We planned to eat at McDonald's and skip meals, all for added savings. Lord knows the trouble we would have found if God had not intervened in a very profound and supernatural way.

In those days, young ladies wore pantyhose, modest dresses (cut below the knee), and high-heel pumps. Dressed in our Sunday best, we arrived at Detroit Metropolitan Airport with great anticipation for a weeklong trip to New York City. Our carefully packed suitcases were placed in the trunk of my mother's new, powder-blue Mustang. But for safekeeping, Diane held a large, round hatbox that secured a coiffured wig her flamboyant brother had styled for sister's exciting trip to The Big Apple. Ronnie was a make-up artist for Ebony magazine, featuring monthly "before and after" pictorial centerfolds of glamorous black women. Her wig box also contained a pair of comfortable white canvas tennis shoes.

After parking, to our shock and dismay, the trunk of Mom's car wouldn't open!

"The luggage must be jammed against the lock," said Mom, looking annoyed. "I'll back up on the curb, and you two rock the bumper."

"Great idea!" My heart skipped a beat with this glimmer of hope.

Diane and I looked ridiculous rocking the bumper up and down. But after trying the trunk key again, we were on the verge of tears because it didn't open.

"You two go on ahead," said Mom. "I'll get to the Ford dealer first thing in the morning and ship your suitcases by noon at the latest."

We dashed off with glee and finally secured our seats on a midnight flight to LaGuardia, arriving at 2:45 a.m.

"We're going to freeze at this hour in the morning," I warned. Anticipating the cold, we hid two flimsy airline blankets in the wig case to use as warm shoulder wraps in the chilly early morning air.

The next afternoon, we aimlessly walked around a few busy streets in Manhattan wearing uncomfortable dressy outfits. Diane looked ridiculous wearing a dress with ugly, worn-out tennis shoes. However, as she strolled in comfort, my feet were painfully pinched inside my too-narrow Sunday pumps. Bored and tired, my burning, blistered feet made me feel ill. There was no money in the budget to purchase comfortable shoes for me. Exasperated and weary from my complaints, Diane made a suggestion.

"I have an auntie that lives here. She's worked for a wealthy Jewish family for the past thirty-five years. Maybe I should call her."

"Yes! *Please* call her right now!" I nearly shouted while pointing to the nearby phone booth. I can still see Diane leafing through the gigantic Manhattan White Pages to locate Aunt Lu's phone number.

After connecting with her, we were immediately invited to the

Adlers' luxurious apartment at 115 Central Park West, which over-looked Central Park. The building is called The Majestic, a New York City historic landmark. It featured a uniformed doorman and an elevator that opened to their private foyer. Their expansive living quarters occupied the *entire* corner of the building. It was the first sunken living room and opulent fairytale I'd ever stepped into.

After polite introductions by Auntie Lu, Phil and Pauline Adler warmly embraced us as special nieces home from college.

With glee, Mrs. Adler announced the menu for dinner. "We're on this new diet. We get to have a *hotdog*," she said in a very thick New York accent. "So, I'm sending you to our butcher. Don't worry. He's just around the corner. We need more kosher wieners, so get going, don't stop for anything." Her delightful accent caused us to stifle a giggle every time she spoke.

Shortly thereafter, we dined on picnic-style hot dogs with deli mustard and a tossed salad with low-fat dressing sitting under a colossal crystal chandelier at the longest table I'd ever seen. It was a highly glossed cherry table that extended the entire length of the elegant dining room. It easily seated twenty guests. Auntie Lu ate every meal with the Adlers since she was more than a live-in housekeeper. In fact, she'd help raise their two grown sons and was treated as a cherished family member. We felt completely at ease.

As a natural storyteller, I delighted the Adlers with the tale of my mom backing up on the curb, bouncing the bumper up and down, and later sneaking the airline blankets off the plane to keep warm. The only one not amused was Auntie Lu. She never cracked a smile. Pauline made me repeat the story, and she laughed just as hard the second time around.

The Adlers were visibly alarmed to learn that we were staying in such a sleazy part of town. Concerned for our safety, they insisted we immediately check out of our hotel and move in with them.

"Let me find you warm coats to wear," Pauline said, leading us to a front hall closet.

My jaw dropped viewing the large walk-in closet lined with fabulous exotic furs. It resembled an actual fur salon.

"My son used to own a fur company, so, what can I say? Just take your pick. You can't go around with just blankets to keep warm!"

Becoming real-life Barbie dolls, Diane and I giggled while trying on the luxurious full-length coats and jackets of many varieties—beaver, sable, chinchilla, lynx, fox, and mink. Finally, we made our selections. Mrs. Adler produced two large shopping bags with handles. She stuffed a mink stole in each tote for the bus ride to fetch our suitcases that had finally arrived at our hotel. Riding the crowded bus, I remember feeling nervous carrying shopping bags containing such expensive furs.

On our first night out on the town, in fresh dresses, Diane and I paraded around Greenwich Village draped in posh mink. Consider that we resembled vagabonds the day before, wearing musty clothing and thin red blankets draped around our shoulders.

The Adlers were involved with theatre management and stage productions. Diane informed me that Phil Adler helped produce *My Fair Lady*, which had a record-long run on Broadway.

The next evening, we were chauffeured by private car to the theatre to see *Hair*. "Now, don't be late!" Mr. Adler had reminded us several times since he would be waiting for us outside of the Biltmore Theater. When we pulled up, he quickly moved off the curb to greet us with a huge smile because we had actually arrived on time. As a proper gentleman, Mr. Adler opened the car door and carefully guided us into the crowded theatre, beaming like a proud uncle.

Strolling down the aisle of the crowded theatre in our mink stoles, we felt like royalty escorted to VIP front-row seats. The musical *Hair* was electrifying. We had never been to a Broadway performance. During one lively song and dance routine, handsome black actor Ben Vareen was bopping at the edge of the stage, flirtatiously staring into Diane's eyes. Little wonder. Diane was a tall, striking bi-racial beauty. This unabashed attention made us both blush and squirm in our seats.

Pauline Adler enthralled us with Broadway stories. One night, we hung out in her bedroom for a pajama party. While seated on her bed, she stood in front of a tall dresser sharing fascinating tidbits about Lauren Bacall, Julie Andrews, and other famous celebrities.

"Did you ever meet Liz Taylor?" I gushed.

"Yes, and she's more beautiful in person!"

Several nights in a row, we were treated to a variety of other Broadway shows, five in all. I flush at the cost of theatre tickets and the Adler generosity to provide such an extravagant holiday for two impoverished college chums. In private, I remember whispering to Diane, "I don't want to sound ungrateful, but I am getting a little tired of going to Broadway shows every night." Isn't that ridiculous? We went from blanket-shawls on a shoestring to extravagance provided by a sweet Jewish couple treating us with dignity and grand style. It was the grace of God to lavish us with such goodness even though we didn't deserve it.

On Sunday, Auntie Lu went missing. Later that evening, I commented about her being gone so long. Diane replied, "Oh, Auntie Lu spends all day and night in *church* every Sunday. She's very holy."

"Are you kidding? *All day?*" I was utterly amazed at the thought of spending that much time in *church*.

Looking back now, I'm certain that no-nonsense, sanctified woman gathered all the Pentecostal church ladies to travail in tongues for her wayward niece and friend who had stolen airline blankets on a lark.

Smiling, I realize how God miraculously jammed that trunk to redirect my path. When my mother arrived back home, my dad used the same trunk key, and it popped right open!

The Lord surely has had His Hand upon my life. Even though I made plans oblivious of His presence, He clearly redirected my steps for a higher purpose. The Lord orchestrated a divine appointment with Auntie Lu and the loving Adlers. He placed my friend and I in the spiritual lens of a humble and sincere praying Christian. After crossing Aunt Lu's path, she surely prayed for the hounds of heaven to dog us down for all of eternity.

After I departed for home, I sent a bouquet of flowers to Mr. and Mrs. Adler and Aunt Lu, sincerely thanking them for their kindness, generosity, and gracious hospitality. Diane stayed on another few days.

Those eight astounding days in New York City, being privy to an opulent lifestyle, was a true eye-opener for me. But. What impressed me most was how humbly they lived and gave to others. The seeds were planted to aim high and set my sights on a more excellent way of living. Making a dedication to aim high, the Lord honored my desire for a more excellent life. Throughout the next forty years, I've lived an amazing life. Surely God answered the fervent and righteous prayers of Auntie Lu.

A few years later, Diane was instrumental in connecting me to my future husband, a handsome and successful businessman. Daryl Sanders had recently retired from the NFL, so I didn't know him as a football star. During the early few years of marriage, we enjoyed traveling in executive jets while staying in luxurious five-star hotels in Paris, London, Madrid, Acapulco, the Canary Islands, and Morocco. We enjoyed a rewarding lifestyle while Daryl was a successful business executive of a Fortune 500 corporation.

After becoming a born-again Christian, I realized the pleasures of this world couldn't compare to the happiness and peace of intimately knowing Jesus Christ as Lord and Savior. By far, *my most exciting and prosperous excursion throughout my lifetime has been my adventures with the Holy Spirit.*

Jesus has never ceased to amaze me or fill me with joy, even in the midst of difficult trials or painful setbacks. God is in the perfecting process; He is far more concerned with the condition of our heart than with the comforts of this lifetime. I'm deeply thankful for the blessings the Lord has provided for my family, and I am eternally grateful for Auntie Lu, who surely prayed that I'd meet Jesus one day, and I did!

"The mind of man plans his way, But the LORD directs his steps" (Proverbs 16:9, NASB).

"For the Son of Man came to seek and to save the lost" (Luke 19:10, NIV).

Traveling the world...
Daryl and I were in Madrid on a business trip
with his Fortune 500 Company, and as young
lovers, we decided to duck down to
"Casablanca" (after the movie) and ride the
"Marrakesh Express" (after the song).

Agadir, Morocco, 1970

CHAPTER TWO

Morocco with Pamela Courson and Jim Morrison of The Doors

Memories exist like snapshots of scenes similar to dreams. A vivid dream while sleeping, replayed upon awakening, might consist of three or four nonsensical images, which quickly switch from one scene to the next like a slide show. Somehow the pictures are mysteriously related, and if you ponder them long enough, the dream might make sense and bring resolution to something perplexing or reveal something prophetic in nature.

Three vivid snapshots of Pamela Courson Morrison remain in my mind from a brief Moroccan resort stay with her on the beach of Agadir in 1970. Perhaps these scenes, months before the death of rock star legend Jim Morrison, will satisfy the curiosity of his fans wondering why and how these famous lovers perished long before their time.

My future husband was a handsome twenty-nine-year-old corporate executive. He was the VP for a large incentive travel company that had multi-million-dollar accounts with General Motors and other large corporations.

Together, we traveled on the Marrakesh Express from Casablanca to Marrakesh. Days earlier, we were in Madrid for his business meeting. As young lovers feeling adventurous, we secretly slipped off to discover parts unknown by his Fortune 500 Company located in Dayton, Ohio.

Traveling in corporate jets with Daryl seemed like royalty compared to the American Airlines employee travel discounts offered by my job in Detroit. Instead of grungy taxi service to a budget hotel, Daryl and I sped off to a five-star hotel in a chauffeur-driven, shiny, black Bentley.

Arriving in a place as primitive as Agadir, located on the Atlantic Ocean in southern Morocco, I wondered what type of special "VIP vehicle" awaited our arrival. The first clue was the military presence on the tarmac. Ominous Muslim soldiers draped with machine guns across their chests stood by as our private jet taxied to a stop. Moments later, a charming Arab gentleman warmly greeted us with a huge toothy grin and escorted us to a fancy horse-drawn carriage. And off we rolled along the dusty road to a fabulous beachfront resort. I smiled all the way, sensing this was surely going to be an adventure.

An earthquake had leveled Agadir in 1960, we were informed. The long stretch of beachfront offered only two newly built hotels. Our adobe-type, three-story hotel was of lesser magnitude compared to the secluded Club Med located nearby. One could only imagine the rich and famous people who were behind that privacy wall that separated the two hotels.

Our first-floor, ocean-front suite stepped out into sand, but Daryl needed to make a trans-Atlantic office call to "check back in" before taking our first stroll on the expansive and isolated beachfront. So, I wandered down to the hotel lobby hoping to locate a gift shop offering swimwear. I traveled to Madrid not needing a bathing suit. That's when I encountered Pamela Courson Morrison.

As I stood at the counter waiting to pay for my new swimsuit, the French-speaking switchboard operator was attempting to place Daryl's long-distance call; she kept repeating Ohio and mispronouncing the O, which sounded like an E each time.

I called out, "It's O in O-hi-O that he is saying to you."

The attractive gal with long, auburn blond hair quickly turned to face me.

"You're an American," she said, astounded.

"Yes, we just got here. That's my fiancé trying to call his office."

We both chuckled, listening to Daryl's obvious frustration on the opposite end of that switchboard. The exasperated girl never did get it right, but the transatlantic call went through.

"What the heck are you doing in Morocco?" yelled the CEO when Daryl finally surfaced five days later. George Gilfellen was the best man at our wedding eighteen months later, but at the time, he had no idea who I was or why his former NFL golden boy had suddenly vanished.

Our seaside resort offered no open restaurant to come and go as you please. Rather, you selected from a menu a day in advance and showed up in the dining room, on time, for a strict eating schedule that offered no allowances for tardy or absentee guests.

The French menu offered lobsters prepared in more ways than I ever knew existed. Every time I thought I had selected boiled, served with butter Lobster tails, I got some exotic dish instead. With no live waiter to interpret, you hoped for the best when checking off your selection written in French.

Since it was late October, there were few guests, so it felt as if we had the entire place to ourselves. One evening, following another elaborate lobster in cream sauce concoction, Daryl and I relaxed in a quiet lounge area facing a fireplace that was not yet lit. The girl with long, auburn hair arrived, appearing as if she had just awakened from a needed nap. But not a living soul remained in the dining room.

"Is dinner already done for the night?" she asked, looking forlorn and obviously hungry.

"I have an apple you can eat," I said, promptly producing a bright red delicious apple I had stashed from the buffet table earlier.

"Thank you!" she gushed, reaching for the extended apple and plopping down on the cotton-duck-covered sofa opposite us.

"This is the girl I met in the lobby yesterday." Daryl nodded politely.

"I'm Barbara, and this is Daryl from 'O-hi-O,'" I added with a big grin.

She laughed easily while hungrily munching on the apple as if in a college dorm all-nighter after the cafeteria had long shut down. Being in a foreign country creates comradery between fellow Americans. We're all considered crazy and need to stick together during emergencies such as this one.

"I'm Pamela Morrison," she said brightly. "I am married to Jim Morrison of the rock band The Doors. Well, we aren't officially married, but we've been together for seven years, so that makes us legally hitched."

Mildly impressed, I smiled and nodded, even though I vaguely recalled his name or status of the rock group. Listening to Motown sounds living in Detroit was like living in Wisconsin and eating cheese from Vermont. Why would you?

When The Beatles hit the airwaves, no other music genre played on the radio with them besides the marvelous Motown tunes cranked out weekly by Hitsville, USA, located on West Grand Boulevard.

Pamela explained that she was in Morocco as "an emotional escape from Jim" since they had hit a rocky place in their relationship. She needed to talk, and, being with complete strangers, perhaps, she felt safe to unload on us.

After finishing her apple, core and all, she said, "Hey, will you be here for a while? I want to get something from my room to show you." Moments later, she returned with a well-worn journal the size of a notebook. It was a book of poems written by her common-law husband, Jim Morrison. I recently read that this notebook was auctioned off for over $200,000 dollars.

We politely listened as she tearfully read the prose with expression, and at other times, with great emotion and intense feelings. Her entire being was entwined in Jim's life for better or worse. As if her only identity revolved around him, but his rambling thoughts revealed a troubled young man expressing futility. The poetry made little sense to someone unfamiliar with Morrison's lyrics and style of music, which reflected his jaded conception of life.

Pamela gently cradled the journal on her lap as if holding a baby. She glanced over at us as if expecting feedback. There was nothing to say because it was beyond my comprehension. I'm not sure what the businessman was thinking other than, *Please get me out of here.*

Pamela explained that Jim had been charged with drunkenness and indecent exposure at a concert in Miami the previous year. That news hit every newspaper in America, which is how his name became familiar to me, not by his celebrated music or being part of his huge worldwide fan base.

"He has drug problems." Her voice reflected genuine regret. "One time, while I sat next to him at the piano, he was about to take another hit of heroin, but I took it instead, just to keep him from overdosing." Her large hazel eyes reflected regret. I sensed she feared her celebrated lover was not long for this world.

Hours later, after sympathetically listening to her woes, we felt a kinship and made plans to meet up again.

The next day, clad in my newly purchased two-piece swimsuit, I water skied in the Atlantic Ocean along with a few robust German guests from our hotel. As our ski boat was underway past the lavish Club Med, I gawked at the exclusive compound, hoping to catch a glimpse of a celebrity. The night before, Daryl and I, decked out in our finest resort clothes, slipped into the private establishment known around the world. We made it as far as the cocktail lounge undetected until the snobby waiter requested payment for our drinks in the form of plastic pop beads. Busted.

So, after showering off the salt water, it was time for a needed afternoon nap. Our ocean-view suite opened right onto the sand. The contemporary bed was a single-layer mattress on a molded platform planted on the tiled floor. As I peacefully slept alongside the man I loved, I felt something crawling up my bare chest toward my neck. Half asleep, I instinctively flicked off the crawling creature while screaming in bloody terror. Daryl and I were instantly on our feet atop the bed as I trembled from head to toe in post-trauma shock. Daryl suddenly spotted the furry-legged tarantula crawling across the tile and grabbed his hefty size fourteen wingtip shoe as a weapon. I couldn't bear to watch as he aimed and shot his shoe at the target. "Whatever it was, it crunched!" he said with triumph. I remained weak-kneed ready to faint.

After the blood-curdling brush with the tarantula and getting bounced out of Club Med, we were all in for more escapades beyond our seaside resort. My conservative businessman seemed game for anything, which made it all the more fun seeing him totally out of his element.

The mystical Moroccan open-air market didn't disappoint, offering snake charmers, monkeys on a string encouraged to jump on people, welcomed or not, donkeys pulling carts piled high with plenty of souvenir stuff to hawk. Seductive black eyes peered out from draped, dark shadows and entryways as we passed through trails of rugs, brassware, woven baskets, handcrafted bead wear, hats, scarves, sandals, and other bright cotton wear.

We bumped into Pamela at the market. Since she was so knowledgeable about illicit drugs, we asked her to purchase some hashish to experience Morocco. Pamela told us to stop by her room that evening for a smoke. After dinner, we wandered up to her room. Handcrafted Moroccan purses and satchels were piled high on her queen size bed. Delighted by the sight of so many beautiful things, I treated myself by handling many items with admiration.

"I own a boutique in LA," she explained before making space for us to sit on the edge of the bed.

Pam sat at the top of her bed against propped pillows. She expertly rubbed the hashish on the top of her left hand, on the space between her thumb and forefinger. The substance became soft before she scraped it off to form something to smoke. She fascinated me.

Here we were, two country bumpkins from Ohio, thinking we were so cool smoking hashish with Pamela Morrison, the live-in girlfriend of infamous lead singer Jim Morrison of The Doors. I had only smoked pot once before, so this was totally audacious.

Unfortunately, that's the last snapshot I have of her. That following summer, Pamela and Jim Morrison were in Paris, obviously reconciled. My heart sank when I learned of his overdose on July 2, 1971, but not surprised. In a published account, Pamela called his longtime friend, Alan Ronay. "My Jim is dead, Alan, he left us, he's dead." She added, "I want to be alone now; please leave me alone."

Sadly, on April 25, 1974, Pamela died of a broken heart fueled by an overdose of heroin. We were the exact same age, born within four days of each other. As it turned out, our futures were determined by the diverse choices made as very impressionable young women.

If only I could turn back the pages of time to guide us to a loving God who saves and delivers from all dangerous addictions. She'd be alive to share priceless wisdom garnered from these last four decades of living surrendered to Jesus Christ as Lord and Savior.

Remembering those mischievous young girls giggling together in the lobby of a Moroccan hotel so very long ago fills my heart with deep sorrow. We were both full of hope for a productive future with the husbands we loved.

With the grace of God, I lived out a productive life, yielded to God and guided by the power of the Holy Spirit. We were both searching for truth within our tender hearts. Her vision was clouded by a senseless heroin addiction that claimed her life and that of a loved one she had sincerely tried to rescue. Tragically, Pamela Courson Morrison didn't survive long enough to discover the truth that sets you truly free.

"You have set our iniquities before you, our secret sins in the light of your presence. For all our days pass away under your wrath; we bring our years to an end like a sigh. The years of our life are seventy, or even by reason of strength eighty; yet their span is but toil and trouble; they are soon gone, and we fly away."

Psalm 90:8–10

DESPERATE FOR PEACE

"Finally, brothers and sisters, rejoice! Strive for full restoration, encourage one another, be of one mind, live in peace. And the God of love and peace will be with you."

2 Corinthians 12:11 (NIV)

CHAPTER THREE

The Phil Donahue Show with Guest Godfrey Cambridge Confronting a Clairvoyant

My fairytale marriage to Daryl Sanders was spent in Dayton, Ohio, for the pre-Jesus, miserable few years. Even with all the luxurious travel and living in a beautiful historic home in Centerville, I was challenged as a twenty-five-year-old young woman attempting to cope with unruly stepchildren who had survived the holocaust of divorced parents.

Daryl married as a teenager and divorced ten years and two kids later. It was a dismal time in my life, adjusting to life with two troubled pre-teens and coping with an ambitious spouse climbing the corporate ladder of a Fortune 500 company that seemed to own his soul. We were a mess. My husband disappeared at 7 a.m. and arrived home for dinner after 8 p.m. each weekday evening. He played golf Saturday and Sunday, so it was up to me to run the household, discipline the children, ages eleven and twelve, and keep harmony in the home. Right? W-r-o-n-g!

Prior to marriage, the fun-loving girl with loads of friends laughed easily and thought the best of everyone. My step-kids were suspicious of my joy and put me through the wringer with test-after-test to prove my authenticity. Pride drove me to become the best step-mom on the planet. I envisioned writing a best seller to prove my success. Right? W-r-o-n-g!

Consequently, to obtain sanity and maintain peace, I turned into a drill sergeant attempting to undo the years of dysfunction and unruliness. After the divorce, Dad lived on a beach in California, dating beautiful women while traveling the globe on corporate jets. Their gentle and soft-spoken mother had become a space cadet in survival mode. It was no surprise the kids were filled with contempt when I stepped on the scene and cracked the whip as Wonder Woman.

Petrified of drinking alcohol or taking prescription drugs for stress, my best coping skills were limited to excessive sleep and seeking out a clairvoyant who might offer *hope* for a future. With no light at the end of the tunnel, I felt stuck. Life was bleak.

Two adventurous friends understood my misery and need for hope. They had introduced me to Mrs. Goodman, a local psychic. My first visit to the fortune-teller was with Sherry Berry, age twenty-eight, on her third marriage to a prominent periodontist. Thankfully, Sherry became my sounding board. She often shared a tape recording of her latest psychic reading with me. This spiritual realm fascinated me. Ten-dollar visits to Mrs. Goodman started off as a lark with a twinge of excitement. The old woman made predictions that often rang true. Since our checks were made out to the "church of God," it seemed that Mrs. Goodman was true to her name as a harmless religious person.

Meanwhile, it wasn't long before flamboyant Sherry, the buxom blonde bombshell and former life-of-the-party, got radically "saved." She began preaching at every social gathering. There were plenty of opportunities for Sherry to get on her soapbox. I felt abandoned by the new Bible-quoting zealot who made me feel condemned. To make matters worse, every Wednesday, Sherry faithfully telephoned at the crack of dawn to coax me out of bed for a weekly Bible study. Convinced she was crazy, I came up with felonious excuses like "sorry, tennis lesson today…" or "sorry, I have a doctor's appointment." She knew I was lying, but I had to save face with some legitimate-sounding excuse. Like Auntie Lu, she was probably praying for the hounds of heaven to track me down.

Several weeks of Sherry's persistence paid off. I relented because I ran out of excuses. Entering the neighborhood Bible study, my guard was up. Like attending corporate social functions with my executive husband, I braced myself for similar rejection from older women threatened by an attractive young wife.

However, I was stunned by the genuine kindness extended to me by the group of Christian women attending this Bible study.

What impressed me most were the earnest prayers uttered aloud while the women sat on the family room floor, creating a circle of united hearts. Hearing such sincere expressions of faith was completely foreign to my ears. Sherry's friend, Eva, was seated to my left. She said "amen," under her breath after every prayer. I wrote her off as a religious fanatic!

But it was the bold, Charismatic Eva who had my number as a

phony-baloney trying to fit in. Afterward, coffee and donuts were offered in the kitchen. Sherry stood beaming at my side because I had finally come to the Bible study. Eva walked up to me and peered directly into my empty eyes.

"So, what did you think of the Bible study?"

"Oh, it was interesting…I sensed true joy and peace with these women," I answered, attempting to sound philosophical while munching on my apple fritter. I nervously glanced around the kitchen, hoping the other gals weren't listening in. I wanted them to think I was virtuous like them. I stood between the sink and the dishwasher, cornered by her discerning probe of my sorrowful life. She was about to blow my cover.

"Joy and peace?" she answered. "So then, would you like that for yourself?"

"Yes, of course," I responded, shrugging my shoulders, wishing I could disappear into the linoleum.

It was a set-up. I was ambushed because Eva quickly produced a small tract from her pocket and opened it to Spiritual Law number one. "Here, read this aloud," she commanded with authority. The Four Steps to Salvation were illustrated with simple, easy-to-understand principles based on Scripture verses—*confess, believe, repent,* and *receive.*

Principle number one stated that "faith in Jesus Christ as the Savior is the *only* step to salvation. The message of the Bible is abundantly clear. We have all sinned against God (Romans 3:23). Because of our sin, we deserve to be eternally separated from God (Romans 6:23). Because of His love for us (John 3:16), God took on human form and died in our place, taking the punishment that we deserve (Romans 5:8; 2 Corinthians 5:21). God promises forgiveness of sins and eternal life in heaven to all who receive, by grace through faith, Jesus Christ as Savior (John 1:12; 3:16; 5:24; Acts 16:31).

I didn't fully comprehend all of what I had just read aloud. But when these two sincere women invited me to receive Jesus Christ as my personal Savior, I bowed my head, feeling genuine reverence. I repeated the sinner's prayer led by Eva. God used my pride by backing me into a corner. It worked. My strong-willed determination to govern my life was now taking a turn toward God's ultimate command. It certainly was a step in the right direction because I had come to the end of myself. I hated the person I'd become. I needed help.

Sherry glowed as we left the Bible study that day. However, as soon as I crossed the threshold onto the porch, I heard a mocking voice inside my head. *So, are you going to turn into a preacher like Sherry and have everyone laugh at you behind your back?* I froze. I would never be outspoken like Sherry and risk losing friends.

When I got into the car, Sherry already had the Bible wide open on the console between us. Her countenance had sobered as she warned, "You can't go back to Mrs. Goodman ever again now that you're a Christian!"

"Why not?" I asked, surprised and genuinely confused.

"Psychic readings are Satanic, that's why!"

"Sa-tan-ic? What's that mean?"

"Of SATAN!" Sherry hissed his name as if spilling out poison from her lips.

"But she's such a sweet old woman. How can that be?" I argued.

"Here. read this passage out loud." She shoved the Bible into my lap and pointed to Deuteronomy 18:9–14, a warning against occult practices.

I began reading. *"When you enter the land the Lord your God is giving you, do not learn to imitate the detestable ways of the nations there. Let no one be found among you who sacrifices their son or daughter in the fire, who practices divination or sorcery, interprets omens, engages in witchcraft, or casts spells, or who is a medium or spiritualist or who consults the dead. Anyone who does these things is detestable to the Lord; because of these same detestable practices the Lord your God will drive out those nations before you. You must be blameless before the Lord your God."*

"Mrs. Goodman has séances and calls back the dead. She is *NOT* of God," Sherry warned with blazing eyes.

I couldn't argue with what I had just read from the Bible. It was the first passage of Scripture I'd ever read in my entire life. Little did I know I'd be quoting this passage of Scripture within forty-eight hours to millions of viewers on the Phil Donahue show, thus launching the prophetic anointing upon my life.

Later that evening, Sherry phoned me at home as a follow-up. She knew it was vital to acknowledge Jesus Christ as my personal Savior. She started the conversation with, "So! What did Daryl say?" I could tell she was grinning from ear to ear with joy.

"Say about what?" I knew what she meant. But pride kept me from wanting to tell the whole world about it.

"Well, *you know*…about getting saved today." Her smile was gone; I could tell that by the disappointment in her voice.

"Oh, that," I said nonchalantly. "We haven't gotten on the subject of religion yet."

Sherry probably felt like hanging up on me; instead, she quietly spoke, "Well, I'm going to pray you do because if 'you confess with your mouth that Jesus is Lord and believe in your heart that God raised him from the dead, you will be saved.' That's what the Bible says, so be sure you do that."

I ended the conversation feeling completely defeated, knowing I would *never* be brave enough to spout off about Jesus like Sherry was known to do with all our friends. I was among the in-crowd who secretly snickered at her zeal.

The next day my brother, David, arrived for a weekend visit.

Whenever family visited, it was a big treat to be an audience participant on the Phil Donahue show, taped live in the morning and aired again at 2 p.m.

My husband often worked out with Phil on the basketball court, so I never needed advance notice or tickets to get on the show. Phil was always kind to me, allowing me to take group pictures with him in his office afterward. During the live show, Phil always stuck the microphone in my face whenever I asked the guest a simple question. I'd say, "So, when did you get your start in show business?" That way, my guests were also caught on camera. It was always so much fun to later see ourselves on television.

On Friday morning, David and I arrived for the show with my usual front-row seats. The guests were actor Godfrey Cambridge and his attractive female companion and "spiritual advisor," a clairvoyant promoting her book about the occult.

God's timing is always perfect. It still amazes me how God orchestrated that encounter. As this woman bragged about certain predictions coming true, the deceptive veil about Mrs. Goodman was lifted. My spiritual eyes were opened during that program. I realized that promoting dependence on tea leaves, tarot cards, fortune-tellers, or relying on horoscopes for direction in life was not Christian.

Godfrey bragged, "I don't leave the house without a reading from her." (Too bad she didn't warn him to get to the hospital before he died of a massive heart attack at the age of forty-seven.)

With sudden supernatural wisdom, I raised my hand to ask the psychic a question. I anticipated how she would answer, so I had already rehearsed my responses in my mind.

Phil asked me to stand to address my question to his guests. The cameraman was over his right shoulder as Phil presented the microphone to me. Millions of viewers were watching his popular daytime show, the forerunner to Oprah.

"Where do you get your power from?" I asked sweetly.

"From God," she said, somewhat defensively.

"So, do you read the Bible?"

"Sometimes," she sneered. Her eyes narrowed, so I sensed she knew where I was headed.

"Well, if you read the Bible, then you should know that Deuteronomy 18 says that anyone who consults mediums or wizards is not of God. The reason I know this is because I've accepted Jesus Christ as my personal Savior, and I don't believe what you're doing is of God at all."

Phil's eyes widened with the thrill of a heated debate. He nearly shouted, "So are you saying that she's of the DEVIL?"

"I didn't say that; God said it." I sat down. End of discussion. I had been calm and poised while addressing her, but once seated, I began to tremble.

Sherry saw the program live that morning. She was surely

smiling when I told the whole world that Jesus was my Savior.

Later that day, I phoned my husband at his office, requesting him to tune in to the taped Phil Donahue show. "Don't worry; I am in the first ten minutes of the show. There is something you need to hear me say."

Television had become a profound way to declare my new-found faith in Christ Jesus. A supernatural launch of miraculous signs that enlightened my life as a Christian.

The decades to follow became an extraordinary prophetic journey with the supernatural, proving that the Holy Spirit is *for real*.

"Ask and it will be given to you; seek and you will find; knock and the door will be opened to you" (Matthew 7:7, NIV)

A HEALING MIRACLE

Just then a woman who had been subject to bleeding for twelve years came up behind him and touched the edge of his cloak. She said to herself, "If I only touch his cloak, I will be healed." Jesus turned and saw her. "Take heart, daughter," he said, "your faith has healed you." And the woman was healed at that moment.
Matthew 9:20–22 (NIV)

Chapter Four

Robert Alexander Sanders, Our Miracle Son, "Bo"

Following an outpatient laparoscopy procedure, my OB/GYN surgeon gave my husband some grave news. It would be a few hours before the anesthesia wore off, so I remained oblivious to my fate.

Daryl stood waiting in the hospital corridor outside of the surgery theatre. Dressed in scrubs, Dr. Thomas Magnotta removed his green surgical mask to speak.

"Hello, Mr. Sanders," he began with a somber expression. "Well, your wife is doing fine. Her ovaries look normal." He paused before speaking again. "You already have two children, right? So, it wouldn't bother you if you couldn't have any more kids?"

"What do you mean?" Daryl asked, perplexed.

"Well, for an X-ray purpose, I attempted to inject dye into her fallopian tubes, but the dye ran off onto the floor. We attempted the dye injection three times, and each time the dye ran out onto the floor. Her fallopian tubes are definitely blocked. Further probing revealed deterioration."

"What about surgery?"

"There is a new procedure coming out right now. Medical science is experimenting with the use of artificial fallopian tubes, but you need healthy tissue to adhere to the artificial implants. This won't work for your wife, so don't give her false hope. She will never conceive."

Ever the optimist, my husband did not accept the doctor's report. At home, he gently informed me that I would need "surgery" to conceive a child.

During recovery that same morning, I became extremely cold, but I was not awake enough to cry out for a warm blanket. In fact, when I did wake up, the inside of my mouth had painful bleeding cuts from clenching my teeth down on my cheeks during the drop in my body temperature. Therefore, the thought of necessary "surgery" and going under anesthesia again was too frightening to consider.

Easter Sunday came in March that year, a month following my surgical exam. We were in Michigan for a weeklong holiday visit with my mother. We'd been married for two years, so my family members were anxious for us to have a baby. "So, when are you going to have a baby?" teased Aunt Bonnie during Sunday brunch. I didn't tell my mother or her younger sisters that I needed surgery to conceive.

Actually, I was far more bewildered not attending church that day. It was the first Easter Sunday that really meant something to me. For the first time in my life, I had a longing to celebrate what Jesus had done for me on the Cross of Calvary. That Sunday morning, I said nothing to my husband about desiring to go to church since he had not yet returned to his childhood faith at that point in time. But I felt sad for not being able to attend church.

Later that day, our family of four drove back to Dayton. I slept the last leg of the trip stretched across the front seat of my husband's big Oldsmobile '98. My head rested on my husband's comfortable knee. My ever-bickering stepchildren were in the backseat, so I was able to tune them out by sleeping.

When we exited onto the Centerville ramp, Daryl pulled into Woody's supermarket. He awakened me to ask what was needed at the store besides milk, bread, and some lunchmeat. We'd been gone for nearly a week.

I remained reclined on the front seat, gazing up at the cobalt blue sky laced with billowing white clouds. It was a perfect day for a miracle. After all, it was Resurrection Sunday.

Having a baby meant surgery, according to my husband's misleading report. I was dreading going under anesthesia again. Since I had never actually prayed before, I was reluctant to seek the Lord about my dilemma. All the Christian ladies prayed out loud at Sherry's Bible study group. These women expressed sincere prayers, which were spontaneous, like natural conversation. When I joined their prayer circle, I was still too timid to pray aloud.

At that point in my walk with Jesus, I didn't want to presume on God. *Why would He hear me?* I hadn't done anything worthy to dare call upon His name. I felt unworthy and filled with shame for all my un-confessed sins. I was a babe in the Lord, unschooled in the principles of Christianity. So, my first prayer expressed from my spirit was that of a little girl coming to her heavenly Father.

I closed my eyes and opened my heart. "God? If you are really *real,* then maybe you can *heal* me."

Nothing could have prepared me for God's response to that simple childlike prayer. A sudden jolt of mild tangible energy surged through my body. It was so real that I stiffened with fright before hearing a soothing inner voice say, *"Be still, this is of God. Do not be afraid."* I relaxed to experience liquid warmth slowly travel from the top of my head and downward. When this warmth reached my womb, it separated into two electrical pulses before settling on each fallopian tube for a few seconds. I felt something similar to sparks hitting your hand from those fourth of July burning sparklers throwing off a shower of sparks. This phenomenal experience lasted only about a minute.

When Daryl got back in the car, he saw my stunned face.

"What's wrong with you?"

"I'll tell you when we get home" was all I could manage to mutter.

Later, when we were alone, I explained what had happened. Daryl looked at me with pity. From the sympathy in his eyes, I could tell he thought I was delusional from too much religion.

The next day, I telephoned two of my friends to share my

amazing "God experience." Both women quickly changed the subject and didn't comment. Apparently, these two also thought "religion has gone to her crazy head."

The following Wednesday, I attended the Bible study again. Afterward, while talking to Sherry and Eva, I stood in the exact spot where I had accepted Jesus Christ a few months before. I debated whether or not to tell them because I was afraid they'd think I was loony as well.

"Something strange happened to me on Easter Sunday." I began hesitantly, unsure of myself.

"Oh yeah? Tell us about it." Sherry said, waiting expectantly. By the time I finished the testimony, she and Eva were both shouting, "You're healed! You're healed! Praise the Lord you're healed!" They began joyfully dancing, arm-in-arm around in a circle. They attempted to grab me to join in, but I jerked back at their wild reaction!

I knew something supernatural happened to me because it was tangible. The surge through my body felt like warm energy. *But healed?* I didn't dare go that far! But as the girls twirled jubilantly around the kitchen, I spoke a second prayer from my heart. *"Lord, I want their same kind of faith someday."*

In the following weeks, I didn't give much thought to the Easter Sunday "healing." One day, I ran into Sherry at Food-a-Rama, our favorite grocery store in Centerville. When she saw me at the end of the aisle, she shouted with glee, "Are you pregnant yet?"

She was grinning from ear to ear as usual.

We moved to Bridgeport, Connecticut, in 1974. Sherry cautioned me about finding the right church to attend. In fact, she had instructed me to bring back the Yellow Pages following a prior house-hunting trip. She circled the best "Gospel preaching" denominations listed in the phone book.

"You can't just go to any church," she warned. "It has to preach the doctrines of Christ." I had no clue what she meant. But we did try out a few churches she had circled in the Yellow Pages.

On our cross-country pilgrimage to Connecticut in early May 1974, I was experiencing my monthly menstrual cycle. I was definitely not pregnant yet. But I was now hopeful since Sherry finally convinced me that I had actually been *healed* on Easter Sunday.

Between May and June, we conceived! I started experiencing lightheadedness each time I ate food. I began announcing, "I think I'm pregnant."

After a few weeks, Daryl snarled at me. "You are going to make yourself *sick* with this kind of crazy nonsense! You are *not pregnant*, so stop talking about it!" He knew it was *impossible* for me to be pregnant, according to the doctor's medical report. So, naturally, he was concerned about my mental health. He handed me money to test at a lab near where I worked as a travel agent.

When the pregnancy test came back *positive,* I waited to tell Daryl in person. I wanted to see the look on his face when I gave him the good news. I greeted him in the driveway when he arrived that early evening. When I shared the victorious news, his face was as if he'd just seen a ghost. He was spooked beyond words. He shook his head in disbelief. He said, "How can you be? The doctor said it was *impossible*." That was the first time he had confessed the doctor's *true* report.

During those next few months, Daryl returned to his childhood faith and thanked the Lord for a true miracle. Our precious son, Robert Alexander, was born on February 3, 1975, at Bridgeport Hospital. We call him "Bo."

Bo is a gifted young man. He oil-paints and composes music as a music engineer. He graduated from an audio engineering school in Manhattan. He built his own recording studio. He also has a two-year associate's degree from Case Western Reserve in Cleveland. He was planning to become a mechanical engineer but followed his love for music instead. In a private high school, he was an all-A-student and played varsity soccer. In grade school, he always represented his private Christian school in each citywide mathematic competition.

He's a handsome, gentle, and kind-hearted young man who is discovering his path in life. We have sincere hopes that his life and all of his music and artistic talents will bring glory to the Lord in a unique and extraordinary way someday. Our son was a joy to rear and remains a blessing to us. He's a true gift from the Lord.

"God, who at various times and in various ways spoke

in time past to the fathers by the prophets, has in these last days spoken to us by His Son, whom He has appointed heir of all things, through whom also He made the worlds; who being the brightness of His glory and the express image of His person, and upholding all things by the word of His power, when He had by Himself purged our sins, sat down at the right hand of the Majesty on high, having become so much better than the angels, as He has by inheritance obtained a more excellent name than they."

Hebrews 1:1–5 (NKJV)

CHAPTER FIVE

A Brush with Death, But, Perfect Love Casts Out Fear

We remained another year in Connecticut after our son was born. Our lovely five-bedroom colonial home on Canoe Brook Lane overlooked a lake lined with tall pine trees. One day that idyllic setting turned into a living nightmare.

At seven months of age, Robert loved to scoot around in his round walk-about on wheels. The hardwood floors created an unobstructed pathway to travel from the kitchen, down a hallway, through the dining room back to the kitchen. I sat at the dining room table writing out nametags for an upcoming Christian Women's Club luncheon.

My stepdaughter Tammie and her friend Martha had come home from middle school a few minutes earlier. Completing some chores was required before leaving the house again, so the teens immediately went to the basement laundry room to fold some clothes. The door leading to the cement floor basement was right off the kitchen. As a family, we were careful about keeping that door shut. However, that day, when Martha followed Tammie downstairs, she left the door open. Soon our curious baby inched toward the edge of the stairs when he heard their chatter below. He fell down the stairs onto the cement below.

My brain translated a bucket bouncing down the flight of stairs, but when Tammie started screaming, I realized my baby had crashed and he might be dead. Seconds later, I met tearful Tammie holding him. He wasn't making a sound, and his head was teetering. My immediate panic was that his neck was broken. We rushed upstairs to the kitchen wall phone. I had just called to doctor's office to make an appointment, so the address book was open to the phone number. My pediatrician came right on the line. He began firing questions at me… "Is he conscious? Is there any blood on his head? Is there bleeding coming out of his nose or his ears?" To each question, I kept shouting, "I don't know! I don't know!" He instructed me to drive straight to Bridgeport Hospital and try to *keep him from going unconscious.*

It was raining out, but I ran every red light with caution. Tammie held baby Robert and kept frantically blowing into his face each time his eyes closed to dose off. She managed to keep him from going to sleep, which probably saved his life.

After a series of rapid questions, the young emergency room physician intimated that I was *overreacting* because my seven-month-old baby's head was not swollen. However, after the X-ray showed a hairline fracture on his skull, he quickly apologized. He immediately sat me in a wheelchair to hold my baby as he personally wheeled us onto the elevator. When the doors opened to the seventh pediatric floor, I remained in complete shock. We were led into a very long, dark corridor.

The only illumination providing light was a huge, colorful,

brightly lit stained-glass scene on the wall at the far end of the hallway. I came out of shock when I viewed Jesus embracing a few children. It was a Bible scene from Matthew 19:14, "Let the little children come to me, and do not hinder them, for the kingdom of heaven belongs to such as these."

Seeing Jesus touching children pulled me back to my faith in an instant. I began to weep, and at that precise moment, the Lord gently spoke to my heart. *"I love your son more than you do. He will not die, be at peace."* God's peace flooded my soul and comforted me like a warm blanket in freezing rain.

The nurses carefully lined his metal crib with furry lambskins to prevent him from banging his now swollen head. Swelling relieves the pressure inside the brain, so it was a good sign, according to the pediatric neurosurgeon. My husband and I took turns staying with him while rocking him until he slept. My mother flew in from Detroit to help out.

The result of that near-death scare was now my cross to bear. I became a crazed mother that never left my baby unattended in fear that something might happen to him. Whenever I left the room, I made sure someone watched over him in my place. *Fear hath torment.*

"Therefore, if anyone is in Christ, he is a new creation; old things have passed away; behold, all things have become new" (2 Corinthians 5:17, NKJV).

"When the Spirit of truth comes, he will guide you into all the truth, for he will not speak on his own authority, but whatever he hears he will speak, and he will declare to you the things that are to come."

John 16:13

And hope does not put us to shame, because God's love has been poured into our hearts through the Holy Spirit who has been given to us.

Romans 5:5

CHAPTER SIX

Mary Magdalene Sets Me Free

There was once a time when I was uncertain about my identity with Christ Jesus. Although we became faithful members of a loving Christian church with wonderful fellowship among our adult Sunday school class, I still struggled.

I had been a Christian for over a year without any positive transformation in my life. I kept looking for the "new creation in Christ" to emerge. But sadly, I was the same old creature who erupted with anger when things didn't go my way.

Fortunately, Jesus rescued me from my *self*. Throughout a dreadful year of *me* unsuccessfully solving the conflicts in our family, I doubted my salvation experience. Tempted to throw in the towel because I hadn't changed one bit, caused doubt that Jesus was real.

Only when I stepped off the throne and stopped calling the shots did I experience a flood of *genuine peace*. The weight of the world lifted off my shoulders. No longer in control, I completely trusted Jesus to take care of things. From the moment I "let go and let God" gain *complete* control of my life, Jesus provided glorious grace.

This amazing transformation came one day by a revelation in a hand-written letter from my brother, David, who lived in Detroit.

Before I read his letter, I felt defeated as a born-again Christian because I hadn't changed one bit. As I opened the envelope, I began thinking about a story Billy Graham told about himself in a televised sermon.

Dr. Graham had explained that knowing Christ as *Savior* (just to get to heaven) was like having fire insurance. However, allowing Jesus Christ to become the *Lord* and *Master* was the key to victorious living. Each Sunday, as a twelve-year-old lad, Billy was antsy sitting on the church pew. He watched the wall clock above the pulpit slowly click by while the pastor preached the Sunday sermon. Then, one day, he made Christ *Lord of All.* The following Sunday, he couldn't get enough of that very same preacher!

As I read my brother's letter, something broke inside of me. Whatever it was he wrote caused me to realize that I was seated on a throne, "calling the shots," while my Savior Jesus was in orbit, floating around my universe. Yes, I knew Jesus as Savior. But was He *Lord* of everything? As soon as I surrendered the throne to the King of Kings, my Lord Jesus took command of my life. Jesus was now seated on the throne as King Jesus. I actually felt like heavy bricks were lifted off my shoulders. I wept tears of relief in this freedom. Finally, Jesus was crowned Lord of all! Suddenly, I related to how Billy Graham went from only knowing Jesus as *Savior* to making Christ Jesus his *Lord* and *Master.*

Years later, my sister-in-law, Lorraine, asked me if I remembered getting a certain letter from David. My eyes widened because it was the letter that saved my life. "Yes!" I exclaimed. "Tell me what you know about that letter David wrote me."

Lorraine shared how David sat at the dining room table composing that letter to me. Years earlier, I had led my brother to the Lord, so most of our conversations were about Jesus. However, he had never written me a letter.

While writing from the dining room table, he stopped for a certain *God thought* to continue. "Lorraine, you know that song in the movie *Jesus Christ Super Star* that Mary Magdalene sang about *not knowing how to really love Jesus?*" He began to hum the tune waiting for her to sing the words.

Lorraine has a beautiful voice and has sung countless solos in church cantatas. She knows the lyrics to every Shania Twain song out there, as well the words to most Christian and secular pop music. She was baffled by the tune. She shrugged her shoulders, returning a blank stare.

It was an important point my brother was attempting to make. Frustrated, he threw down the pen and rose from the table. He flicked on the radio. That beautiful song by Andrew Lloyd Webber was playing at that exact moment! Dave rushed back to his letter and wrote out the lyrics.

Back when that movie came out, I was deeply moved by that song. I saw the movie seven times, inviting various friends to go with me.

Daryl said, "Why do you keep buying movie theatre tickets?

Why don't you just buy the soundtrack?" God used that rock opera to stir my emotions and soften my heart, especially when the Crucifixion masterpiece by Rembrandt flashed on the screen.

The movie script was written from the viewpoint of Judas, with a secular intention of proving Jesus was merely a mortal man. However, the heavenly melody of Mary Magdalene's song is an exact copy of a theme from Mendelssohn's violin concerto in E minor. Felix Mendelssohn, a devout Christian, also composed *Hark the Herald, Angels Sing,* and other iconic hymns. Inspired by the Holy Spirits over a century earlier, the *anointing still ignites hearts* to bring forth inspiration and life.

MARY MAGDALENE

I don't know how to love him.
What to do, how to move him.
I've been changed, yes really changed.
In these past few days, when I've seen myself,
I seem like someone else.
I don't know how to take this.
I don't see why he moves me.
He's a man. He's just a man.
And I've had so many men before,
In very many ways,
He's just one more.
Should I bring him down?
Should I scream and shout?
Should I speak of love,
Let my feelings out?

I never thought I'd come to this.
What's it all about?
Don't you think it's rather funny,
I should be in this position.
I'm the one who's always been
So calm, so cool, no lover's fool,
Running every show.
He scares me so.
I never thought I'd come to this.
What's it all about?
Yet, if he said he loved me,
I'd be lost. I'd be frightened.
I couldn't cope, just couldn't cope.
I'd turn my head. I'd back away.
I wouldn't want to know.
He scares me so.
I want him so.
I love him so.

Andrew Lloyd Webber, 1970

That languishing song touched my soul because I had fearfully struggled relating to Jesus. *I didn't know how to love Him.* He was more than a man; He was the Lord, God Almighty. His unconditional love moved me to open my heart. *Trusting* Him with my entire life required the realization that I could not love Him with my own ability. Exposing my pride, admitting my failures and weaknesses to ask for help became the first step in trusting Him to make things better.

"Jesus stood and cried out, saying, "If anyone thirsts, let him come to Me and drink. He who believes in Me, as the Scripture has said, out of his heart will flow rivers of living water"

John 7:37–38, NKJV

No one born of God makes a practice of sinning, for God's seed abides in him, and he cannot keep on sinning because he has been born of God.

1 John 3:9

CHAPTER SEVEN

Sherry Berry Pinpoints the Source of Panic Attacks

Life is never certain. Just when we peacefully settled into a wonderful, Christ-centered church with our teens excited about their youth program, God uprooted us. It was a scary time because my husband was suddenly unemployed with no certain future in sight. We needed to move from Connecticut.

Two years earlier, my husband made a major career change working as an executive for a Fortune 500 company in Dayton, Ohio, to purchase into an old, established Cadillac dealership in Bridgeport, Connecticut. However, this plan fell through when the owner reneged on selling, going back on his former "gentleman's handshake" agreement.

We pursued a few options that included going to Dallas Theological Seminary or pursuing another Cadillac agency opportunity in Columbus, Ohio, but nothing was etched in stone.

While waiting it out, we moved into my childhood home with my widowed mother in Dearborn.

Scott, my fifteen-year-old stepson, was already enrolled in a Christian boarding school on Long Island in Stony Brook, NY. My stepdaughter, Tammie, age sixteen, made the move with us.

My first panic attack occurred in a chiropractor's office as a first-time patient. When the nurse escorted me into the exam room, I felt perfectly fine. "The doctor will be right in," she said, smiling.

She departed, closing the door. It suddenly felt as if a casket lid had shut down on me. Unable to breathe, my heart began pounding out of my chest. I bolted from the exam room and rushed down the hallway, desperate for oxygen. The nurse was back seated at a station facing me as I clawed her desk, desperate for air. Her eyes bulged at my bizarre behavior. "I can't breathe!" I managed to gasp. Then my breath returned, allowing me to feel normal. Feeling very embarrassed, I rushed back to the exam room to grab my purse before departing and waving her a meek apology.

Similar episodes followed, causing me to think I was getting early signs of *emphysema*. I had never heard of an *anxiety disorder*. Consequently, when an episode suddenly comes on, I fully understand why sufferers of this depilating disorder become homebound with the terror of it happening in public places.

During our short and temporary stay in Dearborn in 1976, I paid a visit to my Ohio friend, Sherry Berry, who was instrumental in leading me to the Lord a few years earlier. We were seated in her church for a Sunday morning service when I felt this scary sensation coming back on my chest. As I felt my breathing become more labored, I noted there were no windows in the sanctuary. I leaned over to whisper to her. "I'm having trouble breathing in here. If I suddenly run out for some air, it's because I'm getting emphysema." I was thirty years old.

"It's just Satan," Sherry responded, sounding annoyed. "Just rebuke him." She spoke with true authority before placing her hand firmly on my back. Then she began quietly praying in a foreign language. I had never heard anyone speak in tongues, but the heaviness immediately lifted from my chest. I became free to enter into the lively praise music and enjoy the uplifting preaching without fear.

Later that evening, in her lovely home, Sherry explained that the Baptism of the *Holy Spirit* was something I needed in my life. I agreed. She prayed for me and began singing over me in a beautiful heavenly language. I felt a flutter in my heart as a witness that God had truly touched me with a *Baptism of the Holy Spirit*.

A few days later, my own unique heavenly communication was released within my human spirit. A beautiful language erupted from my innermost being, which truly felt like rivers of living waters flowing out from my belly. It is this ability to pray in tongues that makes me certain that there is a part of the Godhead that resides in me—Father, Son, and Holy Spirit.

Today, all these years later, now 2022, our son Scottie is also moving in the Holy Spirit with a deep compassion to reach street people in an unsavory area in Columbus, Ohio. His vocation in chemical dependency is through a Christian agency that makes available residential treatment. He offers a "prayer and pizza" get-together every Friday night. Scott shares a Biblical message to the downtrodden coming in off the dangerous streets. He has water baptized many weary and lost souls into salvation with Christ

Jesus. His heart of mercy is precious to us and to the Lord.

Scott wrote, "*The only way the chains of addiction will be broken on Sullivant Avenue, in this community and others like it, is through the power of the Holy Spirit. The chains of addiction are wrapped too tightly here—to such a degree that other methods to get clean just won't work. We are standing on God's promises to miraculously break chains of addiction, to heal hearts, minds, and physical bodies of those trapped in addiction.*

In August of 2022, God gave me a vision. From an elevated position of twenty or thirty feet and directly above the center of Sullivant Avenue at the corner of Richardson, on the Hilltop, I looked down the center of Sullivant Avenue toward the east. I began to see the Blood of Christ, starting in the middle of the street, spreading across Sullivant, covering buildings, and then down the alleyways and over houses, spreading to other streets. The Blood was not deep, just a layer. Once everything became red, a large white dove, the size of a car, descended on Sullivant."

The Holy Spirit is real.

Scott's older sister, Tamra Farah, met her husband at Oral Roberts University. Barry is the son of the late Dr. Charles Farah, former Professor of Theology at ORU. They are busy using their incredible sphere of influence to help better the world by promoting conservative and pro-life values. Through strategic initiatives, supporting Christian advocacy, they both write for national publications and broadcast weekly podcast teachings and exhortations through *Culture Shift by Barry Farah.* Through the years, the Farahs have both served on the board of directors of various authentic faith-based coalitions impacting the world. I keep encouraging them to run for Congress!

God has been faithful to keep His mighty Hand upon our blended family that experienced many emotional challenges for all of us in the early years of marriage. The Holy Spirit is *real*!

> *"And they were all filled with the Holy Spirit and began to speak with other tongues, as the Spirit gave them utterance."*

Acts 2:4, NKJV

Let the word of Christ dwell in you richly, teaching and admonishing one another in all wisdom, singing psalms and hymns and spiritual songs, with thankfulness in your hearts to God.

Colossians 3:16

But to this day the Lord has not given you a heart to understand or eyes to see or ears to hear.

Deuteronomy 29:4

CHAPTER EIGHT

Merlin R. Carothers, "From Prison to Praise" Leading to a Miracle Healing

One afternoon, while living at Mom's for a few months, I placed my fourteen-month-old baby down for a nap. He felt warm, so I gave him a dose of baby Tylenol, which he promptly threw up. He awakened an hour later, crying and on fire. As I held him, his little body went into a grand mal seizure that didn't stop until we arrived at Oakwood Hospital twenty minutes later. His temperature was 107, so physicians thought he suffered from spinal meningitis. The source of the infection was in his ears. Thankfully, it was cleared up by an antibiotic and antihistamines.

After we moved to Columbus for another major career move, ear infections plagued my son for the next year. Symptoms started with a runny nose causing bacteria to the inner Eustachian tube, resulting in an infection.

My hands constantly felt my toddler's head for a body-temperature read. If his nose started to run, no problem; I had a cupboard filled with grape-flavored liquid Dimetapp and a vast assortment of antihistamines and other fever-reducing medicines. An allergist tested him with needle pricks down his back to determine food or element allergies. No allergy shots were required, so Mommy was on guard twenty-four hours a day like a hovering lunatic.

A best-seller entitled *From Prison to Praise* by Merlin Caroth-ers kept being recommended by various church friends. But the book was sold out each time I tried to buy it. One morning, during a five-day fast, I walked into my local Christian bookstore and immediately spotted the book staring back at me. I can remember that moment as if it was yesterday. I came home and read the en-tire book in one afternoon.

Since I was *imprisoned by fear*, Merlin Carothers opened my eyes to the principle of *praising God* in the midst of pain and dif-ficult circumstances. That night, I was almost asleep under the bed covers when the *Holy Spirit* spoke to my heart. An inner voice instructed me to take a *step of faith* for my son's healing.

What He instructed me to do felt like a command to journey through a deep forest in the middle of the night without a flashlight or compass to find my way back out. The challenge was a severe test of faith. The Holy Spirit instructed me to empty out the two shelves of my baby's medicines. I couldn't move and probably stopped breathing for a few seconds.

I reluctantly got out of bed to carry out the task. Shaking in my boots comes to mind. Our trash compactor was located in the garage. Once you pressed the button, that was it. The glass bottles and soda cans were completely crushed up to neatly fit in a com-pact bag.

My heart pounded as I dumped out countless bottles of medi-cine. I purposely left a container of baby aspirin on the shelf "just in case" my son developed a temperature. After pressing the button to hear all those glass bottles and plastic prescription containers getting crushed, I felt triumphant.

After climbing back into bed, I pulled up the bed covers up around my neck. *You didn't get it all* is what I heard in my spirit. I froze with fear. *No, Lord, I can't throw out the baby aspirin!* I remained paralyzed for several minutes. In slow motion, I got out of bed feeling like I was about to skydive out of a moving airplane. Trembling, I reached the kitchen cupboard in tears. I continued crying as I placed the baby aspirin in the trash compactor. *Letting go is a terrifying moment in faith.*

About a week later, my precious baby boy developed full-blown symptoms of another ear infection. Remaining on guard all night, I prayed for hours from his wicker rocking chair before taking sleep on the floor below his crib.

Early the next morning, my husband challenged my sanity and insisted on taking his son to the pediatrician. Daryl came home with the usual diagnosis. "The doctor said there is fluid behind his ears which will most likely lead to an infection." Before leaving for work, Daryl handed me two prescribed scripts for an antihistamine and an antibiotic. We were starting all over.

Throughout that day, I kept feeling my son's forehead for a possible temperature rise, a telltale sign of infected ears. The ultimate test of faith came later in the day. Baby's nose was still running, and his head felt hot.

In that moment of fearfulness, I lifted the receiver off the kitchen wall phone to dial up the pharmacy. Suddenly, I felt a sudden burst of faith rise up in righteous indignation. I stomped my foot and yelled out, "NO!" before slamming the phone back unto the receiver. It was a defining moment of faith and of triumph over fear.

My son *never* had another ear infection for the rest of his life.

CHAPTER NINE

Mike Evans and a Supernatural Healing

Those early years of discovering Jesus were adventurous and somewhat scary. As new converts, we were also venturing into another career move in an unfamiliar community.

In 1976, we opened the Daryl Sanders Cadillac agency on Sawmill Road in Dublin, a lovely suburb of Columbus, Ohio.

The busy first month in our modest home was spent unpacking, cleaning, painting, and enrolling our two teens in Worthington Christian high school. Our eldest boy, Scott, had spent his freshman year at the Stony Brook School on Long Island. Ned Graham was also enrolled there, so it was encouraging to know the school met the excellent Christian standards of Dr. Billy Graham.

One sunny day, I ventured out of the house with my baby, now seventeen months old. I placed Robert in the stroller for our first outing. I spotted two moms in a front yard a few houses down the street. Their small children played on the sidewalk while they stood chatting.

As a newcomer, I felt eager to make new friendships with other young mothers. As I approached the two women, I grinned at them with my usual friendliness. My long brown hair blew in the breeze; I felt carefree and excited to meet them. It was a beautiful summer day.

"Hi, I'm Barbara Sanders; we just moved in a month ago." The two girls stared at me with blank expressions. They seemed to shrivel with intimidation before getting struck mute. I expected a "hi, welcome to the neighborhood," or "oh, your baby is so cute; what's his name?" They were sullen and did not speak. I had heard of "getting the cold shoulder," but it had never happened to me until that moment.

As I walked away, feeling shunned, a painful lump formed in my throat. Tears rolled down my cheeks before I let my heart talk to the Lord about being snubbed.

Lord, obviously, those girls aren't Christians. I forgive them for being unkind to me. I promise to represent Jesus in a loving and caring way to anyone who doesn't know you, but I vow never to cultivate friendships with anyone unless they belong to you, Lord.

Perhaps the Lord hardened their heart to get my attention about casting my valuable pearls too recklessly. I encircled the subdivision, feeling very lonely. I missed my Connecticut Christian friends. This was a new city, and so far, my own neighbors didn't accept me.

During that sad stroll, I spotted a van in a driveway with a PTL (Praise the Lord) bumper sticker. I made a mental note of it and continued on home. While resting on my porch steps, I leafed through the envelopes collected from the mailbox. Suddenly, a loud voice erupted from the side shrubbery blocking my view of who was talking to me. The exorbitant woman burst forth, still talking rapidly as she rushed toward me.

"Well, there you are!" she gushed. "I've been watching all month to get a glimpse of you." Her friendly face beamed as she appeared in full view. "I live four houses down. I'm Betty Wilson. Welcome to our neighborhood! It's so nice to finally meet you." She smiled with genuine kindness. Amazed to see God *answer my prayer* so quickly, I was actually stunned with silence for a brief moment.

As a woman in her fifties, Betty didn't seem threatened by my attractive appearance. As we chatted, I quickly learned she was a genuine church lady. Of course, she was. She seemed to know a lot about the subdivision, so I inquired about the house with the PTL bumper sticker. I also asked if there might be a neighborhood Bible study.

"Oh, yes, some gals meet every Thursday up on that end of the sub; that's probably the house." She paused while lowering her voice. "But they believe Christians should *speak in tongues*, so I don't know if you'd be interested in that group." I smiled, getting that timely information. *It was the very group I was looking for!*

The following Thursday morning, I drove off to go shopping. Scott was home babysitting for me. As I drove away with divine thoughts of spending a few hours at the mall, the Holy Spirit reminded me of the Bible study. I turned the car around and stopped at the house I had seen with the PTL bumper sticker.

A young boy answered the door. He said, "Well, it's usually here, but today, they're having Bible study down the street in that first cult-a-sac." He pointed out the direction, and by the number of cars in the driveway, I found the house. Later, I learned that the PTL sticker van was the home of Rosie Cunningham.

Several women were gathered at a kitchen table praying when I rang the doorbell. The surprised hostess graciously invited me to join them. I learned that they had just asked the Lord to "send more Christians to the neighborhood." Emma Lou Roller, Ginger Cermelj, and Rosie Cunningham were among those seated there and remain friends of mine to this day, all these decades later.

Rosie invited me to attend a weekly prayer meeting across town at Pastor Mabel Whipple's church. This gathering was my first exposure to what charismatics consider "being slain in the spirit." When receiving prayer by a pastor or church leader, the recipient "falls out" under the tangible anointing of the Holy Spirit. Your body becomes overwhelmed to the point of falling down under its power. You land on the floor. However, there is usually someone behind to "catch you" from falling too hard. It's a blissful state while you're lying on the floor basking in His glory. This downtime is also considered "soaking" in His presence.

Each week, Mabel taught us an inspired scripture lesson from the Bible. Afterward, she ministered with the laying on of hands and personal prophecy. Decades later, I heard Pastor Rod Parsley share that Pastor Mabel Whipple had personally led him to Jesus when he was nine years old.

An adorable Dominican nun also attended Mabel's prayer gathering wearing her full habit. Sister Angelica was 4'10 inches tall with bright blue eyes. Her joyful face revealed that she loved the Lord with all her heart. I got the biggest kick seeing her fall out under the spirit wearing her penguin-looking, black-and-white nun's habit.

At home, when I shared these charismatic experiences with Daryl, he expressed skepticism about falling out by a touch from the Lord. However, he was about to get a first-hand experience that erased all doubt.

My husband had been running five days a week at a nearby high school track. His left knee began retaining fluid with intense pain. As a former football player for Ohio State University, he visited his former physical trainer. He advised Daryl to ice his knee when swollen and hope for the best. Probable knee surgery was necessary if swelling continued. Daryl stopped running and managed to limp around in pain for several more months.

Rosie and her husband Terry invited us to a seminar hosted by Pastor Gene Speich, founder of Evangel Temple Assemblies of God. Evangelist Mike Evans, President of *Jews for Jesus,* was speaking at this three-day evangelistic event.

Daryl and I had never attended a charismatic meeting together, so we had little expectations. Evangelist Mike Evans began the service by exhorting the large gathering with scriptures from the

Bible. Suddenly, he stopped to respond to the Holy Spirit. Through a *Word of Knowledge,* he announced, "There is a man with a knee injury; please come forward to receive your healing."

When Daryl shot out of his seat, I was amazed to see him act so quickly. As a melancholy, he usually mulls things over before making a decision or responding. He was the only one to go forward. Mike stepped off the platform to pray for Daryl.

He said, "Before I pray for your healing, I have a prophecy for you. There is a call of ministry upon your life. You are going to be a wealthy man, and I pray that money doesn't destroy your trust in the Lord." I don't remember the exact words, but it was something to that effect.

There were two men standing behind him serving as "catchers" in the event Daryl went out under the spirit. Mike placed his hands on my husband before he gracefully fell backward, as gentle as a feather. I remember that it almost looked like he fell out in slow motion. That glorious night Daryl came in the church a cripple—limping with a throbbing swollen knee. But God! He left totally healed by Jesus! He began running again the next day. The Holy Spirit is for real!

> *He jumped to his feet and began to walk. Then he went*
> *with them into the temple courts, walking and jumping,*
> *and praising God.*

Acts 3:8, NIV

CHAPTER TEN

Pat Robertson, Kenneth Hagin, Jr. Costa Deir, Mike Evans & the Supernatural

Outdoor JESUS festivals were popular summer events in the mid-1970s and '80s. Throughout a ten-year span, our church youth group attended the outdoor rallies on Pennsylvania farmland for an outdoor spiritual extravaganza. Makeshift entrance gates were set up on an expansive open field. Thousands of pre-registered attendees arrived in motorcycles, cars, trucks, vans, and RVs from all across the nation.

Visitors stopped at the gates to receive welcome packets containing a schedule of the weekend events. Before cell phones, there was information about a first aid station and receiving or making emergency phone calls. Somehow, the bathroom and showers were set up with running water.

My two teens and three of their Michigan cousins joined our church's youth group to attend JESUS '76. My aunt Katie and my second mom, Mary Koester, accompanied them. I stayed home with my baby boy.

This 1976 event featured the 700 Club host, Pat Robertson, along with a cast of other national ministry guests and various popular Christian music groups.

Denominational barriers were non-existent as Baptists, Presbyterians, Lutherans, Catholics, Mennonites, Nazarenes, and Pentecostals worshipped to anointed music within massive crowds gathered to exalt the Lord.

Numerous big top tents accommodated about a thousand people in each tent to hear a special guest speaker. A large stage was amped up with huge speakers to blast music for miles. Different tents offered specific teachings on salvation, healing, deliverance, and receiving the Baptism of the Holy Spirit, with qualified adult counselors ready to minister to individuals seeking prayer.

A large pond provided a perfect sanctuary for water baptism, and every hour, several converts were dunked to identify with the death, burial, and resurrection of our Lord Jesus Christ.

The atmosphere was certainly electrifying, with about 30,000 Christian believers seeking God on a gigantic campground.

About four years later, I got a chance to attend JESUS '80 with an acquaintance from our weekly AGLOW Bible study. Marianne did not want to "rough it" by sleeping in a tent with the rest of our church moms with kids, so she rented a comfortable air-conditioned Winnebago. Danny and Brian, her two pre-teen sons, joined us. I certainly appreciated the comforts of her generosity, even though I felt like a prima donna when we pulled up.

The featured guest speakers were Rev. Kenneth Hagin, Jr., Evangelist Costa Deir, and Evangelist Mike Evans, founder of Jews for Jesus. Since my husband had received a miracle knee healing through his ministry, I planned to attend all of Mike Evan's sessions!

Mike Evan's first session has held under a large picnic shelter up on a hill above the valley, where the large stage was situated with giant speakers to amplify the powerful music of Second Chapter of Acts, a Dove Award-winning music group.

Marianne and I ended up on a blanket way out near trees because the crowd was so large.

Mike taught on the subject of "Abba Father," and he prophesied that the Holy Spirit would "release a 'double portion' of the Holy Spirit to various people."

Immediately, I got slammed by an unseen force, nearly knocking me over. Since I was already seated on the ground, I quickly braced my arms to keep from falling out. The Holy Spirit ignited my spirit by telling me that I had been a recipient of a *double portion* even though I had no Bible understanding of what that actually meant.

But God knew the spiritual warfare affecting our group. He was equipping me with needed special grace to prayerfully intercede in a very serious situation involving a child of sexual abuse that had not yet been revealed.

Later that day, I sat in on Evangelist Costa Deir, who had preached at a Word of Faith conference in New Orleans. He was a dynamite vessel of God affiliated with Elim Bible Institute in upstate New York. Costa sported a huge handlebar mustache over a mischievous grin. He preached with a tambourine to shake when emphasizing an important scripture or saying something funny. He laughed when giving glory to God—which was often—because he was so full of joy. Costa was an entertaining speaker you'd never forget.

Even though he was engaging with humor, his revelation of Scripture was profound. He had zingers to deliver, and I caught one, big time. He challenged us to operate in the *fullness* of the Holy Spirit. "When you place *blame* on someone during an unresolved conflict, you *neutralize* the Holy Spirit in your life," he cautioned while shaking his tambourine. I got it. I came under deep conviction because I blamed my step-children for causing discord in our family. The Lord had worked on my heartstrings all night long.

Early Saturday morning, Marianne, her boys, and I set out with aluminum lawn chairs for a ring-side seat in Mike Evan's picnic shelter two hours before schedule.

After an hour and two cups of coffee consumed that morning in the camper, I needed a potty break before Mike Evans arrived.

On the way to the restroom area, my heart was heavy, under deep conviction, for placing blame on my step-children. My spirit began silently praying for the *grace* to forgive. I confessed my sin of *blame* and made a conscious *decision* to *forgive*.

It felt like a ton of bricks was lifted off my shoulders. I actually felt an *expansion* of the Holy Spirit, allowing me to now operate in His *fullness* with a renewed surge of power. Costa was exactly right.

By the time Mike Evans arrived, there were about six hundred people expectantly gathered to hear him minister prophetically with a word from the Lord.

During his opening prayer, a woman cried out in an inappropriate interruption. He shushed her gracefully. Then he explained that the Holy Spirit is a *gentleman.* Therefore, we should not get loud when the Lord is present, especially during prayer. That kind of disruption often happens when God's glory manifests. The enemy attempts to bring commotion and confusion whenever the Lord is doing His deepest work.

Mike Evans ended his hour-long lesson by clarifying the "double-portion" Word of Knowledge from the previous session. He said, "Yesterday, the Holy Spirit told me that *seven* people had received the double portion of the Holy Spirit.

Suddenly, I began to shake uncontrollably. I collapsed back in my lawn chair because the Holy Spirit struck me *completely unconscious.* I left the present to enter another realm as if going under for surgery. Apostle Paul described this as not knowing if he was *in or out of his body.*

When I *"came to"* about forty-five minutes later, the shelter area was vacated except for five or six strangers standing above me with extended hands, touching me in reverence. I looked up to see tears streaming down faces as they wept in awe. God had drenched me in His presence. I had not yet tried to speak with words.

"I will come to visions and revelations of the Lord: I know a man in Christ who fourteen years ago—whether in the body I do not know, or whether out of the body I do not know. God knows—

Such one was caught up to the third heaven. And I know such a man—whether in the body or out of the body I do not know, God knows—how he was caught up into Paradise and heard inexpressible words, which it is not lawful for a man to utter" (2 Corinthians 121:1–4, NKJV).

Marianne and her boys hung in there until I awakened. She was also weeping. Then, all of a sudden, Brian, age 11, went ballistic. He began cursing and viciously punching his mother for trying to subdue him. He had been a problem child for a few years. She looked helpless and searched my face with pleading eyes. My thought was to speak comfort to her, but when I opened my mouth to speak in English, all that came out was *tongues*. So, I picked up my notebook and pen off the ground with the intention of writing out my thoughts to her. But I began shaking so badly that I could not hold on to the pen. She left with the boys to return to the camper.

Still shaking, I could barely walk. It probably took me over an hour to reach our campsite. When I finally arrived and climbed aboard, Brian was still enraged. After sitting down, I made another attempt to speak to the situation. However, this time, when

I opened my mouth to speak something comforting to Marianne, only a prophetic word came out!

"My daughter, do not become fainthearted. Walk in faith...do not fear...this is my battle...be diligent to pray and don't give up on your son...your children belong to Me."

I was thirty-two years old and completely baffled by the prophetic realm that had taken complete control of me. Soon thereafter, I began to feel earthbound. I rushed from the camper to locate Judy, a Messianic believer who was schooled in the area of deliverance.

Fortunately, my comrade from church was at the campsite nearby. She returned with me to pray over Brian. For the next hour, we cast out demons, to the amazement of his mother. He was set free to be the sweet little boy God intended him to be. It was years later that his mother learned a trusted female employee close to the family had been sexually abusing him.

Later in the evening, a very calm and secure Brian solemnly declared, "We need to have a *foot washing*." Marianne looked shocked but also delighted. To our knowledge, Brian had never learned about the sacrament of foot-washing prior to that very moment! He needed to wash his mother's feet because of the defilement he caused by dishonoring her.

We filled a dishpan with warm, sudsy water and produced some fresh towels. What followed was the most powerful healing of emotions that I've ever witnessed in my life.

When this little boy got on his knees to wash his mother's feet in humility, she wailed with grateful tears of anguish. She washed Brian's feet in return and cried her heart out over him with unconditional love. They both cried from the depth of their souls.

When this tender-hearted child washed my feet, it felt as if it was Jesus touching me. It was so holy and sacred that I could not find words to describe the moment. I wept with tears of gratitude for the healing God had done in Marianne's family and in me.

Those three glorious days were dramatic beyond comprehension.

Those two young lads grew up to become accomplished professionals making their parents very proud. I was privileged to witness Brian's glorious wedding when he married a lovely Christian girl. They are happily married with sweet children, a true blessing from the Lord.

God is good, and the Holy Spirit is FOR REAL!

CHAPTER ELEVEN

Children's Hospital
Mending Hearts as a Volunteer

One cold February afternoon, I stood at the kitchen sink washing dishes praying and talking to the Lord. My son was now four years old. I felt an unction to pray for hospitalized children around the world. During my dialogue with the Holy Spirit, I added, "And Lord, you really need more Christian doctors and nurses to work in hospitals…"

So, how about you? The Holy Spirit didn't miss a beat.

I cringed because hospitals made me queasy. The last person I visited in the hospital made me nauseous at the sight and smell of medicinal procedures. Therefore, a hospital was the *last place* I'd ever volunteer my time. But I knew the Voice of the Lord. Challenged to the core of my being, my heart managed to stay closed to the idea. Peace eluded me as each day passed.

A week had gone by when a severe blizzard hit, closing down schools, stores, and most roads. "Okay, Lord. If there is a volunteer coordinator on duty at Children's Hospital to take my call, I'll know that I am to become a Candy Striper."

As the phone rang in the volunteer office, I secretly hoped no one picked up.

"Hello, this is Mrs. Taylor speaking. How can I help you?"

I thought, *She would have my maiden name to make it all the more convincing.* She was delighted to tell me about volunteerism at Children's Hospital.

After my training orientation the following week, I made a commitment to start off volunteering one day a week. Like putting my toe in the water to see if it was okay to go knee-deep in unchartered water.

My first assignment was in social services in an ancient building located behind Children's Hospital.

"Oh, thank you for coming!" Kathy gushed. "Can I get you some tea? Coffee?" The social worker was elated at the sight of me, and I'd quickly learn why.

Near Kathy's desk, on the cold marble floor, where I would sit for hours, were countless stacks of six by nine index cards needing filing. Personal computers had not yet been invented. Each card held important data…age of the patient, name of parents, address, phone, diagnosis, and personal details written by the social worker. About every fourth card, I noticed a red dot. To my alarm, this red dot indicated sexual abuse… at the bottom of the card would read something like "five-year-old female treated for gonorrhea, father and uncle living in the home tested positive…"

After six hours of reading the red-dotted cards, I realized that Franklin County had an epidemic of sexual abuse and these cards only indicated the tip of the iceberg. I prayed for each helpless victim, often with tears and anguish. I had to fight the feeling that

God did not exist if such evil prevailed.

Kathy was in her thirties, about my same age.

Each volunteer Tuesday, I faced several hundred cards with dread. The file cabinet was jammed tight with contact cards, so my fingers had to squeeze open enough room to add another card. My cuticles bled each time I left for home.

One day, I noticed a Christian self-help book on Kathy's desk after she had left for lunch. When she returned, I commented on the book.

"Oh, that's not *mine*. A co-worker must think I need to read it after all I am going through," she said in a deadpan voice.

"Oh? I am sorry…do you want to talk about it?"

She hesitantly began saying, "Well, my mother gave me and my four siblings up for adoption when I was nine. My father had committed suicide. But she kept the two youngest ones. A few months ago, after twenty-five years, I heard from my older brother wanting to meet me. He had located one of our sisters, too." Her voice was filled with despair for some reason.

"Well, that's wonderful," I said, perking up from my dismal spot on the floor. "Have you met them?"

"No, I figured they just want money from me."

I thought that was such a strange response, but I said nothing.

"Then, if that wasn't bad enough, my husband served me with

divorce papers the very same day that my brother called."

I stood up and placed a hand on her shoulder with compassion. "Can I pray for you? I am a Christian, and I believe God will give you the grace to get through this...Jesus loves you, Kathy."

She started to weep while I prayed. She was a dedicated social worker able to counsel many hurting children. Perhaps her own wounded inner child motivated her to enter social service.

We talked for a while. I spoke from her mother's perspective. Kathy only related to her mother from the injured heart of an abandoned nine-year-old.

"You don't remember the hardship she faced after your dad's death. She couldn't afford to keep all of you. It must have broken her heart to give you up."

"But she kept the two little ones," she said with harsh anguish.

"You don't have children, but I do. I know from a mother's heart that placing children in foster care was an act of love. She must have suffered for the rest of her life."

The following week, I noticed Kathy seemed a bit happier. She had made a decision to meet her siblings. I thanked the Lord with all my heart. Mission accomplished.

Before long, I was transferred to the main hospital to do phone-message errands. Patients could only call out on the telephones in the room, so the main switchboard was the only way to communicate with patients or visiting parents.

Delivering phone messages allowed me access to every floor. One day, I stopped in to greet a young patient sitting all alone in her room. She was about eight years old. Her name was Debbie.

"Wow, you must be very popular," I said, smiling brightly. "Look at all those cards covering your wall!"

"No, it's only because I have been here so long, that's why." She sounded glum but did not appear physically ill.

"Well, tell me why you've been here for so long."

"I have a blood clot on my leg, and it won't go away. I've been here for over nine weeks. The medicine isn't working, and I can't go home till it disappears."

"Tell me how that happened," I said, taking a seat on the side of her bed. I knew a blood clot could be fatal if it traveled to her heart, lungs, or brain.

"Well, I was on the playground, and that mean bully Tommy kicked me in the leg." She sneered when speaking his name.

"I know that must have really hurt. I am sorry that happened to you. Have you forgiven Tommy for doing that to you?"

Her head lowered in conviction. "No…but…I know I should," she said hesitantly, sounding as if she had a genuine conviction from the heart.

"Well, perhaps by forgiving Tommy, the medicine will start to work, and you can go home. I'd like to pray that you forgive Tommy and that the medicine works to dissolve your blood clot."

The following Tuesday, I stopped in to see Debbie. Her bed was empty because she had gone home. Mission accomplished.

On one phone delivery, I walked into what seemed like a death trap. Without knowing where I was going, I delivered a phone message to the nurse's station in the Intensive Care Unit with several children on life support. Every half hour, distraught parents were allowed in for about five minutes to sit next to the bed of a child sustained between life and death. It was visiting hour when I walked past several bedside parents.

If ever I came close to fainting, it was when the medicinal smells, ominous sounds of beeping monitors, IVs, breathing tubes, and the sad faces of hopeless parents invaded my senses like a bad dream. I think my heart stopped until I escaped that death chamber.

When I left the fourth-floor ICU, I vowed to *never* push open the double doors of horror again!

A few weeks later, I stood next to the switchboard operator waiting for more phone messages to deliver. I'd usually wait till I had a least five before taking off. After the call, she said, "That is the saddest thing I've ever heard."

She informed me that the grandparents were babysitting their four-year-old grandson when their daughter's husband had been hit by a motorcycle. After rushing to the hospital, the four-year-old was struck by a car running behind them through the parking lot. This little boy was up in ICU. Hearing this tragedy, with a four-year-old of my own, my heart was about to break.

After delivering several phone messages on that run, I entered the elevator to return to the switchboard. As if in a trance, I pressed the fourth-floor button on my way down. I passed the waiting room filled with about ten or eleven adults waiting to re-enter ICU for visitation.

After walking through open double doors of the ICU, a nurse stood next to the Johnson boy. She looked up at me as I approached the foot of his bed. I braced myself to view this little boy. I am crying now as I write this scene, which happened over forty years ago.

"Is this the little boy hit by a car?" I asked softly. She nodded yes.

This precious little blond child was unconscious. His head and face were swollen beyond recognition, with tubes going into his ears, nose, and mouth.

"How's he doing?" I asked like an idiot. The little boy was obviously near death.

She shrugged her shoulders. "What do you think?" she said, shaking her head with obvious remorse before walking away.

I gently touched his feet, covered by a blanket. I closed my eyes and silently prayed for healing and asked Jesus to take him to heaven if he didn't make it. Never have I ever felt so helpless.

When I came back through the double doors, every head in the waiting room jerked up. Any nurse coming through might have information concerning a child belonging to one of them. Dressed in my red and white Candy Stripe apron, I looked official.

"Where is the Johnson family?" I asked with a tone of authority. Every hand quickly pointed to the grandparents sitting close to the doorway entrance.

I turned to them—a weathered couple who appeared as if they had led a hard life. He was smoking a cigarette. "I am so sorry this happened. I just prayed for your grandson, and I want to pray for you now." Their grief-stricken faces nodded in agreement. I fell to my knees at their feet.

They clutched my hands as I prayed aloud for everyone to hear, including the two young physicians around the corner watching me.

By the time I finished praying, they were weeping with gratitude. I got up to head for the elevator. The two doctors seated in the adjacent office craned their necks to stare at me. Their faces registered shock as I walked past them confidently, my long ponytail bobbing up and down.

Back on the elevator, I began shaking from head to toe. By miraculously lifting me out of my comfort zone, Jesus placed me in a supernatural state to pray for the Johnson family. He heals the brokenhearted and grants grace to those suffering with grief.

With tremendous sadness, I learned that their grandson died a few days later. This sweet little boy was in the arms of Jesus. His grief-stricken grandparents were touched by a loving God through just an ordinary girl with a ponytail on a mission that day.

> *"But he said to me, 'My grace is sufficient for you, for my power is made perfect in weakness.' Therefore, I will boast all the more gladly of my weaknesses, so that the power of Christ may rest upon me."*

2 Corinthians, 12:9

"There is no fear in love; but perfect love casts out fear, because fear involves torment. But he who fears has not been made perfect in love."

1 John 4:18, NKJV

But I say, walk by the Spirit, and you will not gratify the desires of the flesh.

Galatians 5:16

CHAPTER TWELVE

Myles Munroe,
Jungle Jack Hanna,
and the Snake Pit Mission Field

The terror of snakes was passed on to me from my dad. At the impressionable age of eight, I watched my frightened father use a shovel to hack up a harmless garter snake in a woodpile behind my grandfather's house. That fear became a demonic stronghold, which nearly passed onto my son two decades later.

After my grandma Lambert died at age forty-nine, our family moved in with Grandpa to help rear my mother's younger sisters, who are close in age to me. As a child, after a hard rain, my two young aunts, Claire and Bonnie, would torment me by dangling earthworms in my face because I screamed at the sight of anything that slithered. Whenever it stormed, I waited several days before venturing outside.

Unfortunately, those fears carried over into my adult life. One summer day, on top of a stepladder, I attempted to hang a tree swing near a sandbox for my little boy. Home from college, Tammie assisted me as three-year-old Bo watched us.

As I flung the roped rubber tire over the large tree branch, I spotted a black snake slithering along at the base of the tree. Without a word, I leaped off the ladder's top rung. Racing into the house, I silently screamed, not wanting to scare my son and pass on my terror of snakes to him. Once I got inside the house, I shook from head to toe. Later that day, per my request, my husband took our little boy out to locate and handle the non-poisonous snake to make sure Bo wasn't afraid.

The next morning, I washed dishes at the kitchen window while Bo ate his cereal at the table. Outside, Sam, our big goofy Newfoundland dog, was near Bo's play area and tree swing, frantically scratching at the railroad ties that were boxed in the sand. Without thinking, I said, "Oh, that dumb dog is digging for that snake hiding in the sandbox."

"Mommy, why don't you like snakes?"

Caught off guard, I hesitated before answering his innocent question. How would I explain "fear" to a three-year-old?

"Well," I began with halted words, "you see, Mommy is a little bit afraid of snakes. But you shouldn't be afraid because snakes don't scare Daddy. He's strong and brave like you."

Bo looked at me and boldly stated, *"Fear ye not."*

What do you say to a three-year-old quoting Scripture? Busted. A year or so later, I discovered that my father had, indeed, passed on his fear of snakes to his grandson through me.

After Tammie transferred from the Ohio State University to Oral Roberts University in Tulsa, her leadership maturity quickly manifested while being recruited to step into the position of Spirit-Life Director of her dormitory floor, which entitled her to free tuition.

In her newly appointed position, Tammie got involved with intercessory prayer with other ORU team leaders. Every Friday night, fellow student, Myles Munroe, taught the principles of prayer to a group of dedicated prayer warriors. Tammie often quoted profound "spiritual tidbits" from Myles, who became an outstanding bestselling international author and Christian leader before his tragic death in a plane crash.

Our country home was located near a correctional institute for teenage criminals too young for women's prison. The first year we moved to our waterfront home, two incarcerated teens escaped, running along the dried-up riverbank to travel upstream on a frigid day in November.

They ended up in our yard, but we weren't home. Sue, my next-door neighbor, rescued the nearly frozen girls, who were also bleeding from climbing up jagged rocks. While they warmed up under blankets and drank hot coffee, Sue secretly called the police. As a social worker, the Good Samaritan was not frightened in that precarious situation. Upon returning home a few days later, Sue telephoned me to report the gruesome ordeal.

"Boy, it was a *good thing* you weren't home last weekend." She gave a blow-by-blow account as I listened, completely spell-bound.

"The girls in that prison are really dangerous. Most of them are in there for murder. They'd just as soon kill you as look at you." As a social worker, I considered Sue a voice of authority on those matters. Her warning fortified my dread about that mysterious compound.

One day, when Tammie was home on spring break, she and I drove by the correctional institute. We were accustomed to praying out loud with each other, so it was not unusual for spontaneous prayers to be lifted up.

"Lord, send a missionary into that prison to be *a light* to those girls," I pompously prayed while traveling past the ominous gates.

Tammie glanced over at me. She challenged me by stating, "Myles Munroe says, 'Unless you're willing to be that missionary, don't ask God to send someone else.'"

I felt convicted to the core of my being. My cheeks flushed at the thought of going inside those prison walls. It seemed like such a dangerous place, shrouded with mystery. Whenever I drove by, I never saw a single soul walking among the ancient stone buildings located along the O'Shaughnessy Reservoir in Delaware County.

A few months after my enlightenment by Myles Munroe, our local newspaper featured a photograph of a volunteer teaching sewing to some of the girls inside those prison gates. I studied the photograph intently. It was my first glimpse into the obscurity surrounding that state correctional institute. The smiling faces of the teenagers melted my heart. It caused me to realize that this institution was filled with eager young girls in need of mother figures to teach them basic homemaking skills. The Lord pulled on my heartstrings to get involved. The following week, I had an appointment with Kathy, the Volunteer Coordinator.

On the morning of my late afternoon appointment with Kathy, I took my son, now five, for a haircut in town. Next door to the barbershop was a pet store. I always took Bo inside to visit the puppies. I also made sure Bo viewed the reptile aquariums while I secretly glanced in the opposite direction. That day, I noticed Bo rushed by the tanks, so we returned home without him looking at the reptiles. I made a note of that, thinking it was strange behavior.

My son loved to play Superman in the bright red and blue costume my mother had made for his fifth birthday. He told all his buddies in kindergarten, "Oh, my grandma will make you a Superman outfit, too." However, that day my darling little boy was decked out in a cowboy hat, boots, and holster with a gun. He was outside climbing on a dwarf size tree, and the Lord spoke to my heart. *Take him with you tonight.*

My first response was fear-based. *Oh, maybe he'll fall from a tree if I don't take him with me.* My stepson, Scott, age nineteen, worked a summer job while home from college, so I had a built-in babysitter arriving later. A presumptuous thought invaded my head, *Oh, this cute little cowboy is going to help the girls warm up to me.* However, both notions were false. The Lord had something profound planned for me, *which forever changed my life.*

My husband Daryl had traveled out of town on business, so I fixed something kid-friendly to consume before my 7 p.m. appointment with the volunteer coordinator. While standing in the kitchen preparing food, I heard the front door slowly creak open. Seconds later, Bo appeared in the kitchen doorway. It was such an odd entry because Bo always barged through the door as a typical kid. It caused me to glance in his direction.

His little face was blanched with fear.

"Mommy, there is a *snake* outside in the grass."

"Oh, that's nice." I tried to sound nonchalant. "What's the snake's name? Did you talk to him?" I attempted to be cool, calm, and collected even though my knees felt like Jell-O.

"Oh no, Mommy. I *hate* snakes. I'm afraid of them," declared my son with a quivering voice. My heart sank. Stark fear permeated the room like the smell of sulfur. In plain view stood the crippling fear that had paralyzed me all of my life. It was the same uncontrollable fear that kept me from flower gardening, camping, or strolling in a wooded park. I knew this identical fear would forever thwart my son, who loved playing army out in the woods with his little neighborhood buddy, Michael.

Oh, if only Daryl was home. He could march him right back out there to nip this thing in the bud, I thought, trying to think of another solution.

I lifted Bo into my arms and plunked him down on the kitchen counter to look him squarely in the face.

"Now, Bo, look at Mommy. You are *not afraid* of snakes," I

affirmed. "You and Daddy have picked up garden snakes before. So, you are *not afraid* of snakes!" I also pointed out that my little niece Bethany was terrified of our dog and used her example of irrational fear.

Bo kept declaring his fear, and the more we argued, the more it reinforced the stronghold. This futile discussion continued for several more minutes, and neither side budged.

Exasperated, I said, "Okay, but will you pray with Mommy? If I pray about being afraid of snakes, will you pray with me, too?"

My sweet little boy nodded in agreement. For the first time, I prayed about being delivered from a lifelong fear of snakes. When I ended the prayer, I started crying, and so did Bo. I tenderly held him to my chest as we wept. Little did I know that within an hour, that prayer of deliverance would be put to the test with a twelve-foot-long boa constrictor. God doesn't mess around.

In his cowboy attire, Bo accompanied me to my appointment with Kathy, a large, jolly woman who loved to talk. Her lively personality helped dissolve my apprehensions about becoming involved. But best of all, Kathy had deep faith as a born-again Christian.

Soon Bo grew weary of us yakking and fell asleep on her office sofa. Kathy sat behind her desk in front of a large window with a partial view of the campus. A large group of girls was gathering outside, so I jumped up to get a better look at them. Aside from the newspaper photograph, it was my first real glimpse of the young women.

"What are so many girls doing outside?"

"Oh, Jack Hanna is out there with some exotic animals from the Columbus Zoo. Jungle Jack comes here often to put on shows for the girls."

I leaned into the window to see Jack Hanna holding a humongous *snake*.

"Oh, my gosh! Can my son go out there to watch? We just had a big discussion about him thinking he was afraid of snakes. I think this is an answer to prayer!" I fully intended to stay inside.

I woke Bo up with news of Jungle Jack Hanna outside. He was delighted at the opportunity to see him and the zoo animals. However, he was not about to go out there among about fifty girls without tightly gripping my hand.

Kathy happily ushered us outside. I put up a brave front but kept a very safe distance from the snake handler. In fact, I kept my eyes glued on the snake just in case it got loose. After running away, one hysterical girl was being dragged back by a large security officer. I thought, *You poor child, I completely share your sentiments about being forced to be that close to a snake.* Her screams caused me to slide up on the hood of a nearby parked car, so my feet didn't touch the ground.

Following the demonstration, Mr. Jack Hanna balled up the Boa constrictor to fit it into a large, white knapsack. He pulled the rope closed before placing the sack down on the grass.

He announced, "For any of you who want to touch the snake, I'll bring him out later." My eyes remained fixated on the bulging knapsack; all the while, Jack produced other exotic animals to wow the students and my son.

Moments later, Kathy took me and Bo on a tour of the large campus overlooking the Scioto River. She pointed out large buildings that were landmarks from the mid-nineteenth century when a therapeutic Sulphur Spa thrived in the idyllic Scioto River Valley of Delaware County. It was a lovely setting, covering hundreds of wooded acres.

As we rounded back toward her office, the crowd of students had narrowed to about three girls standing close to Jack Hanna and *the snake*.

"Hey! Look, Mom! Let's go touch the snake!" With excitement, Bo darted ahead of me. The emotional chains around my ankles made moving forward feel as if I was pulling a freight train.

Later, Kathy chuckled when she said to me, "Your face turned completely green."

Jack had the boa constrictor stretched across his shoulders. The snake's belly was wrapped across his back and along his chest. Jack held the head of the snake over his right shoulder. As Kathy and I approached, my eyes met the eyes of the snake. Standing about six feet away, I was completely mesmerized. As if mocking me, our eyes locked as his tongue flickered out at me.

"Okay, Mom, I just touched the snake. Now it's *your turn* to touch him."

Fear hath torment, but perfect love casts out fear.

It was a defining moment in my life. My feet felt like they were wedged in cement. I was stuck. Thankfully, my unconditional love for my son provided *supernatural courage* to touch that snake. I knew I had to do it. I walked in front of Jack to contemplate touching the belly of this monster.

A grace from God rose up within me, giving me the courage I'd never known before. I slowly inched forward toward the snake. With one finger, I hesitantly extended my hand toward the smooth, light-colored belly. I quickly touched it as if testing a red-hot iron. But the second time, I boldly placed my entire hand on the belly of that mammoth snake. I held it there for a moment to conquer a major stronghold in my life. Considering this deathly fear of snakes became one of the greatest triumphs in my walk with Christ.

Afterward, I walked around to face the snake again. This time, I stood triumphantly within one foot from its mocking eyes and flickering tongue. The Lord spoke to my inner spirit, "*Now that you have conquered your physical fear of snakes, I am going to take you into this spiritual snake pit. You will never be afraid of anything that comes at you because I will be with you every step of the way.*" The Holy Spirit is real.

"Have I not commanded you? Be strong and courageous. Do not be afraid; do not be discouraged, for the LORD your God will be with you wherever you go"

Joshua 1:9, NIV

"Be strong and courageous. Do not be afraid or terrified because of them, for the LORD your God goes with you; he will never leave you nor forsake you"

Deuteronomy 31:6, NKJV

That which is born of the flesh is flesh, and that which is born of the Spirit is spirit.

John 3:6

And Jesus, full of the Holy Spirit, returned from the Jordan and was led by the Spirit in the wilderness.

Luke 4:1

CHAPTER THIRTEEN

Scioto Correctional Institute: Opportunities to Love

Volunteer coordinator Kathy Kelly welcomed me on as a new volunteer. The following years were some of the most exciting days of ministry that I have ever experienced.

I started out teaching calligraphy to a small class of interested teens. By listening to their tragic stories, I had many opportunities to pray and weep with them as I earned their trust.

Since this correctional facility was technically a high school, in one building, there were two side-by-side kitchenettes set up for home economic classes. Therefore, I taught cooking a few times a week to countless girls from various classroom settings.

One evening, one of my thirteen-year-old students was missing, so I called the cottage security attendant. I was informed that Takeesha was "in a straight jacket because of a suicide attempt earlier that day."

The officer informed me that Takeesha had fought with her cousin, another student in my class. I asked if Takeesha could come to class anyway. "Really?" she asked. I assured her it would be okay. She was released, and I purposely put Takeesha and her cousin together in the same kitchen to make Rice Krispies treats.

During a fifteen-minute break, I privately ministered to Takeesha about the power of forgiveness. Knowing her Bible, she answered, "I know Jesus said to forgive seventy times seven in one day." We prayed, and she forgave her cousin. After the girls returned to their cottage, the correctional officer called me.

"What did you do to this girl?" asked the stunned officer. "Takeesha had been depressed all day. Yesterday, she tried to hang herself with her bra from a rafter in the ceiling. She was in a straight jacket when you called for her. Takeesha returned from your class smiling, and I hear her talking and laughing with her cousin right now."

Most of the girls came from destructive home situations: physical and sexual abuse, domestic violence, alcoholism, and rampant drug use. I expressed compassion and always spoke to them about the love of Jesus.

I taught them catchy scripture songs so they could get the Word of God within their hearts. Many of them had never been to church or ever heard of the Ten Commandments. I had the privilege of leading many tender hearts to the Lord. I also opened my home, along with my heart. So did my entire family.

Many of the girls asked to go to church with me. I was granted permission to pick them up on Sunday morning and escort them to service with our family. With permission from Kathy, we water baptized countless young women in our swimming pool throughout the summer months.

Whenever four or five teenage girls came for dinner, I put out my best china and stemware to treat them with dignity and honor. And yes, it was true that many of them had committed murder in the second or third-degree while strung out on drugs. Away from the corruptive influences and off of drugs, these girls were typical teenagers. My heart went out to them.

Soon, I recruited my prayer partner, Shar Joyner, and together, we converted a vacant space in a large campus building into a volunteer center. This two-room facility had a kitchenette and a large living room. From our own personal resources and generous friends in business, we put together a nice living room with new carpeting, a sectional, custom draperies, fresh paint, and a stereo to play praise music. Within a few weeks, the new volunteer center resembled a suite at the Hyatt! It was beautiful. Soon, other church organizations began conducting Bible studies with the troubled teens, too. I oil painted a lighthouse located on an oceanfront to hang on the wall because it was a Jesus center that offered light and hope to so many troubled hearts.

Throughout those few years, we led countless teenagers in singing praise choruses from printed music sheets filled with scripture songs.

When the girls showed up for Bible study, about fifteen at a time, there would be one or two girls who were stern and attempted to snarl at us. They were defiant. At first, the girls wouldn't join in the singing, but they'd show up the following week. Their hard demeanor would tempt me to avoid them. However, the Lord showed me that they were the ones who were the most desperate for His love. I'd go out of my way to extend kindness, even though they would usually glare at me. Within weeks, these same "toughies" were calling out requests of their favorite songs. When these tough nuts finally cracked, their faith was genuine. Hearts were melted because God was in our midst. Shar provided hot cider, frosted cupcakes, and very big matronly hugs.

By recruiting local bands every few months, Shar organized Christian rock concerts in the large auditorium with the help of other Christian volunteers. Even though I couldn't hear the lyrics through the blaring rock music, many girls responded to the message and received Jesus Christ as their personal Savior.

In addition, faithful Shar arrived early every Sunday morning to pick up about ten or twelve teens for church. In her fifteen-passenger Chevy van, Shar drove the girls back to her country home for breakfast. They were treated to a closet filled with outfits and high heels of every size to dress up for church. More than anything, these lonely girls were seeking love and attention from a mother figure. Following church service, Shar brought them back to her house for Sunday supper. Shar was a dedicated soldier. She had been a victim of domestic abuse and was no longer married. She operated a "safe home" for domestic-violence victims. She is one of my true heroes in the faith, and she has been deeply missed since Shar went home to be with the Lord a few years ago. Her daughter-in-law called me with the sad news that Shar had passed away peacefully in her sleep while visiting her only son and grandchildren. I cried for months, mourning her death. She was a true champion for Jesus.

During that time period at the correctional institute, one bright sixteen-year-old named Michelle came to live with our family as a ward of the courts. We agreed to take Michelle to "Ninety Alcoholics Anonymous meetings in ninety days." Many times, Daryl accompanied Michelle to an AA meeting when I was unable to drive her into the city. As a recovering alcoholic, Michelle kept us on our toes at all times. We adored her, but she was a challenge. We paid for her to attend a private Christian school with our son, Bo, so she could finish high school. She lived with us for almost two years and is still considered one of my true daughters.

Through meeting me, her brother John received Jesus Christ as his Savior. John went through the Teen Challenge rehabilitation program, and Dr. John is now a licensed psychologist at a Christian counseling center. You never know what the big picture is when God asks you to go where "angels fear to tread."

If I had been too fearful of moving forward, there would not have been a harvest of souls entering the Kingdom of God. Fear keeps us from moving mountains. Fear is a great enemy of faith. Conquer your snakes. Take a step of faith and see where the Lord leads you. God will never lead you unless you're willing to go. The Holy Spirit is real.

> *"Above all, love each other deeply, because love covers over a multitude of sins"*

1 Peter 4:8, NIV

CAUGHT UP IN THE SPIRIT

*"It happened when I returned to Jerusalem
and was praying in the temple, that I fell into a
trance and I saw Him saying to me, 'Make haste
and get out of Jerusalem because they will not
accept your testimony about Me.'"*

Acts 22:17–19 (NKJV).

CHAPTER FOURTEEN

Pastors Rod Parsley, Jim Custer, Mabel Whipple: The One Foundation & Unusual Friendships

Whenever Pastor Mabel Whipple attended a conference at World Harvest Church, Pastor Parsley honored her like royalty. I loved her, too. The matriarch introduced Rodney to the Lord when he was a youngster. A decade earlier, Sister Mabel introduced me to demonstrations of God's supernatural power at her weekly Bible study. Throughout my personal connection with her, I was about to learn another amazing dimension of the Holy Spirit.

My friend Bonnie White organized an all-day ladies' seminar on a Friday at Pastor Whipple's church. I was asked to speak about *worship*. Following that teaching, I continued to operate in the *spirit of worship* for the next few days. In fact, the entire weekend, I found myself humming, singing, whistling Christian songs, or composing *new melodies* while singing in tongues. I did very little talking. It felt like being suspended in a spiritual bubble while going about my household duties.

On Monday morning, I went jogging, returning home breathless and sweaty. I collapsed on my bed to rest. While lying on my back, I fell into a *dream state* while being partially *awake*.

It was the first *trance* I had ever experienced. It seemed like a twilight sleep, being half awake and half asleep.

In this unfamiliar spirit realm, I observed a fully-clothed man suspended above me at the end of the bed. He had reddish hair and looked vaguely familiar. Loosely wrapped with rope from his neck down to his ankles, he struggled to free himself. The rope was loose enough to trash about but tight enough to keep him bound.

"Lord, *please* help him. *Please free* this man." I felt his agony and became very concerned. The Holy Spirit answered, "I cannot free him. You have the authority on earth to free him. Pray for him and give him the book, *The Kingdom of Self* by Earl Jabay."

Who is he? I wondered.

Just then, the phone rang, startling me fully awake. I did not find out the identity of this man tormented by a rope!

Rosie Cunningham was calling me to chat. Interestingly, she is the former neighborhood gal who introduced me to Pastor Maple Whipple when we first moved to Columbus years earlier.

We ended up discussing the "pros and cons" of the parochial school where Rosie's four kids attended and the Evangelical Christian School where my two older kids attended.

"What does Pastor Jim look like?" It was such an odd question.

Pastor Jim was the head of the largest Evangelical church in town, which included the Christian school. As I described him, I realized the man bound up was Pastor Jim!

It was with fear and trepidation that this charismatic book was given to Pastor Jim. His large and influential church did not believe that Christians spoke in tongues. Their doctrine stated that this phenomenon *ended* with the Book of Acts.

Daryl suggested I include a note to say, "Dear Pastor Jim, since you're active in pastoral counseling, perhaps this book, written by a chaplain counselor, might be a helpful aid..." Our weekly Bible study Christian friends laid their hands on the book and prayed about the outcome.

While entering the church office to drop off the book and note with his secretary, the enemy's condemning voice challenged me. *Who do you think you are? You are nobody. He'll never listen to you.*

A week later, I received a kind, hand-written note from Pastor Jim thanking me for "a timely" book on a subject that had been near to his heart. For the past month, he'd been studying the subject of "self."

Ironically, within a few years, Pastor Jim and Pastor Rod Parsley became *fast friends* through their mutual connection with National Christian Broadcasters network conferences held annually.

When my husband formed a non-profit ministry called One Foundation, he invited Pastor Jim to serve on the board of directors. He agreed and quickly suggested that Daryl include Pastor Rod Parsley, which was surprising. "Well, after all," Pastor Jim admonished, "Rod's got the largest charismatic church in town.

We should have him on the board."

One Foundation had five black and five white pastors representing several different denominations. Their mission was to come together to help the struggling inner-city churches that minister to the poor and disadvantaged. God was glorified by this noble effort.

God is seeking *unity* in the body of Christ, whether we speak in tongues or we don't. He searches the hearts of men and proves Himself strong when we labor as One Body for His kingdom.

Our Lord Jesus is glorified when we put our doctrinal differences aside and worship together in one accord. The Holy Spirit is for real!

> *"Now may the God of patience and comfort grant you to be like-minded toward one another, according to Christ Jesus, that you may with one mind and one mouth glorify the God and Father of our Lord Jesus Christ"*

Romans 15:5–6, NKJV

> *"The steps of a good man are ordered by the Lord, And He delights in his way."*

Psalm 37:23, NKJV

Pastors Rod Parsley, Jim Custer, Mabel Whipple. . .

DIVINE CONNECTIONS FOR CHURCH PLANTING

"Eye has not seen, nor ear heard, nor have entered into the heart of man the things which God has prepared for those who love Him."

1 Corinthians 2:9 (NKJV)

Your word is a lamp to my feet and a light to my path.

Psalm 119:105

The one who conquers will have this heritage, and I will be his God and he will be my son.

Revelation 21:7

If the Spirit of him who raised Jesus from the dead dwells in you, he who raised Christ Jesus from the dead will also give life to your mortal bodies through his Spirit who dwells in you.

Romans 8:11

CHAPTER FIFTEEN

Author Judson Cornwall, "Let Us Pray," and Congregational Corporate Singing

Before his blessed heavenly homecoming, the late great Judson Cornwall authored countless books on various subjects such as praise and worship, praying the scriptures, and developing intimacy with God. He is a patriarch in the faith movement and is dearly missed.

His three books entitled *Let Us Worship, Elements of Worship,* and *Let Us Praise* are considered Christian classics on the subject. He has had a great impact on the world by introducing corporate worship to the body of Christ. He was birthed in this knowledge through his personal worship experiences at Bethesda Missionary Temple and his decades of teaching there as an honored guest speaker.

On Sunday morning, December 5, 1948, the congregation of Bethesda Missionary Temple gathered in the church basement in Detroit. Their new edition was under construction. After Mom Beall preached a sermon, her son, Pastor James Beall, invited everyone to stand for the benediction.

Suddenly, through a sovereign move of the Holy Spirit, *singing in tongues* broke out and continued for over an hour. Every voice lifted in total abandonment while a corporate *sound* reached a heavenly realm, producing a glory that filled the temple. When this "singing in the spirit" subsided, a *holy hush* fell upon the people.

Next, a prophetic message was sung, birthing what had just happened in this supernatural visitation.

"This is the promise of the coming latter rain,

Lift up your eyes, behold the ripening grain.

Many signs and wonders in His mighty name

Drink, oh drink, My people, for this is latter rain."

Following this extraordinary move of God that morning, many souls were saved. Physical healings manifested as new converts got filled with the Holy Spirit. That Sunday marked the beginning of what became known as the *Latter Rain Revival.*

Two months later, on February 3, 1949, the main sanctuary (seating 2,200) was officially dedicated. Then the unexpected happened next. When the doors opened, people *rushed* in to grab a seat. It was reported that 1,700 people were turned away. Services were held night and day for the next *three and a half years. This revival drew people from all over the world.*

Thousands of the church members were fasting and guarding their seats because of the crowds thronging to make it into the sanctuary. Someone reported, "We hardly left the sanctuary because we didn't want to miss what God was doing. We sprayed Lysol to purify the stagnant air, but God was *so real* it didn't matter."

At the time, Bethesda Missionary Temple was under the auspices of the Assemblies of God denomination. When this unusual revival broke out at Bethesda, the founder, Rev. M.D. "Mom" Beall was banished from this governing organization. Her affiliation with the AOG ended. This exile broke Mom's heart, but with great persecution comes a tremendous increase if you remain standing. Her vision for Bethesda developed into what she considered an "armory to equip world leaders to plant churches and grow into mighty fortresses for the Lord."

There are countless thousands of people who have been touched by Mom Beall and the ministry of Bethesda Missionary Temple, currently known as Bethesda Christian Church.

To think that in 1934, this young mother of three children started preaching in a small storefront location.

Today, Bethesda is a 200,000-square-foot church and education facility occupying hundreds of acres. In addition, the ministry has launched countless missionaries currently serving Haiti, East, Central, and South Africa, Uganda, Indonesia, Far East Asia, Ecuador, South America, and other parts of the world that are still planting churches and preaching the Gospel to the lost.

But as it is written: *"Eye has not seen, nor ear heard, nor have entered into the heart of man, the things which God has prepared for those who love Him"* (1 Corinthians 2:9, NKJV).

The Spirit himself bears witness with our spirit that we are children of God.

Romans 8:16

You, however, are not in the flesh but in the Spirit, if in fact the Spirit of God dwells in you. Anyone who does not have the Spirit of Christ does not belong to him.

Romans 8:9

CHAPTER SIXTEEN

Evangelists Fred & Florence Parker, Pastors James Beall, Patricia Beall Gruits, Moses Vegh, and the Birth of Prophetic Church

The tall, attractive bi-racial couple passed by our seats as Sunday morning service was about to begin at Christian Assembly in Columbus. The attractive, light-skinned woman, accompanied by a mocha-skinned black man, could have easily passed for being white. Somehow, though, I knew she was of a mixed African-American bloodline. That discernment was key to this life-altering testimony.

My brother, Dr. David Taylor, and wife, Lorraine, were visiting us from Detroit that weekend. This was not our home church, but we were attending a baby-dedication service for Dr. Don and Susan Furci. After our dear friends waited many years for a baby, their newborn, Bethany, was being dedicated on June 5, 1978. It was to become a memorable occasion in more ways than one.

Following service, a group of us were in a circle chatting it up in the narthex.

Imagine the boldness of the white-looking woman interrupting our conversation to shake our hands. Introducing herself as "Florence Parker" from Windsor, Ontario, her diction resembled the

Queen's proper English. Florence smiled brightly, proudly promoting Bethesda Missionary Temple, located across the Canadian bridge into Detroit.

Florence explained that Pastor Jim Beall had received several speaking invitations from Pastor Sam Farina. Since she and her husband, Fred, were in town for an Ohio family reunion, it seemed only fitting to visit the church that thought so highly of her pastor.

As Florence walked away, the Holy Spirit whispered, "Florence can help Diane; go talk to her." I froze with intimidation. My spirit was willing, but my flesh felt weak.

Beautiful Diane, my college friend on our adventurous New York City trip years earlier, was unsuccessfully battling emotional problems. Jesus was her cure, but baffling conversations with an incoherent young woman made no sense. Each time I hung up the phone with her, I cried.

After graduating from college, Diane taught in a public high school in Detroit, but she couldn't hack the pressure. My heart agonized over my friend's failing mental health. All too frequent trips to the psych ward had me very worried. Our special time together in NYC was now all the more meaningful because that was the last time I remember her being mentally stable.

Our church group continued to yack, but my mind paid no attention. Gripped with trepidation, I prayed that Florence and Fred would not depart before I mustered up the courage to address her unique skin color. I kept glancing over at the Parkers, patiently standing near the exit doors as if waiting for something to happen. Finally, taking a deep breath, I dashed over to speak to Florence.

"Hi," I began tentatively. "We just met a few minutes ago. I was wondering if you would consider contacting my friend, Diane. She lives in Detroit, too. Maybe you could invite her to your church. She's bi-racial, too. She has mental problems and desperately needs the Lord."

Florence lit up like a moonbeam. "Oh, yes, of course, I will; just give me her phone number." She quickly produced a small address book for me to view. Flipping through the open pages, she said, "Look; first, I write the person's name in pencil. After they get converted to Jesus Christ, I ink them in. See?"

Actually, it *was* amazing how many inked-over penciled names Florence had in her directory. She also recorded my address before handing off her business card and introducing me to Fred, who was just as friendly and outgoing.

Thanking her, I felt relieved that the opportunity didn't slip away by intimidation on my part. This bold, evangelistic couple was on a mission, obviously *stalling around* with expectations from the Holy Spirit. God is the master conductor, always orchestrating *divine connections* in a heavenly realm for an earthly purpose. Therefore, be on the alert for unusual circumstances to cross your path.

A week passed by before I called Diane. She seemed too incoherent to comprehend if Florence had telephoned her or not.

But, after calling Florence next, she *had* spoken to Diane *and* her mother a few times by telephone.

During our next visit to family members in Detroit, Daryl and I visited Bethesda Missionary Temple for the first time. I attempted to locate Florence, who was teaching Sunday school. We left word with that church member to let Florence know that we'd been in service and regret not seeing her.

At that time in my life, I desperately needed a mentor. My heart yearned for the deeper things of God, but I didn't know where to look for such a person.

One night while bathing, I placed my hands on the side of the tub and rested my weary brow on top of them. "Lord, I need a spiritual Mother; please send me one," I begged from the depth of my soul.

The next day, walking in from the mailbox, my husband handed me a bulging envelope from Florence Parker.

"Well, you finally *met your match*," Daryl chuckled. "She writes twenty-page letters, just like you!"

Florence had taken the time to type a thirteen-page letter reiterating a sermon from Pastor Charlotte Baker, who had recently preached at Bethesda. The subject of her sermon was "manna from heaven." As I read the essence of this sermon, my heart leaped for joy. At last, God answered my prayer with someone who was sincerely interested in my spiritual growth. It actually felt like true *manna* from heaven!

Our correspondence continued for several months with lengthy letters. Florence recognized my need for a firm biblical foundation. She taught the importance of the *six foundation stones* found in Hebrews 6:1–3.

My letters spoke nothing of Daryl or what he did for a living. My spiritual connection with Florence was purely based on our mutual love for the Lord Jesus Christ.

Eight months later, Florence mentioned that her teenage son, Jamie, was attending a youth rally at Hope Temple in Findlay, Ohio. Had we met Pastor Moses Vegh? (Not yet.) Since Findlay was only ninety minutes away, I invited her and Fred to keep driving and spend the weekend with us.

The Parkers arrived on a Friday afternoon. We drove over to the dealership for a late lunch with Daryl. As we pulled in, Fred asked, "Oh, is your husband a *salesman* at this Cadillac agency?"

"No… He *owns* it," I laughed. "He has a Bible study luncheon here every Tuesday. All of his salesmen are Christians, too."

Fred and Florence were equally surprised to learn that Daryl played football for Coach Woody Hayes at Ohio State University in a Big Ten Championship year against the University of Michigan and was later drafted as a number-one draft choice for the Detroit Lions, their home team.

Daryl and I treated them to lunch at Brookside Country Club.

This humble couple seemed unaffected by the social status of our lives. Reaching out to me, a total stranger, Florence had pure motives for meeting the spiritual needs of a lonely young woman living in Columbus, Ohio. She was the answer to my heartfelt desire to mature in Christ.

Florence and I talked about God that entire weekend. The Parkers were counselors among many who were part of a weekly, nine-month course. That class was attended by several hundred adult students each fall. This book is entitled *Understanding God*, a catechism written by Reverend Patricia Beall Gruits. She was known as "Sister Pat."

The Parkers suggested asking Senior Pastor Jim Beall for permission to bring this vital "catechism" course to Columbus. Daryl was open to it being taught at his dealership in an upstairs conference room.

When the Parkers departed on Sunday, tears rolled down my cheeks when saying goodbye. I asked, "Will you bring back this Understanding God course, even if I'm your *only* student?" They answered, "Yes!"

Pastor Jim Beall wholeheartedly endorsed the Parkers to teach the nine-month Understanding God course. Thirty students enrolled the first year.

For the next nine months, the faithful Parkers drove five hours from Windsor to Columbus every Tuesday. They taught that evening and spent the night in our home. This continued for a few years, and our lifelong friendship developed.

As a bonus, these two anointed prophets from God set our dysfunctional house in *order* in a loving, constructive way with humor and godly wisdom.

Our two teenagers were struggling with me as an authority figure. Unfortunately, I was not spiritually mature enough to recognize their emotional needs nor wise enough to deal with the conflicts in our home. Our family needed intervention, and thankfully, the Parkers straightened us all out!

We began our frequent pilgrimage to Detroit to attend Bethesda Church leadership conferences and teaching seminars. We encountered Pastor Moses and Bette Vegh and Pastors Paul and Eleanor Stern. All four anointed leaders grew up in Bethesda under the prophetic wisdom and guidance of Mom Beall.

Pastor Paul and Eleanor were newlyweds sent out as missionaries from Bethesda. All five of their children were born in Africa. When they returned home, Mom Beall admonished them, "You two are trailblazers...you will die on the vine if you stay here." They accepted the challenge by pioneering the Rock Church in Danville, Illinois.

Biblical foundation stones were properly laid in our lives through the diligence of the Parkers pouring into our lives. I am forever grateful.

More than anything else, my heart longed to *worship God* in spirit and in truth, just as I *experienced* corporately at Bethesda Missionary Temple, Hope Temple, and the Rock Church.

Pastors Jim and Harry Beall, Pastor Patricia Beall Gruits, Pastor Moses and Bette Vegh, and Pastor Paul and Eleanor Stern counseled us. These strong leaders were the guiding force behind birthing a prophetic church of worship that remains standing strong on the Word of God and biblical principles.

> *"I will pray with the spirit, and I will also pray with the understanding. I will sing with the spirit, and I will also sing with the understanding"*

> **1 Corinthians 14:15, NKJV**

> *"Yet a time is coming and has come when the true worshipers will worship the Father in the Spirit and in truth, for they are the kind of worshipers the Father seeks. God is spirit, and his worshipers must worship in the Spirit and in truth"*

> **John 4:23–24, NIV**

CHAPTER SEVENTEEN

Bethesda Missionary Temple, Mom Beall's Prophecy, Her Lasting Legacy

"You a preacher?" asked the elderly woman seated in a wheelchair. Mom Beall intently gazed at Daryl as we were about to walk past her. We were in Detroit attending an "Understanding God" seminar conducted by her daughter, Rev. Patricia Beall Gruits, the author of the nine-month Bible course. It was early spring 1979.

Mom Beall, a delicately frail woman, was parked at the rear of a very crowded church conference room filled with pastors and lay leaders from all over the country. My tall, handsome husband, dressed in a dark, three-piece navy suit, looked very distinguished walking up the aisle at my arm.

"No," Daryl laughed, rolling his eyes. "I'm a car dealer!"

"Well, you will be," she chuckled with a twinkle in her eye. But we kept moving toward the dining hall with the hungry lunch crowd, not comprehending her prophetic peek into our future. Her words eventually came true. However, she made sure we comprehended the weight of her prophetic prediction.

Rev. Myrtle Dorthea Beall, the founder of Bethesda Missionary Temple, must have sensed we didn't value the significance of her prophetic word to us about Daryl becoming a preacher. So, from that point on, she kept a watchful eye over us throughout the three-day conference. That evening she personally invited us to sit beside her at dinner. She told me her amazing testimony during our mealtime together.

Mom Beall passed from earth to heaven in September 1979. We were blessed to hear her minister several times since she usually gave closing remarks following her son's sermon. A second pulpit stood on the platform, low enough for her to speak from her wheelchair.

One Sunday morning, we sat in a packed 2,200-seat auditorium after another weekend conference. After Rev. James Beall delivered an eloquent message, we sang a closing song before Brother Jim delivered the benediction. We were all standing, waiting to be dismissed. I felt uplifted by the rich deposit of God's Word heard through various guest speakers. Feeling grateful to be in the company of so many gifted ministers from all over America, it had been a tremendous event, as always.

Suddenly, Mom Beall wheeled to her podium to say something. "When we sang that last chorus, the Lord brought the story of the lost coin to my mind," she began reflectively. The microphone amplified her soft, tender voice. "Scripture tells us that the woman searched and searched her house until she finally found the missing coin. She was so overjoyed that she called her neighbors to rejoice with her. Jesus said that the angels rejoice when a lost sinner is found…"

Before she said another word, I began to tremble. I had read that familiar parable many times. The Holy Spirit quickened my understanding of His wondrous love in a deeper measure. Something like warm energy shot through my body, stirring my emotions. I began to weep. Within seconds, the entire congregation could be heard weeping, too.

A few thousand people reverently and quietly slipped out of their seats onto their knees, using the back of their seats as a makeshift altar. I could not stop crying, even when I tried. In fact, I continued crying throughout our four-hour drive back to Columbus. My eyes were nearly swollen shut by the time we arrived home. But I felt renewed, refreshed, and thankful for the cleansing experience. God had certainly done a deep work in my heart. Daryl was equally touched as well.

Thirty-five years later, I remain in reverent awe of the anointing of God expressed through this compelling woman. Mom Beall's anointed words caused the Holy Spirit to sweep through that auditorium as a sovereign visitation from heaven above. It was the most profound experience I've had with God in a corporate setting. If this dear, saintly lady uttered a few syllables to cause an entire auditorium of people to humbly sink to their knees in tearful repentance, I could only imagine what the revival must have been like during the three-and-a-half years it lasted in the 1950s. After that experience, I'm convinced the revival fire has not died.

Our friendship with the entire Beall family grew because we frequently traveled to Bethesda for Sunday morning service or conferences.

We began discussing the need for a New Testament Church that taught the principles of Christ Jesus along with a special emphasis on Water Baptism and circumcision of the heart.

Realizing her end was nearing, Mom Beall assigned resident prophet, Manley Higgins, to personally exhort us with his unique prophetic mantle whenever we visited Bethesda. He'd spot us in the crowd and make a beeline toward us. In a good way, he'd always made me tear up by his exhortations about our future ministry.

Therefore, I spent a lot of time in the bathroom wiping off my smeared mascara because this elderly gentleman always spoke life into our spirits. One time he said to me, "You're like Mother Sarah; many are going to nurse from your breast as you feed them what God produces in you." At that time in my life, I had no idea that he was speaking prophetically.

Following one such prophetic moment with Brother Higgins, I washed my tear-stained face in the ladies' room. In my haste to get back into service, I left my purse in the restroom. Right before the offertory, Mr. Comedian Harry Beall held it up in jest. He announced, "Sister Sanders left this very nice Gucci bag in the ladies' room, so we took the liberty to take all the cash out of it for this morning's offering." Everyone laughed, so they knew he was just kidding.

That laughter was a pleasant relief from the heaviness of feeling a call into full-time ministry and not having any clear direction. Obviously, Mom Beall knew something we didn't know and made sure Brother Higgins gave us direction. The plans would soon be made known.

> *"Ask of me, and I will make the nations your inheritance, the ends of the earth your possession."*

Psalm 2:8, NIV

> *"...of which I was made a minister, according to the gift of God's grace which was given to me according to the working of His power."*

Ephesians 3:7, NIV

"Bless the LORD, O my soul, And forget not all His benefits: Who forgives all your in-iquities, Who heals all your diseases, Who redeems your life from destruction, Who crowns you with loving kindness and tender mercies, Who satisfies your mouth with good things, So that your youth is renewed like the eagle's."

Psalm 103:2–5 (NKJV)

"You are my hiding place; you will protect me from trouble and surround me with songs of deliverance."

Psalm 32:7 (NIV)

CHAPTER EIGHTEEN

Pastors Charles Green, Garlon Pemberton, Mom Beall, with Peter Jenkins, author of A Walk Across America

A few years following Mom Beall's death, I had an opportunity to chitchat with Rev. Garland L. Pemberton, a minister close to her throughout his entire lifetime.

At the personal invitation of Pastor Jim Beall, Daryl and I attended a Louisiana conference hosted by Rev. Charles and Barbara Green, the founders of Word of Faith Temple, New Orleans.

Evangelist Garland Pemberton, a big jolly man, sat on the platform at every meeting, clicking his ballpoint pen whenever he agreed with the guest preacher's high points.

Rev. Garland L. Pemberton was born in Cameron, Texas, in 1917, but he planted numerous churches throughout Louisiana and Mississippi during his lifetime. He died in July 2008.

Sometime in the early 1950s, Garland attended an outdoor revival tent meeting in the southwest. He was curious to hear "the preacher woman" from Michigan.

As Mom Beall approached the pulpit, she suddenly glanced over at Garland, seated nearby. "You're going to be close to me until my end," she said matter-of-factly and kept walking. Naturally, he was startled. But, true enough, after thirty years of a close friendship with her, like another favored son, Garland Pemberton delivered an emotional eulogy at her funeral.

One afternoon, at this 1981 Word of Faith conference, I slipped into a vacated chair next to Garland during our lunch break. "Tell me some more stories about Mom Beall."

His face lit up. "Well, let me tell you about her trip to New Orleans in November 1975. A blizzard had hit Detroit, so we worried that it wasn't safe for Mom to travel, but she insisted on coming." His deep southern drawl was engaging as he continued the story.

Sunday morning, he picked her up at the High Rise Holiday Inn. "Mom, you don't look like you slept very well last night. How are you feeling?"

"I'm okay, Brother Garland. I *have* been up praying half the night. But God put a word in my mouth that '*All of America* will hear.'"

Garland said that author Peter Jenkins and his fiancée, Barbara Pennell, a postgraduate college student from New Orleans, were in service that Sunday morning.

A few years before, *all of America* had read his *New York Times* bestseller, *A Walk Across America*. Peter and Barbara had come to a standstill about their future plans for marriage. Deeply in love but filled with doubt, Barbara had been praying "for a sign from God" whether or not she should marry Peter. *Marriage* meant traveling with him for his final trek across America, which included thousands of miles of territory to finish in the Pacific Northwest.

In his book, Peter shares the circumstances of this seemingly hopeless situation with Barbara. After hearing that she was praying for a *sign* from God at Word of Faith church that morning, Peter was *not* hopeful. This is an excerpt from *A Walk Across America*. The following passage is how the book ended.

"There was nothing more to be said between us, and all I could do was wait. I knew this situation was impossible and nothing could happen; God never did anything like that."

The six or seven ministers entered together from their room at the side of the stage. I was shocked to see the pastor, Reverend Charles Green, push in an old lady in a wheelchair. The pastor always delivered the sermon on Sunday mornings, but today he told us Mom Beall had come all the way from Detroit to speak a special message. A microphone was bent down for her since she had to speak from her wheelchair. She had founded a church in Detroit called Bethesda Missionary Temple over forty years ago, and it had grown beyond five thousand members.

Mom Beall was at least eighty years old, and her hair fluffed light red. I looked at her with prejudiced eyes, and she looked sickly and pale. I had just reached the part where I believed in God, and now an old woman in a wheelchair was going to preach. It seemed even more impossible for anything to happen to save

Barbara and me now. I wanted to step out of the side door and not waste any more time.

When Pastor Green finished his introduction of Mom Beall, the whole church erupted with deafening applause. Whoever she was, everybody seemed to know her and was anxious to hear what she had to say. Mom Beall began to speak. Her voice was as quiet as a leaf dropping to the ground, but it was so truth-tuned that every word was loud and clear. She captured everyone's attention instantly—even mine.

This wheel-chaired grandmother began telling us about all the snow in Detroit but said that the Lord God in heaven had told her to come to New Orleans regardless of the weather or anything else. She didn't know why she was to come, but she had learned to obey.

She spoke, "Everyone, please turn to your Bibles to the book of Genesis, Chapter 24." The pages in hundreds and hundreds of Bibles turned with a sound like walking through a pile of raked leaves. Whoosh, whoosh, whoosh.

The old and wise lady began to tell us a story from the Old Testament. It was like sitting at your grandmother's feet and listening to her kind and gentle voice as she began to tell a story.

The story was about Abraham and his son, Isaac. Abraham was old and about to die, but he wanted to find a wife for Isaac. He sent his best servant to Mesopotamia with many camels and gifts. Mesopotamia was Abraham's homeland, and he wanted Isaac to have a wife from there. The servant stopped in a city called Nahor to water his camels and get a drink. It was hot and dry when the servant reached the well. He prayed, "O Lord God, let the maiden who says she will water my camels be the one whom thou has appointed for thy servant, Isaac."

Mom Beall continued the story sweetly. I sat fascinated and had forgotten about the aching situation with Barbara and me. I had to know how the story would end.

"A beautiful maiden named Rebekah came to the well with a water jar balanced on her slender shoulders. When she saw Abraham's servant at the well, she drew water for him to drink. She quickly began to draw water for his thirsty camels. The servant knew this was the girl for Isaac. When she left, he followed her home with the jewelry of silver and gold. Soon, he would ask her if she would come back with him and marry Isaac."

The next day, Mom told us, "Rebekah's family called her to them because the servant was ready to ask her and give her the gifts."

At this point, Mom paused, ready to emphasize a point as dramatic as any I had ever heard. Her pause was long, and over a thousand people were totally silent.

Although Mom was over eighty, she now looked full of the most powerful energy in life. A radiant glow circled her entire body; she pounded the arm of her wheelchair with her right fist and half-yelled and half-quivered, *"Will you go with this man?"*

The simple phrase, one of the thousands in the Bible, burst through me with a surging power; it echoed and shot through my body like holy electricity-this was Barbara's sign! I knew it as I glanced over at her for the first time since Mom's story had begun.

Again, with fantastic power, Mom shouted those words from Genesis: *"Will you go with this man?"* The impact of the message pushed Barbara back into her cushioned chair. She was sort of slumped down, her eyes staring nowhere. She had prayed all night, yet this direct message from God seemed to shock her.

"Will you go with this man?" Mom's lily-white hand banged the wheelchair, emphasizing each and every word. Barbara gasped as though each word hit her heart with the force of a sledgehammer pounding on iron.

She sat up straighter, blood flushed her pretty face, and her hair seemed to stand out fuller than before.

"One last time," Mom cried, *"Will you go with this man?"* I couldn't believe this was happening. I looked over at Barbara again. She knew that I knew. Her eyes were wide and clear except for the crystal tears that gathered in the corners. She leaned close to me and whispered, *"Peter, I'll go with you."*

Very slowly, we stood as the service ended. I wished I could slap myself in the face just to be sure all this had really happened. Even though I now believed in God, this kind of thing was impossible. Yet, in that church on that November 16 of 1975, among a thousand people, God had pointed his finger at the two of us.

The lights of the tall sanctuary dimmed, and everyone began to leave. Coming toward us against the flow of people was a smiling man with dark hair. When he got to us, he stopped abruptly. He handed me a plastic container, which I recognized as a cassette tape, and said, "We record all our services here at Word of Faith. Perhaps you'd like to have this." God had not only given us the sign Barbara had prayed for, now He was offering us proof!

"Thanks," I said, stunned. Barbara was staring ahead, deep into what had happened to us. She had not noticed the tape. As we stepped through the doors into the blaring Louisiana afternoon, Barbara leaned toward me and said with wonder in her voice, "Peter...Peter, did that really happen?"

I felt the cassette in my pocket. Someday we would listen to it and hear those words again that joined us together.

"It sure did," I said. "It sure did."

I reached down to take her hand. From now on, that's the way we'd be—hand in hand.[1]

Peter and Barbara were married in February 1976. On July 5, 1976, they started their two-year honeymoon hiking and camping across the remaining U.S. territory that included Louisiana, Texas, New Mexico, and into Colorado.

In 1975, Mom Beall's eldest daughter, Patricia Beall Gruits, "Sister Pat," as she is affectionately called, opened a medical clin-

---

1 *A Walk Across America*, Peter Jenkins, Harper Perennial 1979, p. 287 Spring Hill, TN.

ic and maternity ward in Haiti with her husband, the late Peter Gruits. Following her husband's sudden death, Dr. Gruits continued their ministry, Rhema International, along with their four sons and wives.

Up until her death in June 2019, Sister Pat continued to write books, teach seminars, and preach the gospel throughout the world. Mom Beall left quite a legacy. Both sons, Jim and Harry Beall, have passed away, too.

I marvel at God's power at work through the simple obedience of a young mother who studied Scripture and taught the neighborhood children and their parents prior to WWII. This dear, faithful woman, with the approval and blessings of her husband, sparked a mighty revival that impacted the world.

After Mom Beall prophesied Daryl becoming a "preacher," she must have sensed he didn't really believe her. So, she invited us to sit with her at dinner that evening.

Seated next to her, I heard how she left the Catholic faith. She was engaged to Mr. Harry Beall, even though he was a not-so-strict Methodist. Since she was such a *devout* Catholic, she naturally assumed he would convert to her religion. But he didn't budge, even though they were very much in love. Like Peter and Barbara, they came to a standstill in their relationship.

Young Myrtle and Harry were invited to dinner at a relative's home. It was to be their *last date* as an engaged couple before Myrtle planned to break off the engagement over their religious conflict.

While waiting for dinner to be served, Myrtle picked up a small devotional off the coffee table and began reading the story of Ruth. Her eyes met the challenge spoken by Ruth. *Where you go, I will follow; your God will be my God.*

"Those words jumped off the page and into my heart. I couldn't stop thinking about what I had read. I ate those words all through dinner with each bite of food."

She quietly surrendered to Mr. Beall's God, and they were soon married. She followed him and his God in simple but sacrificial submission. Like Ruth, her obedience revealed that the Holy Spirit is *real.*

> *"Eye hath not seen, nor ear heard, neither have entered into the heart of man, the things which God hath prepared for them that love him."*

1 Corinthians 2:9, KJV

"But the Helper, the Holy Spirit, whom the Father will send in my name, he will teach you all things and bring to your remembrance all that I have said to you."

John 14:26

"Nevertheless, I tell you the truth: it is to your advantage that I go away, for if I do not go away, the Helper will not come to you. But if I go, I will send him to you."

John 16:7

CHAPTER NINETEEN

Bermuda's Jesus Perfume with a Power to Deliver

We strolled among charming English cottages laced with blooming flower boxes and other historic colonial buildings of St. George in Bermuda.

Daryl and I were part of a small group of fellow Cadillac dealer tourists sometime in 1979. Since the island has the perfect all-year-round climate to grow flowers, it was little wonder that every gift shop offered a myriad of native perfumes, making it difficult to pick a souvenir perfume. However, discovering a fragrant perfume based on the life of Jesus Christ made the decision a quick and easy one.

"Look!" I exclaimed while turning to my husband, browsing through the shop. "This bottle of Passion Flower perfume represents Jesus Christ!"

Spanish missionaries were some of the first to assign meaning to the Passion Flower when they came across it on voyages to South America.

The legion card attached to the perfume explained that the Passion Flower's unique corona represents the crown of thorns of Christ Jesus. The ten sepals and petals symbolize the Apostles who did not betray Christ (excluding Peter and Judas). The five anthers are the five wounds on Christ's body, and the three stigmas represent the nails. The leaves represent the spear that pierced His side. The tendrils are the scourges that flayed His flesh.

We quickly purchased a small bottle of Passion Flower perfume by Lily Perfumery of Bermuda for my mother and another bottle for me. I lovingly referred to it as my "Jesus perfume," beholding the contents in the highest esteem and only wearing it on very special occasions. My mother preferred her favorite brand of Estee Lauder and returned the souvenir gift to me.

Months later, my friend Marianne requested that I come to her home to pray for a woman named Kathy, who was severely depressed and possibly suicidal.

Marianne's husband, Dr. Sol Hoffman, a renowned heart surgeon, learned of this troubled family through one of his patients. He asked Marianne to pray for this situation because Kathy's mother-in-law was concerned for her four young grandchildren.

Kathy had previously been institutionalized for weeks at a time at Harding Hospital, a private mental institution in our community. This grandmother was distraught with worry that Kathy might not ever recover and her son Gary would have to raise her four grandchildren on his own.

Praying deliverance for the mentally ill was new territory for both of us, but since Dr. Sol had personally requested that Marianne and I pray for this young woman, we certainly wanted it to be a successful mission. Marianne and I were prayer partners, and we possessed genuine faith that Jesus was the only key to deliverance.

While getting dressed earlier that morning, I heard the Lord speak to my heart. "Wear my perfume, and I will go *before you* as a sweet-smelling aroma." I reached for the open bottle of my Jesus perfume and gave myself two quick squirts before heading out the door to prayerfully partake in this strange and mysterious prayer mission for a depressed woman named Kathy.

The Hoffman residence was a spacious and stately brick co- lonial located about thirty minutes from my country home. The front entrance opened to a large foyer and center stairway. To the left was a large formal dining room. To the right of the entrance was a living room that I needed to pass through to reach the library wing at the far side of the house. Selma, the Hoffmans' house- keeper, answered the door with a warm greeting before leading me to Marianne and Kathy, comfortably seated on the leather sofa in the library.

Marianne looked relieved to see me. One glance at Kathy and I understood why. I had never seen anyone that oppressed and sad. Kathy was a pretty blonde woman, but her dark, sunken blue eyes were dull and listless, and her face was a shroud of hopelessness.

Marianne greeted me with a hug before introducing me to Kathy. I smiled at Kathy, and for a moment, I was speechless but quickly regained my momentum by the revelation that this girl was hurting and Jesus was her cure. The library felt stiff and for- mal, so I suggested we move to the more comfortable family room where our weekly Bible study took place with several other Christian women.

After switching to the cozy family room, Kathy sat next to me on the cushy sofa, and Marianne sat on the floor to face us. Kathy turned to me and dreamily exclaimed, "What kind of perfume are you wearing?" It was the first sign of life we had heard from her because her face lit up when she asked about my perfume. I brushed it off and began asking questions about her salvation to make sure Kathy was a believer in Christ Jesus before continuing our quest to set her free.

After determining Kathy had accepted Jesus Christ as her personal Savior, I requested Marianne get two other Bibles for the next phase of ministry. After we each had a Bible, I turned back to the open one on my lap. Directing us all to the Book of Psalms. I explained that *worship* was the Key of David, and whenever we lifted up our voices by singing a Psalm aloud as an act of worship, there would be a lifting of our spirits to a heavenly realm.

"Now, Kathy, don't feel self-conscious," Marianne added with a chuckle, "I sound like a bullfrog when I sing."

I led them to Psalm 9 and began melodiously singing the words to demonstrate what I meant. Soon we all were harmoniously lifting our voices in song to the words, "I will praise you, O Lord, with all my heart; I will tell of all your wonders. I will be glad and rejoice in you, I will sing praise to your name, Oh Most High."

I explained that praise of God is an act of the *will*, and David often proclaimed "I *will*" to bring his soul into agreement with his spirit.

As Kathy's story unfolded, we learned that she began experiencing severe depression for nearly two years. Probing into her life uncovered books on the occult that arrived (two years earlier) through the "Book of the Month" Club and were on her bookshelf at home. Through prayer, she denounced any involvement with these books and confessed other things that might have been "an open door" to demonic oppression. It was only the tip of the iceberg, we'd later discover.

Within two hours, her husband rang the doorbell to fetch his wife for admittance to Harding Hospital. After Selma led Gary into the family room, Kathy said, "Gary, I am fine. I really don't need to go." One look at her bright and cheerful face confirmed that she was okay, and he left her with us with a sigh of relief.

I followed Kathy home in my car, and together we burned the two occult books in her gas-lit fireplace. As she escorted me to the door, she once again gushed, "Oh my gosh, the *perfume* you are wearing is beyond words. In fact, when you walked into Marianne's house this morning, I could actually *smell you before* I saw you. Your perfume permeated the entire house!"

Well, that was certainly confirmation to the Word of Knowledge that morning about "going *before* me as a sweet-smelling savor." I know that a perfume scent can *linger* after a woman leaves a room, but that was the first time I experienced it going *before* a person.

Two days later, the Lord said, "Take My other bottle of perfume to Kathy as a gift."

When I stopped by her home, she was delighted to receive the perfume and confessed that she was still struggling. In fact, the day before, she had gone for a much-needed haircut since she had not gone out of the house in many months. In the middle of getting her hair cut at a beauty salon, she experienced another full-blown panic attack. Gary received her frantic 9-11 call to rescue her.

Obviously, Kathy needed the power of the Holy Spirit to ward off all future anxiety attacks. That afternoon, through biblical instruction and prayer, she experienced the fullness of the Holy Spirit with evidence of speaking in tongues. She never again experienced another panic attack.

However, Kathy was a victim of a horrific childhood, and over the next several years, she went through intensive Christian counseling with an expert in dissociative identity disorder.

Thankfully, Kathy was never again institutionalized and raised her four children in church without depression or despair. Her oldest son is a successful doctor.

About six years after our first meeting, on a Sunday evening, I was in church wearing my Jesus perfume. I had not seen Kathy in a couple of years but kept tabs on her spiritual progress and occasionally talked to her by telephone.

When Kathy entered our church foyer, she was about twenty yards away from me since I was on the opposite side of the sanctuary. I was delighted to see her bright blue eyes and smiling face rushing toward me. She shouted out with glee. "You're wearing our perfume! I could smell it as soon as I opened the door!"

I love Jesus. He is so amazing!

Walk in love, just as Christ also loved you and gave Himself up for us, an offering and a sacrifice to God, as a fragrant aroma.

Ephesians 5:2, NIV

I saw Satan fall like lightning from heaven. Behold, I give you the authority to trample on serpents and scorpions, and overall the power of the enemy, and nothing shall by any means hurt you. Nevertheless, do not rejoice in this, that the spirits are subject to you, but rather rejoice because your names are written in heaven.

Luke 10:17–20, NIV

Jesus answered, "Truly, truly, I say to you, unless one is born of water and the Spirit, he cannot enter the kingdom of God."

John 3:5

For if you live according to the flesh you will die, but if by the Spirit you put to death the deeds of the body, you will live.

Romans 8:13

CHAPTER TWENTY

Dottie Rambo, David Schoch, Charles Green, and Gospel Singer, Sharalee

Together, Daryl and I prayerfully sought direction for our future. We attended a large charismatic church and taught the *Understanding God* course to about thirty to forty adults from various churches throughout the community. More and more, we were feeling a tug to enter full-time ministry.

We had sold the Cadillac dealership and made investments with the capital gain since Daryl was very much a businessman with an entrepreneurial spirit.

Pastor Jim Beall encouraged us to relocate to New Orleans and consider coming under the spiritual direction of Pastor Charles Green for ministry training.

We arrived in New Orleans for the annual June conference in faith, expecting to hear a prophetic word to clarify our future and confirm if we were to stay. It was an exciting time of faith at work.

Guest speaker, Prophet David Schoch, taught on the restoration of the Tabernacle of David. Brother Schoch stressed the fact that our first and foremost service is to *worship God in spirit and truth.* We are created for His glory, and it is by our offering of praise that we approach the throne of Grace. The gates of Zion are the gates of praise!

A few years before this particular New Orleans June conference, Dottie Rambo had arrived in a wheelchair, barely able to walk from pain. It was Prophet David Schoch who prayed for her healing. Following her healing, she wrote "We Shall Behold Him," a national sensation.

Dottie Rambo *adored* David Schoch, so naturally, we were all thrilled when he gave her another encouraging personal prophecy before she departed a day earlier than we did.

On the last morning of the conference, Pastor Schoch was scheduled to teach again. Daryl and I both sensed he would deliver a prophecy over us. Dottie had left the night before to fulfill a ministry commitment in another city.

During his message, Pastor Schoch spoke of his ministry trip to Calcutta, India. After landing, the stench was so terrible he almost got back on the airplane! I remember thinking, *Oh no, Lord. Please don't send us to India!* He gave a timely message about commitment and serving the Lord, even in *deplorable* conditions.

He stopped in the middle of his delivery and pointed out to us. He said, "Daryl and Barbara, the Lord spoke to me about you this morning in prayer. The Holy Spirit says to *return* to Columbus and not budge. Do not knock on any doors or make phone calls to recruit support for your vision. *People will come to you* and ask to be taught, and the church you start will be initiated by the Lord, not by man."

Pastor Green was disappointed. However, the Word of the Lord was clear, and he blessed our lives with wholehearted enthusiasm.

We met Jerry and Sharalee Lucas, who were living in New Orleans. They desired to start a church with us. Jerry was from Ohio and played basketball for Ohio State University before starring in the NBA with the New York Knicks.

Sharalee was a gypsy at heart, rarin' to go anywhere with Jesus! I loved her zeal for the Lord. Her national ministry through several Christian music recordings was impressive. It seemed like an ideal fit. They traveled to Ohio several times and stayed in our home to pray and discuss the *vision.* When Sharalee was offered a tentative television position on the 700 Club, they changed ministry directions, and we blessed their journey.

A few months after that New Orleans conference, Dottie Rambo arrived in Columbus to minister at an area church. She acknowledged us from the platform, excited to see us in the audience. Then she began to prophetically speak about our future.

She proclaimed, "Daryl and Barbara, the Lord says to *sit*, like a tree frog at the bottom of a big tree. Just *sit* like that ole tree frog, *just wait* on the Lord. Do not do anything; people will come to you." She had such a Southern way of saying 'tree frog' that it made us chuckle.

Afterward, when we told her that her *beloved* David Schoch had basically prophesied the same thing, she began to weep with joy. She hugged us and began sharing about her prayer ministry with other people. She told us of her special friendship with Elvis

Presley and how he often called her to pray for him. As a token of appreciation, Elvis gave her his white-fringed performance outfit worn in Blue Hawaii. "I'm the only one who owns one of his outfits," she said, glowing.

As a fashion plate, she dressed like a true diva. So, owning this Elvis outfit was a true gem.

One morning, in New Orleans, her daughter Reba and husband Donny McGuire led anointed praise and worship. I stood next to Dottie in the front row. I glanced down at Dottie's glitzy open sandals to see a shiny gold nail on each big toe. She surely was the female counterpart of flamboyant Elvis. I admired them both so much.

Weeks before that New Orleans conference, the Holy Spirit instructed me to present Dottie with a beautiful porcelain Madame Alexander doll sitting in a rocking chair. I sold this collection in the lobby gift shop I operated in the historic Worthington Inn. I felt a little foolish giving a grown woman a *doll*. When she opened my gift, she exclaimed, "How did you know I collect these same porcelain dolls?! I love it! Thank you so much!"

Within days of seeing Dottie in Columbus and getting another prophetic word about "waiting" on the Lord, Daryl was golfing with three businessmen friends.

While driving around on the cart, the guys began asking him questions about the Bible. One man suggested starting a men's Bible study. Daryl agreed with one condition. "You drum up the men

Dottie Rambo, David Schoch, Charles Green, and Gospel Singer, Sharalee

to attend. I don't want to make any phone calls to make it happen."

Within weeks, Daryl began teaching an early morning men's Bible study at a restaurant in the village of Worthington each Friday. All he had to do was show up with a thirty-minute prepared lesson each week. There were about sixty businessmen on the roster, and about forty faithful men showed up each week for a timely message based on biblical principles. The discipline of diligent Bible study and keeping the lesson to thirty minutes was preparation for becoming a pastor.

The following year, Daryl and I planned to attend our third Word of Faith conference in New Orleans in June 1983. That same month, our daughter, Tammie, would marry Barry Farah, son of Dr. Charles Farah, a theologian at Oral Roberts University. It was a beautiful outdoor ceremony followed by a white tent reception on our lawn overlooking the water.

Easter Sunday, 1983, fell in March that year. I awakened at dawn to watch the sun come up over the large reservoir of water behind our country home. I sang in the spirit, giving adoration to the Lord before praying, as I usually do, but never quite that early!

Later, before dressing for church, I flipped the channels on the TV to find a Christian program. *Three* different church choirs were singing Dotti Rambo's song, "Behold the Lamb." Sandy Patti won a Dove Award the year she recorded it, further making the song famous.

What must that feel like? Our nation of church choirs was performing "Behold the Lamb" that Easter Sunday. That inspired me so much that I sat down and wrote Dottie Rambo a hand-written letter that morning. When I signed the benediction, I wrote, "May you stay safe and free from fear." I fully intended to write, "May the Lord bless you and keep you in His loving care."

Those words startled me, but I didn't have time to ponder them because the prophetic took over with a personal word to Dottie. It was an uplifting word of encouragement that confirmed her life was in danger. She was battling extreme fear, but God was protecting her.

That June, after we arrived in our New Orleans hotel, we found written instructions from Pastor Charles Green that the Friday evening service was *not* at the church. We were directed to a downtown theatre as a surprise. When we arrived, the huge marquee wrapped in lights read, "Tribute to Dottie Rambo."

The legendary Dottie Rambo, by far, is the most prolific Christian songwriter of our time. Her husband, Buck, and their daughter, Reba, recorded as The Rambos, and I adored their music. Dottie, a Grammy and Dove Award winner, wrote over 2,500 songs in her lifetime. With too many awards to list, there isn't a famous Christian recording artist who hasn't recorded one of Dottie's award-winning tunes.

Sharalee was co-producer of The Dotti Rambo Tribute, so imagine how tough it was selecting music from so many anointed songs in Dottie's vast repertoire.

The awesome Word of Life church choir performed the musical tribute with various guest soloists, including Sharalee, an anointed Gospel singer/songwriter in her own right.

That Friday night musical tribute was exhilarating. Dottie sat in the audience, being memorialized in such an honored way. It felt like a tribute to Dottie Rambo at the Oscars! I couldn't wait to congratulate her.

After the show, Dottie stood in the crowded lobby greeting guests. I approached her from behind and placed my hand on her back. She turned with a gracious smile as she did with all her fans. After hugging, I solemnly spoke, "I have a word from the Lord for you, Dottie."

She turned somber before responding. *"I know."*

Sharalee could not sleep that night. Later, she said, "I thought it was all that music rolling around my head keeping me awake. But, as I prayed, the Lord gave me a prophetic word for Dottie about overcoming fear."

The next afternoon, Sharalee took Dottie to lunch to deliver the message from the Lord. However, after chatting through a pleasant lunch, Dottie gave no indication that she was under spiritual attack. Confused, Sharalee leaned forward to challenge, "So, what are you *afraid* of?"

Dottie's eyes filled up with tears. She managed to choke back a sob from the depth of her soul. "I can't cry as *hard* as I want to in this crowded restaurant."

That evening of the Word of Life conference, Dottie performed a few of her glorious songs before testifying of her deliverance. A year earlier, she'd moved to Los Angeles to be near Reba and Donny. However, soon after arriving in LA, she began battling spiritual warfare in strange manifestations from this domain of darkness.

Anticipating this upcoming June prophetic New Orleans conference, Dottie explained her why. She said, "I told the Lord I needed '*two*' prophetic words from Him to guarantee my safety to bring me peace." She beamed, "Sharalee gave me one prophetic word, and along came that sweet Barbara Sanders with the second one!"

Following dinner for all the conferees in the gymnasium, Sharalee and I privately ministered to Dottie at an empty table. She told us that her telephone rang nightly, with a mysterious person breathing on the other end. Also, a strange knock on the front door, late one night in the wee hour, was added terror. Demonic spirits pestered her while sleeping. The devil surely hated this anointed vessel that had the entire world singing "We Shall Behold Him" on Easter Sunday and for decades to come. Together, we prayed for Dottie to remain in perfect peace. She was very grateful for our loving support. We pledged our continued prayer.

The devil's playground is in Hollywood, so little wonder that Dottie Rambo was under spiritual attack. Her return home to Nashville, located in the Bible belt, ended any further demonic harassment.

Over the next twenty-five years, she helped nurture her long-awaited grandchildren in the ways of Christ Jesus. This treasure of life was her greatest legacy of love from the Lord.

The world grieved her untimely death. She tragically died in a tour bus accident on Mother's Day, 2008. She is now in heaven, and that brings us sweet comfort.

Dottie's early life was not easy, but the universe gained precious pearls from her suffering. Her gospel music is sung all over the world. Her musical genius abides in her daughter, Reba, and Dottie's three grandchildren, Dionne, Destiny, and Israel.

Dottie Rambo touched my life those three years we fellowshipped in New Orleans. I will never forget her.

"I will praise thee, O lord, with my whole heart: for thou hast heard the words of my mouth. I will sing praise to thee in the sight of his angels" (Douay-Rhelms Bible).

"I solemnly charge you in the presence of God and of Christ Jesus, who is to judge the living and the dead, and by His appearing and His Kingdom: preach the word; be ready in season and out of season; reprove, rebuke, exhort, with great patience and instruction"

2 Timothy 4:1–2, NIV

CHAPTER TWENTY-ONE

The Birth of
Zion Christian Fellowship

Within three years of connecting with the leadership at Bethesda through the Parkers, we were discussing the need for a New Testament Church that taught the principles of Christ Jesus along with a special emphasis on Water Baptism and circumcision of the heart. *The Lord knew the big picture when we met Fred and Florence Parker.* That connection was the birth of a church called Zion Christian Fellowship in 1985.

Through Pastor Moses Vegh from Hope Temple, he linked us up with his music Minister, Dean Demos, and his wife, Patty, to start this work.

The Apostolic network that ordained us included Pastor Jim Beall, Pastor Moses Vegh, Pastor Paul Stern, and Pastor Willard Jarvis from Columbus.

After church meetings in schools and career centers, we built a beautiful sanctuary. In 1989, we dedicated our beautiful newly constructed church building. To my husband and the planning committee of Zion Christian Fellowship, I admonished, "I don't care who comes from the Beall family, just as long as Brother Higgins is here." Along with a delightful delegation from the Beall family, Brother Higgins was also present with a special place of honor, representing the heart of Mom Beall, who surely would have been very proud of us.

Zion Christian Fellowship continues as a prospering church, still known for beautiful worship and evangelistic outreach to the community. I am forever grateful for the vision birthed by God and fulfilled for a prophetic church that continues reaching the nations and impacting lives for the Kingdom of God.

CHAPTER TWENTY-TWO

Reinhard Bonnke in Africa with Missionaries Jon and Molly Stern

Next time I'll kill him...

Our young missionary friends from Kenya were home on a two-month furlough. During this allotted time, Jon and Molly Stern traveled to various cities throughout America to give a report to churches that supported them through the year.

We welcomed Jon and Molly's yearly visit and looked forward to their testimonies from "the bush." They arrived with a precious newborn baby girl, Lydia, and their three-year-old son, Paul, named after his grandfather Rev. Paul Stern, a father to us in the ministry.

Their stay in our home allowed them time to relax and share intimate details of their mission in Africa. We tried to make them comfortable, serving them home-cooked meals and pampering them as much as they would allow.

Nothing much had changed since we had seen them last; they were as committed to serving in a remote village of Kenya. They had been there for several years and seemed content to make their home among the primitive natives, adjusting to cultural barriers and severe demonic opposition at times.

On Saturday evening, they put on a home video tape of their uncivilized village, with scenes showing their clay floor church with simple wooden benches and a thatched roof. I watched in fascination as the women in the church boiled a huge pot of tea mixture outside on an open fire for a special event.

The people in the church were barefoot, chanting songs in their language, sitting on simple benches, rocking back and forth. I would never have known they were Christians. It surprised me to know that there was very little traditional Christian music and their style of worship was so backward.

Jon and Molly had beautiful voices and sang *More Than Wonderful*, a song made popular by Larnelle Harris and Sandi Patty. As the video played, I whispered to Molly, "Don't you and Jon ever sing? You have such beautiful voices..." Molly's response surprised me but gave me a clue to the opposition they were up against in this remote village.

"Oh, no, the people in our church *hate* our style of music. They really can't stand it. They won't let us sing." I was flabbergasted, to say the least, and wondered how they could continue year after year without seeing much breakthrough or rewards for their sacrificial efforts, especially being denied such a powerful anointing that they possessed in leading worship.

Jon was born in Nigeria, the second of the youngest of four children. His parents, Eleanor and Paul Stern, lived in various parts of Africa before pioneering the Rock Church in Danville, Illinois.

Molly's parents were members of the Rock Church in Danville; her father was a respected physician in the town and a pillar in the church. Jon and Molly met as teenagers, and both felt called to the mission field early in life. It was a match made in heaven!

The video continued to play on the TV screen, and suddenly little Paul appeared with a full-body cast covering his entire torso. It surprised me because I had not heard he had been injured. Molly said, "Didn't you hear what happened to us last year?" I was completely miffed by what I was seeing on the video and anxiously waited to hear more details. I felt bad that I had not been able to pray through an obvious crisis in their life. I surely hoped she didn't feel abandoned by my lack of knowledge about something so serious.

A simple explanation was given after the video ended. Jon was in his Renault vehicle, getting ready to back out of his yard. He was talking to a native member of his church who was walking alongside the car as Jon was backing up. Paul wandered outside and stepped behind the car without Jon realizing he was there. He backed out of the yard, driving over Paul. The young man, seeing what had happened, screamed at Jon. In a panic, Jon put the car in forward, driving back over the tiny body of his three-year-old son a second time! Molly happened to be looking out of the kitchen window as the horror unfolded right before her eyes.

The lifeless child was scooped up and rushed to the nearest hospital, two and a half hours away. The long ride over bumpy and dusty tureen was a nightmare for this young couple as they prayed their child would live and not die. Little Paul was not bleeding externally, but they feared he was bleeding internally. They clung to Jesus, their only hope, praying every torturous minute along the way as their little boy whimpered softly in great agonizing pain.

As it turned out, miraculously, only his pelvis bone was broken, not crushed, and no other organs were damaged. It seemed unbelievable, considering the weight of the car and getting run over not once but *twice.* They praised God for saving the life of their little boy, but Jon was never the same after the accident. Pauly's grueling months, wrapped in a lower-body cast, was a small price to pay for the healing that was taking place in his broken pelvis. It was an amazing story that was still unfolding.

The following night, Jon preached at our Sunday evening service. In a strange voice with no intonation, he shared his longing to birth praise and worship in his village. But felt Jon was up against many spiritual oppositions, mainly the chief Witch Doctor.

Jon told us that a visiting American minister observed that their village was so steeped in superstition and fear that their church would probably *never* embrace spiritual worship, or at least it would take about "nine years" for them to release so many traditions and major obstacles to revival.

I remember thinking, *Nine years?* More like *nine minutes* with the powerful anointing that is upon Jon and Molly for praise and worship.

I kept listening to Jon's voice as he spoke, trying to discern why he spoke in a monotone voice with hardly any enthusiasm. He seemed to be going through the motions, but something was missing...what was it? The Lord interrupted my thoughts and said, "Give him that banner," directing my eyes to the one that read *"Through Our God We Shall Do Valiantly."*

My heart skipped a beat. I could hardly believe what I was being directed to do because that banner was my favorite banner.

That banner represented my heart for the city of Columbus. It was a *war* banner made of heavy-duty outdoor flag material and could be taken on an actual battlefield.

It was the color of blood red with a huge silver shield representing the armor of God. In the middle of the shield was the Cross of Jesus Christ. The Lord spoke prophetically about that banner and once told me that scripture above the shield that read *"Through Our God We Shall Do Valiantly"* was one that would "take Columbus."

I understood the military terminology since I always considered myself a *warrior* for the Lord. It was the very essence of my belief in God and scripture that represented nations *conquered* for Jesus.

There was a lot of sentimental history attached to that banner as well, so little wonder I couldn't bear to part with it. In fact, I could hardly believe God asked me to give it away. I was heartsick for a few minutes.

When our church members prayed outdoors as a declaration march around fourteen acres for the future church building, that war banner led the way.

When we had an official groundbreaking ceremony to begin building, the world's tallest Elder (6' 8) stood behind the leadership, holding up *"Through Our God We Shall Do Valiantly."* When it was my turn to overturn the earth, I plunged the silver shovel into the ground with my typical exuberance. I flung the dirt high into the air with a shout of praise to the Lord. All the dirt flew up over the banner, landing on top of Elder Bob, who didn't see it coming! We all laughed, including the tall Bob, and I got teased to death over it. That story was made famous by Dr. Sam Sasser and retold in his book of comical Church happenings entitled *Holding Sister Sue's Leg Up in Prayer.*

But on a somber note, the Lord asked me to give away that signature banner. I wasn't quite grasping the spiritual significance of His request. My heart was being tested, and I almost missed a powerful blessing that would impact a nation.

I began to negotiate with the Lord. I thought, *Well, I'll ask Daryl if I am not supposed to give this banner up...if not, he'll intervene.* I inched closer to my seat, whispering in my husband's ear, secretly wishing he would not approve. He leaned back to quietly reply, "Well, of all the banners in the room, *that one* was the only banner Jon commented on this morning before Church started; he really likes it..."

I quietly got up and directed our pianist/worship leader to sing *"Through Our God We Shall Do Valiantly"* as soon as I gave her the signal to begin the song.

The stage was set. Jon ended the service, and I took the microphone to make a presentation speech. I directed everyone to Psalm 10 and read the passage out loud. I explained that the Lord wanted Jon to take the banner back to help do *spiritual warfare* in the village against those who were resisting worship. My husband went over to get the banner to present it to Jon after I explained that God desired for them to take our special banner back to Africa to do spiritual warfare in their village.

When the banner pole passed from Daryl's hands to Jon's hands, an explosion in Jon erupted that surprised all of us. At the top of his lungs, he started shouting praises to God. Helen, on the piano, played, *"Through Our God We Shall do Valiantly,"* and the entire congregation sang while Jon continued to shout victoriously. No longer the meek and mild Jon, he was now a powerful warrior roaring with a voice of triumph as he stood holding up the banner.

It was truly a time of celebration and victory, but I was not aware of just how significant parting with that banner would be until many months later.

Molly and I and the children had driven to church in a separate vehicle from Jon and Daryl. On the way home, she looked over at me, smiling brightly. "You will never know what you did for Jon.

He finally got set free from fear tonight..."

"What do you mean?" I asked, puzzled but not surprised, considering how oppressed he seemed while preaching.

"Well, the night Pauly got run over, Jon was on his way to a huge tent rally with Evangelist Reinhard Bonnke. Jon had been on the planning committee all year. He was on his way to the first service of thousands when the accident happened. Since we were at the hospital the entire weekend, we never got to attend the rally that Jon had worked so hard for...the devil warned Jon, 'If you do another revival, the next time I'll kill him.' So he's been under this oppressive cloud of fear ever since the accident, but tonight I saw it break."

We parted the next morning with tears of joy at the goodness of the Lord. We hugged goodbye and prayed for protection over their family. The banner was carefully rolled up and squeezed in the back of their hatchback, which was loaded down with luggage, baby stuff, toys, books, and a large cooler. They were headed to upstate New York to speak at Elim Bible College. They would travel back through Columbus the following week on their way to Danville, their home church.

The following year, Jon told me that a boil broke on his leg as he drove out of Columbus that day. A week later, when they rode back through, he broke out in hives the moment they reached Columbus.

The war was raging. When they arrived back in their African

village, Jon organized a procession with all his church members. Triumphantly holding up *"Through Our God We Shall Do Valiantly,"* they marched through the village, fearlessly shouting praises to the Lord and sending up victorious prayers. Within a few short days, the Witch Doctor packed up and moved away.

Two years after hearing that glorious report, we met with Jon and Molly and their three children, who were healthy and strong. Their kids are now married with children and still serving in Kenya.

Jon gave us another victorious update about their work in Africa. After faithfully serving in the bush for many years, the Lord led them to a mega church in a large city.

This congregation met in an outdoor stadium that seated about ten thousand. Pastor Jon stood on the platform with the senior pastor waiting to be introduced. The pastor was a British missionary who preached every sermon through an interpreter.

After the music ended, the pastor invited Jon to say a few words and lead the congregation in a familiar song. The praise and worship team had already sung all their praise music selections in English.

Now, here is Jon, a blonde, blue-eyed young man invited to lead ten thousand natives in a familiar praise song in English. Jon took the microphone, which was well amplified throughout the stadium with gigantic speakers. Jon began a familiar praise song, but he sang it in their native language of Swahili.

"Wow! Did they get excited?"

Jon smiled brightly, "The crowd went totally ballistic. A roar erupted that could be heard for miles. They continued to shout and praise God at the top of their lungs."

I rejoice at that story because Jon and Molly were faithful to serve in a small village for many years. The Lord led them into the fullness of ministry without an ounce of fear. Praise His Holy Name. The *"Through Our God We Shall Do Valiantly"* banner reigns in this stadium church to this day.

Jon and Molly, along with their now widowed mom, Eleanor Stern, pioneered an orphanage for hundreds of children who lost parents to the AIDS epidemic. Over sixty years ago, Mom Beall had prophesied that Eleanor would open an orphanage in her older years. God is always faithful to His Holy Spirit-inspired prophetic word.

CHAPTER TWENTY-THREE

Evangelist Judson Cornwall and Ohio State University Coach Woody Hayes

Each year he was still alive, Judson Cornwall came to minister at Redeemers East in Columbus. This charismatic church was founded by Pastor Willard Jarvis, the faithful patriarch over leaders in our city.

The Redeemers East conference was usually three days in length, and I drove across town to attend the daytime sessions on my own since Daryl was working.

One Wednesday, following Judson's anointed teaching session, I heard the Holy Spirit say, "Invite Judson to lunch this Friday with Woody Hayes."

This request was bizarre beyond words since I had no idea if Woody was in town or if his schedule would permit a spur-of-the-moment lunch with a total stranger. Yet, in faith, I asked Judson if he'd like to go to lunch with a retired football player and Daryl's college coach.

Two days later, Daryl, Woody, and Judson enjoyed lunch at the Athletic Club on the Ohio State University campus. Daryl said, "Those two history buffs really hit it off. They are the exact same age...they talked non-stop." The two authors exchanged publications with a promise to read each other's books.

Later, Willard chuckled when he told us, "Lunch with Woody Hayes was the highlight of Judson's trip back to Columbus."

The following month, Daryl and I were in New Orleans, attending a five-day conference at Word of Life with Pastor Charles and Barbara Green.

After the morning conference session, a buffet lunch was served in the gymnasium set up to feed over 1,500 conferees in attendance. As I was about to bite into my sandwich, I glanced at the man seated on my right. To my delight, it was Judson Cornwall.

"Well, hello, Doctor Cornwall," I said, smiling brightly. "I'm Barbara Sanders, the lady who fixed you up with Woody Hayes last month in Columbus."

With my cup of coffee following lunch, I joined Judson sitting by himself after the hosts, Barbara and Charles, dashed off tending to other ministry guests. Every day, we shared evangelistic testimonies for about twenty minutes, just the two of us.

After I shared an exciting testimony about God, with a twinkle in his eye, he'd say, "Well, now I have one for you."

Apparently, he thought I was spiritually mature enough to handle a whopper. Actually, if it hadn't come straight from the lips of Judson Cornwall, I probably wouldn't have believed it.

Judson considered himself a traveling Bible teacher and author whose ministry spanned the globe. He was not "pastor material." However, when Senior Pastor Fuchsia Pickett required hip surgery and needed to vacate her post at Fountain Gate Church in Plano, Texas, he stepped in as her temporary replacement while she convalesced at home.

The church was thriving with strong leaders. After a few weeks, he was asked to stay longer because Dr. Pickett's recovery was slower than expected.

He said, "The negative backlash surprised me. Church members blamed *me* for the drop-in attendance and offerings. I actually got accused of trying to take over the church."

So, when seven leadership couples left the church, the foundation was shaken. Everyone blamed Judson for the painful church split.

One night, asleep next to his wife, he was startled awake by a heavy demonic presence taunting him. The hideous evil presence did not frighten him because calling upon Jesus would make it leave the room.

"I repeatedly went through every *formula* I knew for rebuking the devil in Jesus' Name," he chuckled. "After it left, I'd fall back asleep, but it would come back at me, oppressing and taunting. After pleading the Blood of Jesus, the dark, creepy thing lurked in the far corner of my bedroom, refusing to leave. Then I felt something on the side of the bed." He paused for emphasis.

"Go on." I said, wide-eyed, "what was it?"

"Well, I assumed it was our Dachshund attempting to jump up on the bed. I suspect my wife secretly lets our dog sleep with her when I'm out of town," he laughed. "But when I turned to shush the dog away, a three-foot angel jumped up on the bed. Now, I know angels are neither male nor female," he added quickly, "but this angel was dressed in a ballerina outfit and began twirling up and down the bed between me and my wife."

As a former ballerina, I loved this story and hung on to every word.

"The dark creature in the corner dissipated in the presence of this holy angel *dancing* in glorious delight. Then the Lord spoke to my heart. 'Judson, this is what you need to do in the face of adversity. *Tell my church* to dance and rejoice, and I will restore all that's been lost.'"

"Wow," I said. "That is really powerful."

"I was in the middle of writing my first book on praise and worship," he explained, "so this was a principle that I needed to *experience.* In church the next morning, I shared the story with our ailing congregation. I'm not sure they *believed* me, but in faith, we *danced* around the sanctuary even though no one *felt* like dancing. Our hearts were heavily burdened with the church falling apart, but we lifted up weighted-down arms in obedience."

He smiled brightly, his eyes glistening. "Within three weeks' time, the Lord brought fourteen *new* couples, more gifted and with better leadership qualities than the seven couples that had left. They became solid pillars of the church."

That amazing story contains a principle of how praise and worship release God's glory. I am forever grateful for the anointed books Judson Cornwall authored for the Church. Christians and music ministers across the universe have benefited and been enlightened by his teachings that have never lost their relevance.

The Holy Spirit is so very real.

Through God we shall do valiantly: for he it is that shall tread down our enemies.

Psalms 60:12, KJV

Are not all angels ministering spirits sent to serve those who will inherit salvation?

Hebrews 1:14, NKJV

CHAPTER TWENTY-FOUR

Princess Diana and Mother Teresa

Within my circle of friends and family members, I'm best known for my *lengthy* evangelistic letters. It started young. Now, they all get detailed text messages, perfectly punctuated and historical emails, or long-winded voice messages. Some things never change.

At nine years of age, I wrote my first appeal to Mayor Orville Hubbard of Dearborn. My mother told me that Camp Dearborn was "only open to residents." So, I took it upon myself to write the Mayor to *change* the law. My handwritten petition to City Hall was on behalf of my best friend, Sandy, who lived in our former community. I wanted her to attend a two-week camp session with me. We had just moved to Dearborn, and I missed my old pal.

Mayor Hubbard's personal reply was addressed to me. When the letter arrived, my mother yelped. "Why on earth is Mayor Hubbard writing *you*?!" It was Mother's alarmed reaction that caused me to remember writing that petition all these decades later.

If a movie or book moves me, I'm apt to write a letter to the author or actor, even though it might never get mailed. I've written a dozen such heartfelt letters still filed away in my computer.

Daryl and I were enjoying a Florida vacation sometime in 1981, and as usual, I used this downtime to read a Christian self-help book.

I don't recall the name of that particular book, but there was mention of Princess Diana as an example of someone not using her tremendous power of influence for the betterment of society.

The Holy Spirit said, "Send her this book." Perhaps the Lord wanted to let her know how incredibly famous she'd become to be mentioned in a best-selling book.

Oh, dear God, really? I responded. *Where on earth does she live?* Then I remembered a wedding day photograph of her and Prince Charles signing their marriage certificate following the televised ceremony that the entire world watched.

My stepdaughter Tammie and I set our alarms for 5 a.m. to tune into the historic event. My five-year-old son watched right along with us. When Bo saw Princess Diana in the horse-drawn small gilded carriage, he remarked, "Mommy, what if she can't breathe in there?"

Barnes & Nobel carried the pictorial book I needed to locate her *residence* under her signature on the marriage certificate. Princess Diana wrote "Althorp," which later became famous because she was buried there.

The new Princess simply wrote, "Althorp, Northampton." So, that is where I wrote the following letter.

Dear Princess Diana,

I trust this letter finds you well. I am writing to you be- cause the Holy Spirit prompted me to send you this inspiring book. It is worth reading because Jesus Christ has the wisdom to encourage your life.

The entire world is watching your every move and admiring your beauty and your clothing. In fact, you are the most powerful woman in the world right now. Your light is very bright, but please don't go down in history as the Princess, who is only known for your stylish designer clothes. Use your influence to make a difference in the world for humanity, especially for the poor and disadvantaged...

About a month later, I received a handwritten note from England. Princess Diana's Lady-in-Waiting, Miss Anne Beckwith-Smith, wrote me a hand-written thank-you note since she was also Lady Diana's personal correspondence secretary.

Dear Mrs. Sanders,

Her Royal Highness Diana, the Princess of Wales, wishes to thank you for your kind letter and the gift you sent on her behalf. She wants me to be sure to tell you that it arrived on her birthday...

So, imagine visiting her family at Althorp, Princess Diana's former residence, and finding my letter and gift on her birthday. I was most delighted to get that news.

The Holy Spirit planted a *seed* in Princess Diana's life. From all reliable biographical accounts that I've read about her early marriage, it didn't start off well. After all, she was a pudgy, insecure nineteen-year-old when she became engaged to the much older Prince Charles. Everyone needs encouragement, especially those growing up in Ivory Towers.

Years later, Princess Diana obviously found significant confidence and self-worth in her charity work and amazing fund-raising abilities. What a champion of controversial causes she became, like a beacon of light in the world. I admired her.

While writing this story about Mother Teresa and Princess Diana, I came across this article written on August 31, 2012, by Mary C. Johnson, a former nun. It is worth sharing now.

Remembering Princess Diana and Mother Teresa:

They Met at My House

This week marks the fifteenth anniversary of the tragic deaths, just six days apart, of two twentieth-century icons, beloved women who first met at my house.

Some might expect that from my perspective—that of an ex-nun who spent twenty years in Mother Teresa's Missionaries of Charity—that I'd write about the service and inspiration Diana and Teresa offered the world. Instead, I find myself thinking about their clothes.

Diana, of course, was a fashion icon. Mother Teresa was, even among her own sisters, a notoriously sloppy dresser. Mother rarely pinned the sari high enough on her shoulder, and it often hung lopsided around her face, the pins at weird angles. We were all grateful that the morning of Diana's visit, Mother had allowed Sister Dorothy to fuss with her sari until it was more presentable.

My job that Chilly day in 1992 was to keep the paparazzi out. Though Diana's private, unpublicized visit was scheduled for 2 p.m., the photographers appeared outside the convent gates on Rome's Via Casilina before dawn, the glowing tips of their cigarettes visible as we nuns filed into chapel for Morning Prayer. I refused the photographers' pleas for entry, and they lugged their cameras onto neighbors' balconies, adjusted their telescopic lenses, and awaited the limo that arrived right on time.

When Diana emerged, long legs unfolding, eyes bright, we sang. A sister approached with a garland, and Diana shyly bent her long neck to receive the necklace of hand-strung pink netting we'd fashioned from scraps of a child's discarded tutu. The netting was as elegant a garland as we sisters had ever made – normally, we strung garlands from shiny candy wrappers. What did a princess accustomed to pearls and jewels think of our fashion sense?

Mother led Diana into her room, a tiny office/bedroom just off the compound. I waited outside, guarding the door, hoping these two women—so hounded and so ad-

mired—might find solace in each other's company.

They talked for nearly thirty minutes, longer than I'd ever spend with Mother's undivided attention, despite having been a sister for fifteen years at that point. I added the sin of envy to my weekly confession list.

Mother cracked the door, motioning for me to admit the Royal Photographer. He decided to pose the saint and the princess, clasping hands, perched on Mother's cot. I'm fairly certain it's the only royal photo featuring cardboard—Sister Gertrude had taped a thick piece of corrugated boxboard to the wall above Mother's pillow, hoping to ward off dampness.

When the photographer stepped out, Mother told me she and Diana wanted to be alone with Jesus. Mother led Diana across the compound. According to our custom, they both removed their shoes before entering the chapel.

I guarded the open chapel doors as the world's two most-admired women knelt, heads bowed. Mother mumbled words none of us in the gathering crowd of nuns and British Embassy folk outside could hear— and I gazed at their shoes. I'll never forget the sight of Diana's shiny black pumps next to Mother's floppy sandals. Mother's sandals had been mended so many times that I wasn't sure any of the original materi-

al remained. I imagined Diana's pumps as one pair among hundreds in an enormous closet, perhaps chosen for her that day by a maid or a butler. They looked as though she had worn them only for this occasion. Mother had worn the same pair of sandals every day for more than a decade.

I thought of the prayer every Missionary of Charity recites each morning while donning her sandals: I shall follow you, dear Jesus, wherever you may go, in search of souls. Each article of clothing donned has its corresponding, with phrases like "holy habit," "angelic purity," "absolute poverty," and "mantle of modesty." A nun's clothes aren't just clothes; they're symbols of consecration to God and union with the poor, but perhaps clothes are always signs of the one who wears them.

When Mother and Diana exited the chapel and slipped on their respective footwear, I directed a chain of nuns to keep the paparazzi out as Diana's limo drove away. Though the princess left, the press refused to go. The cameramen took turns standing on each other's shoulders, snapping photos of the empty driveway and begging me to let them in.

Finally, near dusk, the superior told me to open the gate. The handful of photographers and journalists who remained could take photos in the compound, but

I had to keep them away from the chapel and convent. I fielded questions with ease until the lone female reporter asked, "What was Diana wearing?"

"A skirt," I said.

"What length?"

"Short."

"What color?"

I shrugged.

"Versace?"

That one flew straight over my head.

The woman curled her lip at me. "Everyone on earth is dying to know what Diana wore to meet Mother Teresa, and you can't remember?"

"She had the most beautiful blue eyes," I said.

Only weeks later, in a Belgian tabloid reprinting a photo from one of those balconies, did I really notice Diana's black and white-checked pencil skirt, her white turtleneck sweater, and black jacket.

If only the reporter had asked me about Diana's shoes...

**Mary C. Johnson, Former Nun, Author,
"An Unquenchable Thirst: A Memoir"**

Since I was most concerned about Princess Diana's relationship with the Lord, I longed to know what she and Mother Teresa *talked* about! It was certainly a spiritual connection and obviously meaningful beyond words.

Sadly, we lost them both *within days of each other*. I remember thinking, *That was so typical of Mother Teresa to quietly depart from this earth eclipsed by a shining star to avoid fanfare.*

Princess Diana's memorial service was televised. Like on her wedding day, I set my clock for 5 a.m. to watch with my neighbor, Brenda, a member of our church. I had baked homemade scones, brewed fresh coffee for a thermos, and carried my picnic basket down the street to watch the service in Brenda's home at 6 a.m.

Nielson ratings reported Princess Diana's funeral drew an estimated *33.25 million* American viewers spread across eight networks on September 6, 1997. Worldwide, it was viewed by *2.5 billion*!

It was a very emotional tribute, and Brenda and I wept throughout the ceremony. At one point in the service, the officiating minister asked *the world* to bow to recite the *Lord's Prayer* together.

Imagine the *glory* released in the heavenly realm as billions recited the Lord's Prayer in holy unison. It's mind-boggling if you think about it. I could imagine white lights radiating all over the dark side of the globe as this prayer unfolded.

As tragic as her life ended, in death, Princess Diana had a

greater impact on the world than in life. Princess Diana accomplished something for the Lord Jesus Christ that no other mortal has done in the history of the planet. In her death, the Lord Jesus Christ was glorified as the nations united in one accord, reciting the prayer Jesus taught us to pray.

Our Father,
which art in heaven,
Hallowed be thy Name.
Thy Kingdom come,
Thy will be done in earth,
As it is heaven.
Give us this day our daily bread.
And forgive us our trespasses,
As we forgive them that trespass against us.
And lead us not into temptation,
But deliver us from evil.
For Thine is the kingdom,
The power, and the glory,
For ever and ever.
Amen.

As I wrote out the Lord's Prayer, the Holy Spirit brought to my remembrance a dream about Princess Diana the night she was in labor, giving birth to her first-born son, Prince William, the future King of England.

Although the world anxiously awaited the royal arrival, the public did not know her exact due date or if she went into labor, but the Holy Spirit was keenly aware!

One night, I dreamt that I was in the labor room reciting the Lord's Prayer over her. When I awakened the next morning, the dream was vivid and easily remembered. When I turned on the news, it was celebrated that she had finally given birth to a healthy baby boy. The world rejoiced for her safe welfare and happiness as a new mother.

The Holy Spirit uses the body of Christ to pray for those in need. May we never lose sight of this mandate from the Lord. We are to use our *sphere of influence* to impact family members, friends, neighbors, cities, and the nations with little thought of what to *wear*. We are to be adorned by a cloak of *thankfulness* for what the Lord has done by dying in our place on the Cross of Calvary. He is altogether lovely.

May we wear the garment of praise in all we think or do in life!

THE LOST SONG

"Let the word of Christ dwell in you richly, teaching and admonishing one another in all wisdom, singing psalms and hymns and spiritual songs, with thankfulness in your hearts to God."

Colossians 3:16 (NKJV)

CHAPTER TWENTY-FIVE

"O Glory to the Lamb" Choir Music Birthed by the Holy Spirit

When I was four or five years old, I often sang my heart out, making up words and melodies since I knew no actual songs.

In the summertime, my sanctuary was at the back of our house, close to a quiet, tree-lined alleyway. I'd stand on the back of the closed toilet seat to sing out through the screened window that featured an extra-wide windowsill. It became my little stage.

Sunlight sparkled through creased tree branches as the lush leaves, chirping birds, and gentle breezes created a sound stage straight to heaven. I sang to God with all my heart in my enchanted asylum. Sometimes, I reached such sacred high notes tears rolled down my cheeks. The angels accompanied me because I could hear them in my heart. I didn't care who heard me. I sounded like an opera singer who sang in a different language.

One day, tragedy struck. That little girl lost her song. I still remember how I stopped singing as if it happened yesterday. It still brings a lump to my throat.

My heartrending consequence occurred while dining with my mother and great-grandmother, Lydia Margaret (Powless) Brant, a full-blooded Mohawk Indian. Her daughter Colleen artfully set a beautiful table with matching dishes, coordinated placemats, linen napkins, and stemmed glassware the color of amber. We did not dine like that at home, so those luncheon dates always made me feel very special.

My great-grandfather, Joseph Brant, was an architect who died months before I was born. Both were full-blooded native Indians. All my life I heard that it was actually Grandma Brant who was a direct descendant of military leader and diplomat Joseph Brant from the American Revolution. He was the famous tribal leader, Chief Thayendanegea, most notable for his alliance with Great Britain during and after the war. As a Christian, interpreting among missionaries, he translated the Book of Mark and the Book of Common Prayer into the Mohawk language. However, our genealogy has never been documented because birth records among the Six Nations are limited.

Out of the blue, Grandma Brant looked across the table at my mother. "Shirley Ann, who sings the *best* of all your children?" She and my mother both played the piano, so she probably hoped her grandchildren had musical talent, too. It was a perfectly innocent question.

I straightened up, expecting my mother to praise my beautiful singing. After all, I was the only one who actually sang aloud. David, a late bloomer, age three, rarely *talked*, much less sang. Baby brother, Dennis, was still in diapers.

"Oh, *David* sings the best," Mother replied with pride. Even though my mother didn't say I *couldn't* sing, that is what my little, tender heart comprehended. I stopped singing.

Twenty years later, when Jesus found me, the lover of my soul, He became my inspiration to sing again. I had lost my song for all those silent years.

God began birthing little songs in me at a ladies' prayer meeting or during my quiet devotions.

Pastor Dean Demos, former choir director at Hope Temple with Pastor Moses Vegh, admonished me about keeping track of my simple, child-like choruses. He cautioned, "Now, Barbara, you won't lose your salvation on Judgment Day, but you'll lose some of your crowns if you *bury* your talents."

In 1987, I was in the midst of planning the first citywide worship conference in Columbus. The keynote speakers were Evangelists Janet Shell and Lora Allison. Janet is a nationally known anointed violinist and preacher. Janet suggested inviting her friend, Lora Allison, as well. They were a dynamic duo still going strong, conducting similar worship conferences all over the globe.

I committed the conference to prayer since I had never organized such an event. One night, after five hours of prayerful intercession, I went to bed. As soon as I laid my head on the pillow, I heard a strong melody in my spirit. Since I did not recognize the tune, I realized it was a *new* song. I quickly got out of bed, humming the melody. After recording in a toy tape recorder, the words immediately followed as I quickly wrote them down.

The choir music is entitled "O Glory to the Lamb." The next morning, I sang it to Janet and later to Dean Demos. He transcribed it into sheet music. It is a beautiful choral arrangement that many choirs have sung throughout the country.

In 1988, Daryl and I attended a national conference at a church in Pasadena, California. While we were there, we also heard about an upcoming international worship symposium, which was honoring Steve Fry, an outstanding music composer whose anointed cantatas have spanned the globe. More than 3,000 Christians registered for that weekend worship conference.

As the music director of this Pasadena church, Dr. David Fischer was also involved with the worship conference coming up the following weekend. When Dr. Fischer greeted us in the hallway, he remembered us from Columbus.

He said, "Barbara. I am conducting 'O Glory to the Lamb' as the *grand finale* on Saturday night with a full orchestra."

Daryl and I weren't able to stay over, but I obtained a video. Dance troupe, Ballet Magnificat, processed with beautiful banners as the choir sang "O Glory to the Lamb." To think that Steve Fry was given a tribute with *my* music is mind-boggling.

Traveling evangelist Rev. Daniel Cason, a music minister, informed me that as a guest artist, he conducted a 400 voice-choir that sang "O Glory to the Lamb" in Philadelphia.

My husband was a keynote speaker at a church conference

in Indiana a few years later. The Pastor informed Daryl that his church choir performed "O Glory to the Lamb" when dedicating their new church!

Prophetic songs are birthed from heaven to bring glory to the Lamb. I am humbled by this testimony because the Lord allowed me to experience a *new song* from the chambers of paradise where angels never cease singing praises to our Lord.

O Glory to the Lamb
Words and Music by Barbara Taylor Sanders
Arranged by Dean Demos

O Glory, O Glory to the Lamb
O Glory, O Glory to the Lamb
His Power and His majesty, our crown
Our Savior has risen from the ground
Praise Him, all ye people
Praise His Holy Name
Jesus, the Messiah has been found
Jesus, the Messiah has been crowned
His blood has been sprinkled on the mercy seat
The sacrifice is complete
Satan is now under His feet
Angels shout for joy
Sin is atoned for all mankind
O Glory to the Lamb
O Glory to the Lamb

Prophetic worship comes from a heart yearning for God. We cannot have a relationship with God without a heart of worship and adoration. Music has been a profound key to my deliverance and walk with the Lord. But before I could worship God in spirit and in truth, I had to make Him *Lord* of my life.

The Holy Spirit is real.

> *"Likewise, the Spirit also helps in our weaknesses. For we do not know what we should pray for as we ought, but the Spirit Himself makes intercession for us with groaning, which cannot be uttered. Now He who searches the hearts knows what the mind of the Spirit is, because He makes intercession for the saints according to the will of God. And we know that all things work together for good to those who love God, to those who are the called according to His purpose."*

Romans 8:26–28 (NKJV)

CHAPTER TWENTY-SIX

Brennan Manning and Unusual Manifestations of Tongues

Those early years in Columbus were spent hanging out with Rosie Cunningham and Emma Lou Roller. For a few years, we drove to Pittsburgh to the annual Catholic Charismatic Renewal conference held on the campus of Duquesne University.

My neighbor ladies were giddy over handsome Father Brennan Manning. After I heard him minister, I also became a huge fan. He left the priesthood to marry some years later. He continues to be an outstanding author and speaker on the subject of knowing the intimacy of God.

During these annual charismatic conferences, we heard other outstanding men and women speak about the power of the Holy Spirit. One mainline denomination senior pastor from a *huge* congregation in Dallas shared a humorous story of how he got finally spoke in tongues. His accent was delightful, so try to imagine this testimony being spoken by a tall man with a Texas-size twang.

He had been seeking the Lord with all his might, but he just wasn't getting any satisfaction because his prayer language had not yet manifested, to his chagrin.

One evening, he was making himself a cup of coffee after a time in prayer. He opened the refrigerator door and reached in for the cream. He suddenly burst out in tongues! He was amazed and thrilled that it finally happened. He looked at the audience with a serious demeanor. "So, if you have received the Baptism of the Holy Spirit but haven't spoken in tongues yet, just get yourself a cup of coffee and reach for the cream…"

One afternoon, I was driving northbound on the main artery in Columbus, making a cloverleaf loop to travel west on I-270.

A motorcyclist was driving south, using the same cloverleaf turn to travel west.

The cyclist was right ahead of my car as we both merged onto the super highway. But the front wheel tire hit the raised lip where the two pavements met, and he crashed, flying at full speed.

I watched in horror as his bike flipped over, and he slid down the highway at high speed. His helmet bounced down in front of him. I cried out to Jesus to keep him from dying.

I managed to pull right over to run to his aid. The car behind me pulled over with two women running towards the accident victim. The young man was crouched down, holding himself. He must have been in shock. I knelt down beside him and placed my arm around his shoulders to comfort him. His leather jacket was pushed up, revealing some minor scratches. I was relieved to see him alive.

"You only have some minor laceration on your back. You're going to be okay."

Suddenly, the two gals were standing over us. When I glanced up, I recognized Sarah from my church, but I didn't know her friend. Sarah burst into tongues, and I joined her. We continued praying with urgency. Then I heard the other gal praying in tongues, too.

Other cars pulled up to help us. A man ran over with a blanket to drape over the young man who had not said a word from body shock.

A few years later, Linda and Tom, newcomers from our church, came in for marriage counseling. Linda looked at me and smiled. "You probably don't remember me, but I was with Sarah the day that guy flew off his motorcycle."

"Oh my!" I exclaimed, giving her a hug. "So that was you? Isn't it amazing that he wasn't killed?"

"Yes, that's for sure. But the funny thing about that accident is that I had *never* prayed in tongues before that moment," she said, grinning. "When Sarah and I ran up to him, I heard the urgency of you two praying in tongues, and all of sudden, I was praying in tongues, too!"

What are the odds of three charismatic women covering a near-fatal accident in prayer? When I saw the man fly off his bike, I burst into prayer, calling out to Jesus to keep him from getting killed. The Christian ladies driving behind me were surely shouting out prayers to Jesus as well.

The Holy Spirit saves lives and rescues in the time of trouble.

And they were all filled with the Holy Spirit and began to speak with other tongues, as the Spirit gave them utterance.

Acts 2:4, NKJV

CHAPTER TWENTY-SEVEN

John Z. DeLorean and Harald Bredesen, Prophetic Encounters

General Motors was never the same after the flamboyant executive stepped off the elevator on the fourteenth floor, sporting a turtleneck and sports jacket. John Z. Delorean defied the conservative dress code of the corporate rulers, clad in dark blue suits and conservative neckties. By lunchtime, every haberdasher along West Grand Boulevard was completely sold out of turtleneck sweaters. If nothing else, the maverick certainly proved to be a trendsetter during his tumultuous days in the auto industry.

It was a hot summer day in 1971 when I met John. He had approached Daryl while we stood in a long line-up at a movie theatre in Bloomfield Hills. It must have been another popular James Bond movie. Dressed like a teenager in shorts and a see-through fishnet tank top, a handsome forty-something man with salt and pepper graying hair, black and bushy eyebrows approached my future husband. I did not retain his name when Daryl introduced us. So, when he walked away, I exclaimed, "Who on earth was *that*?"

"That was *John DeLorean*," Daryl replied in a reverent hush of awe.

I immediately recalled his somewhat scandalous wedding in

1969 when John married twenty-year-old Kelly Harmon, a beautiful blonde model, twenty-five years his junior. Kelly's sister, Kris, was married to Ricky Nelson, and her brother Mark Harmon is the current star of the hit NCIS series on the CBS television network.

A few months later, we doubled-dated with John and his young, beautiful bride. A chauffeur-driven Chevrolet with John in the front seat and Kelly, Daryl, and I parked in the backseat seemed rather amusing. It was a Chevy and not a limousine. Although John was Vice President of General Motors, he was General Manager of the *Chevrolet* division.

During our exquisite dinner at the London Chop House, we sat at a large, round booth with a white linen table covering.

We received plenty of gawking attention from waiters and patrons while I hawked out Kelly's large, alluring diamond ring. I hoped Daryl was taking notes. We were not yet engaged at that early point in our relationship. Gorgeous Kelly was delightful, full of energy, and I felt completely at ease in her company. We were close in age.

Something happened that evening with them that left a lasting impression upon me. While together in the lady's room, a heavy-set black attendant dressed in a crisp white uniform handed Kelly and I tea towels to dry our hands. Surprisingly, this beautiful girl with close ties to Hollywood began chatting with the attendant in such a personable way that you would have thought the woman was a long-lost friend. I was so impressed with the kindness Kelly extended to this common employee. I've made it my life mission to extend the same kindheartedness whenever I encounter less fortunate people struggling in life.

Following dinner downtown, we were let off at the Fisher Theatre. The distinguished Russian ballet dancer Rudolph Nureyev performed that evening.

During intermission at the ballet, Daryl disappeared to the restroom. I felt awkward standing with the two *lovebirds.* I wore a calf-length white wool dress and knee-high purple leather boots that evening. Kelly complimented me on my boots.

I replied, "Thank you, I bought them in Spain." I immediately wished I hadn't name-dropped. I merely worked for American Airlines and made frequent discount airfare shopping jaunts to Europe with my co-workers. I felt as ordinary as the woman in the restroom, but it was my own lack of confidence, not anything they conveyed to me.

Kelly loved telling personal stories about her and John. She made me *blush,* sharing about her "surprise" sitting atop their bed wrapped in cellophane and a large bow around her neck while waiting for the birthday boy's arrival home.

Traveling in the car, Kelly asked if we had seen the movie "The Baby Maker," starring Barbara Hershey. It was about a *childless* couple who hired a hippy as a surrogate to bear their child. From the front seat, John sounded irritated when he said, "Boy, you sure keep promoting that movie for some reason." Kelly dropped the subject, but I sensed she wanted to have a baby. They had been married for about two years.

That same year, they started adoption proceedings for baby Zachary but divorced before the adoption was finalized. Thus, John was the first single male to adopt an infant in the state of Michigan. He was on the Tonight show, interviewed by guest host Joey Bishop about the controversial action. I thought, *Leave it to John DeLorean to accomplish something so cutting-edge.*

We spent a week-long ski trip in Aspen with them before their divorce, but regretfully, I never saw Kelly again except on a Tic Tac television commercial. Kelly assured me by saying, "Daryl was so sad when you had to leave." I needed to depart earlier to get back to my airline job in Detroit.

Ever the playboy, when John married super model Cristina Ferrare, it was national news. The gorgeous Italian beauty had been on the cover of countless magazines throughout her modeling career.

Daryl startled me awake the morning after John's arrest. "Wake up, Barbara. It's all over television. John DeLorean was arrested in Los Angeles." We were completely stunned. He was arrested on October 19, 1982, for alleged cocaine trafficking.

Nearly a year after his arrest, Cristina's glamorous face appeared on the September 1983 cover of Ladies' Home Journal magazine with the feature story entitled *Love on Trial*.

Daryl and I were vacationing on Siesta Key Beach in Sarasota, Florida. The article highlighted Cristina's born-again Christian experience. She confessed to secretly pressing pieces of paper into John's hand during visits at the Terminal Island Federal Prison. She comforted him with certain Scripture verses: "This poor man cried out, and the Lord heard *him* and saved him out of all his troubles" (Psalm 34:6) and "Publicly acquit me, Lord, for you are always fair" (Psalm 17:2). That really touched my heart.

By all newspaper and television accounts, John was doomed to spend the rest of his life in federal prison. All through this terrible ordeal, Daryl and I certainly had been praying for him. But it remained a hopeless situation played out in the press. The feds had video tapes of him accepting cash for a suitcase of cocaine. John had become a desperate man trying to save his failing car company through criminal activity.

After reading the perplexing Ladies' Home Journal article, I gazed out at the sun setting across the beautiful Gulf of Mexico. The sun was setting on John's life, too. I asked God to comfort him and also give grace to his troubled family. By now, Zachary was ten years old and his daughter, Kathryn, was six.

As I departed from the lanai, the Holy Spirit spoke to my heart. *"I have a word for John, if you'll write it."* My spirit took a leap. My heart pounded as I rushed to grab a pen and paper off the coffee table. I immediately began writing out the prophetic message from the Holy Spirit.

Although I didn't keep a copy of the exact prophecy, it went something like, "*My son, surrender your arms. Do not fight this battle in your own strength because this is My battle, says the Lord, your God. Keep your eyes on Me, and I will acquit you... Your fate is in My hands...*" God loved John with mercy upon his troubled soul. As I recorded this inspired message from the Lord, *I had a difficult time believing John would really be acquitted.*

A newspaper report identified John's defense attorney as Howard Weitzman of Los Angeles. I contacted his office by telephone, obtaining the address to mail John the prophecy.

A week later, John left a few phone messages on our house phone before finally reaching me a few days later. "Barbara, thank you for writing me. I have your *prayer* pinned to the inside of my briefcase lid, and I read it *every day* before court begins." He sounded genuinely thankful.

The trial started on April 19, 1984. The same mob of reporters and photographers were outside the courthouse on August 19, 1984, goggling as John DeLorean headed in to meet his fate.

One reporter stuck a microphone in John's face as he exited the car. "What do you think the verdict will be?"

"It's in the Lord's hands," John replied while continuing to walk toward the courthouse.

Later, inside, everyone rose to hear the verdict. The Judge pronounced, "Not guilty."

John shot his hands in the air and exclaimed, "Praise the Lord!"

All these decades later, I recently watched a documentary entitled *Framing John Delorean,* starring Alec Baldwin. John's attorney, Howard Weitzman, appeared in the film. It occurred to me that Howard might have a copy of the prophecy. So, I emailed him through his website.

From: Howard L. Weitzman </hweitzman@kwikalaw.com>
Date: Tue, Aug 13, 2019 8:21 PM
To: 'barbarataylorsanders@comcast.net';
Subject: RE: A Friend of John Z. DeLorean

Barbara,

Appreciate your email. I do not have a copy of the prophecy that you sent to John. I remember its existence and that John would read it, but I've not seen it since that trial took place. All the best.

Howard

Howard Weitzman, Esq.

My husband encouraged me to include Howard Weitzman's return email to document that the prophecy existed.

After John's acquittal, heard around the world, Daryl called Harald Bredesen to reach out to the prison-weary man coming out of two years in loneliness and despair. Daryl told John to be on the lookout for a prophet named Harald Bredesen. *Look out* is right!

Harald was a frontrunner of the Charismatic movement in the late 1950s. He personally led Pat Robertson into the Baptism of the Holy Spirit with evidence of tongues. Pat went on to pioneer the Christian Broadcasting Network and, later, The 700 Club, a worldwide outreach. Harald was an original board of director.

Much of John Sherrill's famous book, *They Speak with Other Tongues* (Chosen Books), is devoted to remarkable stories about Harold's boldness in bringing the gift of tongues back into common Christian usage.

We were honored to host Harald in our home whenever he came to Columbus through our mutual friend, Pastor Moses Vegh.

There was no one like Harald. He was a true character in every sense of the word. We all have endearing stories about Harald's zany personality and spontaneous behavior when evangelizing, which was non-stop.

On one such ministry visit, Daryl was promoting an innovative foam cushion shoe insert that was guaranteed to absorb shock. My husband seemed to think this might be one of those witty inventions that could turn to gold.

Harald said, "Hey, let me try them out in *my* shoes." His eyes twinkled with glee at the thought of something to make your feet feel better. After getting back in his shoes with the miracle inserts, Harald jumped off, carpeting onto a wooden bench to shuffle back and forth on the hard surface. "Yep, these inserts *really do* make my feet feel better," he beamed.

Harald's same spontaneous, Holy Spirit-led lifestyle touched world leaders, presidents, kings and queens of nations.

On a subsequent ministry visit, Harald caught wind that our 16-year-old foster daughter, Michelle, knew how to cut hair from being around her mom's beauty salon. She had been twice incarcerated in the correctional institute down the road from us. Streetwise, she was one tough cookie for her age. I met her when I taught a weekly Bible study there.

Michelle tried to beg off, but Harald insisted she was good enough to cut the small patch of hair growing across the back of his head. His confidence helped boost some needed self-worth in her troubled spirit.

He happily leaned over my kitchen sink for the pre-shampoo. While rinsing his head under the running water, he turned his face sideways to keep yakking at us.

While toweling his baldhead dry, he was grinning, as always. "Just give me a Sunday cut."

Scissors in hand, Michelle looked at me to translate. I shrugged my shoulders.

"What's a *Sunday cut?*" giggled Michelle.

"Well," Harald began, "you only cut enough hair off to make it look as if I haven't had a haircut."

I had a feeling he wanted to play it safe so Michelle didn't get scissor-happy and chop off too much since he had so little hair to begin with.

Zany Harald and John Z. DeLorean?

About a year after his release from prison, John DeLorean flew into Columbus and called us for dinner. We would learn that he did spend some meaningful time with Harald in California.

We enjoyed a three-hour dinner at a quiet French restaurant downtown. The chef came out to shake John's hand, and every-one seated around us was tuned in to our conversation. They were probably astounded by what they overheard.

There was a time when this ruthless auto baron talked only about business, the stock market, or other worldly affairs, as he had done in the past with my business-minded husband.

However, that night we connected with our mutual love for Jesus. John poured out his heart, giving God the glory for all his trials and tribulations. He had the victory.

When John told us that he spent two weeks at Harald Bre-desen's California ranch, Daryl and I chuckled without needing to know details. You'd have to know Harald to appreciate that odd-couple connection.

John quipped, "Yeah, you kept telling me to keep an eye for this guy. I happened to run into Harald at a house party. But when I attempted to talk with him, he was sound asleep on the couch. I thought, who is this character?"

We laughed because all of us have amusing stories about Harald napping during significant events. I think the blazing evangelist had two speeds: Full-speed acceleration or sleeping anywhere he could collapse.

Our dear friend, Marcus Vegh, was the former television producer

for Rod Parsley and, years later, for James Robison. Marcus grew up knowing Harald through his dad, Pastor Moses Vegh. Who didn't adore Harald?

"I collect Harald Bredesen stories," Marcus grinned, eager to share some zingers. "One time, Harald arrived for a national event at a mega church. One morning, a security officer found him sleeping in an empty classroom. Harald could not convince the guard that he was the keynote speaker at that event. He was almost arrested!" Yep, that was our Harald.

"Another time," Marcus continued excitedly, "he was scheduled to present Anwar Sadat with the Prince of Peace Prize from Harald's own foundation. But Harald was nowhere to be found! I frantically rushed around and finally found him sound asleep beneath a projector table."

The King of Egypt was later quoted as saying, "It was the high point of my entire life, more important to me even then the Nobel Peace Prize...that was in the political arena, this was spiritual."

Following our French cuisine, John and I shared a dessert of fresh raspberries and whipped cream.

While reaching for another spoonful of raspberries, I calmly asked a spiritual matter. "John, have you been baptized in the Holy Spirit with the evidence of tongues?"

John smiled sheepishly. "Yes, I have… Harold did that at his ranch." He said it exactly like that. It was so sweet, like a little kid.

I should have known better because that was a *given* being around someone as anointed as Harald, a pioneer in the worldwide charismatic renewal. Harald had everyone speaking in tongues after being with him for five minutes. Anwar Sadat probably spoke in tongues!

After our meaningful fellowship and spiritually connecting with John, we headed back to his hotel. We left our brother in Christ with a loving hug and a promise to pray for his continued journey with the Lord.

As we drove away, I turned to Daryl and marveled at John's solid commitment to Christ. I snickered, "Wouldn't the four-teenth-floor at General Motors flip their wigs if they knew that John DeLorean spoke in tongues?"

"For anyone who speaks in a tongue does not speak to people but to God. Indeed, no one understands them; they utter mysteries by the Spirit" (1 Corinthians 14:2, NIV).

CHAPTER TWENTY-EIGHT

Elisa and Leanne Sanders, The 700 Club Story of their Miracle Adoption

One morning, a small group of church ladies was gathered for our weekly prayer meeting held in a private home. Our hostess was a gal named Judy.

Our music minister's wife requested prayer to conceive another child.

Without missing a beat, Judy chided, "Well, what about *you,* Barbara? Are you planning on having more children, too?"

My response surprised me.

"Well, if I could have identical twin daughters, I'd get pregnant tomorrow..."

Then I turned to Janice, a gal sitting to the left of me. Janice had identical twin daughters attending high school. Grinning at Janice, I said, "It must have been such a blessing to raise Stephanie and Suzanne."

The next day, as I was doing dishes in my kitchen, that comment about having identical twin daughters came to my mind. In fact, I could not get it out of my head for several days. It was to the point that I was being harangued about it, but I didn't know why.

Another week passed by, and as I relaxed in a bubble bath on a Saturday afternoon, those same words came to mind. My husband was reading at the other end of our newly remodeled bedroom. In the process, I got my much-desired Jacuzzi, a soaking tub just big enough for me in the limited space beneath a window.

As I relaxed in my little pink tub, the thought of identical twins came to mind once again.

Okay, Lord, what's up? Why do I keep thinking about twin daughters? I mused.

Within my heart, the Holy Spirit spoke. "Because I put that desire there to fulfill the desires of your heart." It seemed like the Lord said, "Glad you finally asked!"

I sat straight up, startled by such a profound revelation from the Lord.

I called out to my husband. "Hey, honey, the Lord just spoke to me. We're going to have twin girls!"

Daryl put the newspaper down to call back over his shoulder.

"What are you talking about? You mean 'adopt?'"

I thought it was a very odd response.

A few months later, I had a prophetic dream. In my dream, I addressed someone whose face was not revealed. I spoke to this person very emphatically.

"Well, why would God tell me He was going to give me identical twin daughters unless He's intending to?" *End of dream.*

Early the next morning, as we dressed for church service, I shared the dream with Daryl. All the while I continued dressing, the dream was ever on my mind.

Before long, I began plotting how to pull the whole thing off. Now I know how Abraham's wife Sarah felt after being told she'd have a child in her old age. Doubting God, she got her handmaiden, Hagar, to conceive a child with her husband. Soon, this conniving spirit of Sarah completely took over my thought process. Driving to church, I cooked up a plot for in vitro fertilization to pull off twins in a dish. My lack of faith was apparent.

In the early years of pioneering our church, we rented out Sunday space at an adult education career center. My husband, along with a crew of volunteer men, always arrived early to set up the church. They rolled out the piano and organ from the storage room. Yellow molded chairs were arranged theatre-style with a center aisle. A portable pulpit was center-stage.

That Sunday morning, a gal named Beth came rushing over to me, extremely excited. I sat chatting with a lady waiting for service to begin. Beth pulled up a chair to join us.

"Barbara, Barbara! Listen to this!" Beth could hardly contain herself. "I have an urgent prayer request. Remember Jane? She's my friend I brought to church last year. Well, there's a woman in Jane's church with twin girls. They are looking for a good home because the mother is unable to care for them. It is a very bad situation."

Every hair follicle on my body was standing on end. I had goosebumps running up and down my head, arms, and legs. I could hardly believe my ears.

Beth was married to a Viet Nam veteran who was struggling emotionally. Her husband was unemployed, and they had come in for marriage counseling.

However, I also knew that Beth had a hysterectomy and was unable to bear children. A few years earlier, a failed adoption had been heartbreaking for her.

"Were you thinking of adopting these girls, Beth?" Now I was the one barely able to contain myself. But I needed to remain calm and sensitive to her desire to have children.

"Oh, no, I haven't even told my husband, but I would be willing to keep them for a while just to get them out of a risky situation. You wouldn't believe how horrible it is."

I looked intently at her before speaking again.

"How old are they?"

"They're three years old," she said.

"They are identical, aren't they?"

"Yes, you can't tell them apart. It's so funny," she said, chuckling.

I shared my dream with her because I knew these twin girls were ours. The Holy Spirit prepared me through a Word of Knowledge and a prophetic dream.

Beth became elated, and she couldn't wait to call Jane following service.

My dear, analytical husband thought it was too "far-fetched" to be possible. But during the previous months, he couldn't refute that God had spoken to me twice about identical twins.

Our twin daughters were in our home the following Saturday, six days after my dream. With the help of some dedicated Christians, who were in a relationship with the birth mother, the girls were rescued from a deplorable and life-threatening situation.

The little girls were adorable. They had fair complexions with sandy blond hair and hazel brown eyes. Unfortunately, they were not without health problems. Both had severe ear infections when they arrived. At three years of age, they were unable to utter a single syllable of speech because of gross neglect. After hearing tests and speech evaluations, they were deemed eligible for a federally funded pre-school program that my pediatrician highly recommended.

Bo was ten-years-old and affectionately welcomed his two little sisters. When we first approached Bo with the idea of adopting twins, his initial response was, "Well, I won't be alone at Christmas anymore."

An attorney in Jane's church represented Ann pro bono, covering the legal aspect of the adoption. Ann was made fully aware of her legal rights, and she wholeheartedly offered her children to a Christian family so they would have a better life. I spoke to Ann by telephone, knowing that she could easily change her mind and take the children back before our actual court date, several months away.

During our meaningful phone conversation, we talked about Ann's life and her mother's death from cancer when Ann was only five years old. I brought up the Bible account of Hannah and how this courageous mother gave up her son Samuel to the Lord when he was about five years old. Ann also knew the story and shared her thoughts. This mother of twin daughters did the right thing before the Lord, too. I know that Jesus gave Ann supernatural grace to surrender her children to Him. The adoption process took six months to complete in court. When it came our time to sign the legal documents, I wept.

Every day with the twins, renamed Elisa Lynne and Leanne Alexandra, was an adventure because there was so much catching up for them.

A mini-sized yellow school bus pulled into our driveway every morning. Elisa and Leanne were thrilled to climb aboard and drive off, waving bye-bye to me from their window seats. They loved school. Each had a different teacher who was equally qualified to help children delayed in motor skills and speech development. They partook in pre-school activities with down syndrome children and other preschoolers with temporarily delayed development. Mrs. Risky, Leanne's teacher, was a jolly, elderly woman. She said, "Leanne's favorite thing to do in school is to 'cut and paste.' I always know if she doesn't feel good when she doesn't cut and paste during class." Elisa's much younger teacher said to me, "I love her very much. I have never been this attached to any child before her."

Within weeks, we saw a vast improvement in the little girls. Soon syllables were being formed as they ventured into exciting language development. They started out saying "Ba" for banana or "da" for drink. Just as a five-month-old baby learns to make sounds, these little girls were starting to form words in the same way. They were extremely happy to express themselves in a safe and clean environment.

Our generous church ladies gave me a huge baby shower, so Elisa and Leanne were now dressed in the latest fashions—so different from their former tattered clothing.

When Jane and her church friend, Anne, arrived to deliver the twins, I ushered the two women into our daughters' new bedroom. Their room featured an antique double bed with a white lace-eyelet coverlet covered with stuffed animals and dolls. The little girls had a closet full of matching Polly Flinders smocked dresses purchased at an outlet store. When Anne saw all the pretty dresses hanging in the closet, she started to weep. With tears streaming down her cheeks, she said, "Barbara, you will never, never know how bad it was for them…I am so grateful God rescued these little babies."

One afternoon, after returning from school, our adorable little girls rushed into our living room, gleefully singing a nursery song they had just learned in school. They were giggling, bobbing their heads to the rhythm, both singing the same tune, over and over. It was the first time they "found their voices" to sing. They were joyfully looking up at their daddy and me, hoping we'd twirl with them and join their celebration.

We were delighted to unite in the joyous movement of discovery, but we didn't recognize the song! With limited, single-word syllables, the girls sang out the same thing in perfect harmony. Months later, I finally recognized the words of "Ten little monkeys jumping on a bed, one jumped up and bumped his head. Mom called the doctor and the doctor said, no more monkeys jumping on a bed." They both knew what the other was singing even though they sang out nonsensical single syllables! I love to remember that the twins were *singing songs* before they could actually form a sentence!

"Delight yourself in the Lord and he will give you the desires of your heart" (Psalm 37:4, NIV).

PHOTO GALLERY

In the begining after WWII

Portrait by George Romney, England 1776

My English-Irish-Native American Christian Heritage

Joseph Brant, Indian name Thayendanegea, born 1742 in North East Ohio on the banks of the Muskingum River—died November 24, 1807 near Brantford, Ontario, Canada, Mohawk Indian chief who served as a prominent negotiator and diplomat of Northern indigenous people, a Christian missionary and a British military officer during the American Revolution (1775-83).

Brant was converted to the Anglican church after two years (1761-63) at Moor's Charity School for Indians in Lebanon, Connecticut, where he learned English, western history and literature under the tutelage of Eleazar Wheelock, founder of Dartmouth College in 1769. Brant became an interpreter for an Anglican missionary and later translated the Book of Common Prayer and the Gospel of Mark into Mohawk.

In 1710, Queen Anne of England gifted the Mohawks a Bible, the Book of Common Prayer, and a silver communion service as a token of friendship. After the American Revolution ended, Brant unburied these cherished gifts to build a new church called St. Paul's, Her Majesty's Royal Chapel, located in today's Brantford, Ontario.

"Have pity on the poor Indians, if you can get any influence with the great, endeavor to do them all the good you can." Brant's last words on his death bed, spoken to his adopted nephew.

𝒢randmother Elsie (Brant) Lambert, great grandmother Lydia Margaret (Powless) Brant, (holding me) and my mother, Shirley Ann (Lambert) Taylor, circa 1948

My maternal roots trace back to the Mohawks born in the Tyendinage Mohawk Territory, the main First Nation reserve of the Mohawks of the Bay of Quinte First Nation, Ontario.

When my great, great grandparents migrated from Oshawa to Detroit (my birth place), Douglas and Eliza Powless agreed that in moving away from tribal land into the dominant economic world, they would have to forego their cultural practices.

As a symbol and practice of that decision, they buried the regalia that Douglas possessed under a tree at their Oshawa home. They embraced Christianity. Their daughter, my great grandmother, Lydia Margaret, was a devout Christian who married Joseph Markus Brant, an architect. My grandma Brant made sure my parents dedicated me to the Lord in a baby christening ceremony at her Methodist church in Melvindale, Michigan.

Miss Barbara Taylor
age 23

Agadir, Morocco

ZION CHRISTIAN FELLOWSHIP
FOUNDED 1985

O Glory To The Lamb

Words and Music by Barbara Sande
Arrangement by Dean Deme

The First Columbus, Ohio
Worship Symposium 1985

RUSSIA AND UKRAINE MISSION TRIPS

Hospitable, Unified and Beautiful

In Christ Jesus

"A Heart After God" Developing a prayer language from the book of Psalms

"Exploring Avenues Of Prayer" A look at the prayers of Paul

"Becoming A Women Of Influence" Using our God-given position of appeal

"Parting The Waters" Stepping out in faith for the promise

"Knowing the Voice of God" Discernment by reason of use

"Listening Heart" Developing an obedient attitude

"Taking Your Stand" Putting on the full armor of God

"Capturing Strongholds" Taking authority over wrong thoughts

"Loving Your Enemies" Learning forbearance through forgiveness

"Free To Love" Conquering bitterness

"Justified By Faith" Overcoming dead works

"Governed By Grace" Empowered for right choices

"Expressions Of Praise" Spiritual warfare, Part 1

"Expressions Of Worship" Spiritual warfare, Part 2

"Expressing God To Others" How to reach the lost

"Becoming A Sweet F... ...oken vessel

"Risen Indeed" R...

"Rising Ab... ...tations into victor...

"...

"R...

"Fa... ...e Apos...

HONORING MRS CORETTA SCOTT KING,
ON THE 25TH ANNIVERSARY
OF DR. KING'S DEATH,
APRIL 1993.

A HEART
AFTER G...

DEVELOPING A P...
LANGUAGE FROM ...
BOOK OF PSA...

BARBARA TA...
SANDER...

"Before you try to keep up with the Joneses, be sure
they're not trying to keep up with you." *Erma B...*

PUTTIN' ON THE...
DOG & GETTIN' E...

A Madcap Memoir of S...
BARBARA TAYLOR SAND...

Free to L...
Free to L...
A BIBLICAL PAT...
to VICTORIOUS L...

BARBARA TAY...
SANDERS

More Than A Promise

Barbara Taylor Sanders

*Parting Friends, Broken Promises
and A Double Blessing in Disguise*

Awaken...
Your...
Within...

Barbara S...

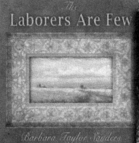

Barbara Taylor Sanders

The
Laborers Are Few

Barbara Taylor Sanders

Foreword by Promise Keepers
Coach Bill McCartney

Barbara Taylor Sanders

HIDDEN

HOLY SPIRIT
FOR REAL
Barbara Taylor Sanders

FOREWORD BY
GRAHAM COOKE

Uniting HEARTS,
Helping HANDS, Igniting HOPE

Barbara Taylor Sanders, B.A.

WISE WOMEN COUNCIL

WISE WOMEN COUNCIL

CHAPTER TWENTY-NINE

Pastor Rod Parsley's Prophesy Over Our Twin Daughters

My mother, Shirley Ann, arrived from Michigan shortly after the twins arrived in late March 1985. It was instant love among the three of them. When Mom got out of the car to greet them the first time, the tiny tots ran toward her with their arms held up.

In early June, after school let out for Bo, we drove to Florida in my minivan to spend two weeks on Siesta Key Beach. On the first day on the beach, we took a large umbrella to shade their unexposed skin from the sun. Jane had informed me that the twins had never been to a park or touched grass with their bare feet. They must have felt like they were in paradise.

At the beach, the twins each wore a red and white polka dot bikini with matching sun visors and little white terry cloth cover-ups trimmed in red. Every single beach stroller stopped to speak to them. Ten-year-old Bo splashed in the shallow shoreline with them as waves gently lapped at their toes. They laughed at everything Bo did, and they never took their eyes off of him. He built them sand castles to their sheer delight of having an amazing big brother. Later, the twins ate their lunch and also napped side-by-side under the umbrella. It was a typical, magnificent "day on the beach."

About four o'clock, Mom and I shook out the towels and quietly loaded up the red wagon to return to our beachfront condo to prepare dinner. We leisurely strolled across the pure white sand, leaving the cerulean blue water behind us. Elisa panicked with no language to protest leaving. So, this little girl communicated the only way she knew how. Elisa ran in front of us and dove face-first in the sand. Both her arms and legs were dug into the warm sand! I'll never forget her clutching the ground with every fiber of her being. Her body language screamed, "*Please*, don't take me from this glorious place!"

Fifteen years later, we celebrated the twin's graduation from high school at a large family picnic in Michigan. All their aunts and uncles gathered, along with about thirty other family members, including most of our first and second cousins.

My favorite picture of them was centered on their large sheet cake. Sweet three-year-old little girls, sitting side-by-side on the shaded lanai during that first trip to the beach. The gloom is completely vanished from their rosy tan faces. Leanne is clutching a baby doll. The beautiful blue Gulf of Mexico is behind them, shining as radiant as the future before them.

Throughout their life, they continued to sing their hearts out, performing duets in church with additional piano lessons. During high school, they partook in musical theatre. When I discovered their high school friend, Andy, could sing, too, I got them booked in churches around town. Their award-winning high school choir was selected to represent Ohio in America's bicentennial in Washington, D.C. In college at Christ for the Nations, their choir accompanied national guest singers like Ron Kenoly. They loved singing in Mark Condon's amazing gospel choir, too. Pastor Parsley teased them about not singing in *his* choir at World Harvest Church.

After our move to Florida, Leanne became a member of the prestigious Ft. Myers Master Choir singing in sold-out performances.

Following college, the twins have enjoyed working on cruise ships in sales. Elisa is stationed in the Mediterranean and Leanne sails throughout the Caribbean. Previously, Elisa was a paralegal working at the largest banking network in Columbus. Leanne also had a very good job working in sales at a successful family-owned company. God has surely been faithful. Our girls are virtuous young ladies who still love to sing.

I wonder where those little girls would be if I hadn't trusted enough to believe the voice of God? My husband has been my rock and totally supportive of my outreach to others. What if we had been too self-consumed with our lives to sacrifice them to take on toddlers with tremendous emotional needs? We answered "Yes" to God, in faith. Raising the twins was not without difficult challenges. However, the Lord has had His hand upon their lives for a very special plan that is still evolving. Our daughters have been a tremendous blessing to our entire family. We are grateful that God plucked them out of the miry clay and placed them in our laps to love.

On Sunday morning, January 4, 2009, Pastor Parsley called "the twins" up to the platform during an anointed time of prayer. Pastor placed his hands upon their heads, and he uttered the spirit of prophecy:

"The spirit of worship is upon you, says the Lord, pouring forth by My Spirit, callings from deep to deep says God. Power in your praise, in the secret place of your private worship, says God, I will break bands of wickedness. I will loose heavy burdens, and the oppressed will go free. And when you are in this place, you will celebrate the shallowness of the depths that were broken loose up out of the river of your belly—rivers, rivers, rivers, rivers, rivers, rivers, rivers of living water."

CHAPTER THIRTY

Pastors James Robison, Moses Vegh, and Marcus Vegh Leading the Way to Russia

One day, perched on a bar stool at our kitchen counter, an astonishing revelation erupted within my heart while talking to Daryl as he stood munching on a sandwich. It was a Saturday afternoon sometime in September 1991.

At this time, Bo, age seventeen, was attending a private Christian school, as were the twins. Elisa and Leanne were now ten years old and completely caught up academically and socially for their age level. My two stepchildren, Tammie and Scott, were both married. Daryl was a senior pastor of our busy, productive, mission-minded congregation. As his wife, our lives were consumed with tremendous ministry demands. We committed to be there forever, sold out to Jesus.

But out of nowhere, the Lord threw us a curve ball, which catapulted our lives from the neighborhood ballpark to the major leagues.

For months, I had been singing or humming the chorus from the song "Ask of Me—Here am I Send Me" by Marty Nystrom.

ASK OF ME
And I will give you nations,
As an inheritance for you;

Holy Spirit For Real

As an inheritance for you
My children,
Ask of Me
And I will give you nations,
As an inheritance for you
Ask of Me.
Here am I,
Send me to the nations,
As an ambassador for You.
As an ambassador for you,
My Father,
Here am I,
Send me to the nations,
as an ambassador for You,
Here am I.
Here Am I, Lord,
Send Me Lord,
Send Me Open my eyes Lord,
let me see
There are millions of people
Ready to hear and receive
Please open my ears Lord,
let me hear
Hear the cry of the nations
From far and near Saying come over there
Won't you please
Are you willing To show them way
Are you willing to go
Are you willing to say
Here Am I, Lord,
Send Me Lord,
Send Me Here Am I,

258

Lord, Send Me Lord, Send Me...

This song had been the theme from summer youth camp that previous June. I sang it hundreds of times throughout the months.

That Saturday in September, I made a seemingly presumptuous statement.

"The Lord is going to send me to Russia," I declared with uncanny certainty. It turned out to be a prophetic revelation coming from deep within my soul. The "yeah, right," look on my husband's face did not stop the prophetic flowing from the Holy Spirit.

"Oh, but you'll have to come, too," I quickly added. "You'll need to go with me because you know the Bible so well, and the Russians will have lots of questions." Daryl rolled his eyes. After all, I did come off sounding like Queen Elizabeth announcing her next goodwill mission to Parliament.

My husband probably thought, *Now, why on earth would God be sending my wife to Russia?* The poor guy—life with a visionary hasn't been easy for someone with his analytical mind. We balance each other. At that point in time, we had lived in harmony for more than thirty-eight years. Through the contrast in our temperaments, we complement one another by embracing our differences. We've learned to honor one another in marriage and support each other in ministry.

God didn't spring that Russian mission trip on me out of the blue. Earlier that year, a lavender paperback Russian New Testament was left on my kitchen desk by my brother while visiting us from Michigan.

Earlier in the summer, I had watched my nephew and three nieces while Dave and Lorraine attended a home-schooling seminar in Tennessee. The Russian New Testament translation was a giveaway gift from host Bill Gothard to remind his conferees to "pray for Russia."

So, I did. Each time I passed that Russian Bible on my desk, I prayed for "missionaries to be sent to Russia." Remember what Dr. Myles Munro said about praying for missionaries? He said, "Don't pray for missionaries unless you're willing to go." I should have considered that the Lord was preparing me to go.

My negative feelings toward all Soviet bloc countries stood in the way of any consideration. The Lord needed to change my heart.

During a business trip to Germany in 1973, Daryl and I passed through the inspection at "Checkpoint Charlie" to enter East Berlin before the Cold War ended and the Iron Curtain was torn down. The burly agent yelled at me to close the door just as I entered the building. The woman was employed by the Russian KGB and acted like it as she rifled through our stuff. My husband's newspaper was promptly confiscated from his briefcase.

After being ill-treated by the rude and demanding communist inspection agent, we were finally allowed to exit without further ado. After going through the outlandish drill, we re-entered our taxicab to cross over the border.

High-powered rifles pointed at our vehicle from a looming

high tower in front of us. The communist guards acted like dictators. After riding past the Wall into East Berlin, we were stopped on the communist side. At that point, we had to step out of the car while the militant KGB used mirrors to inspect beneath the car, opened the trunk, and yanked the automobile seats apart, looking for contraband. On the return, they did the same thing, but this time they were searching for hidden East Berliners trying to escape to freedom.

Our driver informed us that the guards would confiscate my camera if I took pictures of the Wall. The stern armed officials shouted instead of speaking in a normal tone. It was *just like* in the movies.

When we drove over to a nice hotel for lunch, we entered the expansive, marble-floored lobby. Instead of the hustle and bustle of a busy hotel, it was so deathly quiet that you could have heard a pin drop. Several people were standing around or sitting. I noticed how oppressed the East Berliners seemed with downcast faces. I refused to stay for lunch. I couldn't wait to get back to freedom. I also vowed *never* to visit a communist block country again. So, that inner vow became a hindrance.

However, more than twenty years later, I learned that Bill Gothard was featured on television in St. Petersburg, teaching life principles. I changed my tune. I thought, *Boy, Russia really must be desperate to know about God because Bill Gothard isn't on American television.*

A few days after the kitchen counter proclamation about going to Russia, Daryl and I attended a James Robison Crusade held in Columbus. Following the meeting, we greeted one of our dearest friends, Marcus Vegh. Marcus was an extremely talented and bright young man, the son of Pastor Moses and Bette Vegh, our close friends. Marcus was the television producer for James Robison at the time.

With a headset on and a wired microphone coming out of his ear, Marcus joyfully embraced us with a hug. Years earlier, Marcus had been an early pioneer television producer for *Breakthrough* with his dear friend, Rod Parsley.

"How are your mom and dad doing?" I asked after giving him a peck on the cheek.

"My dad just came back from Moscow in an evangelistic meeting with more than 10,000 students from all over Russia!" Marcus always spoke with a huge grin, resembling his handsome, look-alike Hungarian father.

"Well, the Lord is sending me to Russia, too!" I announced with confidence.

"Wow! That's great! James Robison is traveling to Russia next month. Why don't you come along with us?"

The man listening to us was an extravagant gift-giver from our church. Looking at me, Bill said, "If you have a passport, I'll pay your way, but just you, Barbara. I can't pay for Daryl's ticket, too."

I teased Pastor Daryl because he needed to raise the money to *accompany me* to Moscow just a few months later.

The Dew (Rosa) Church
Moscow's Underground Charismatic Movement
1991

We attended the Christian Youth International conference organized by Bob Weiner and hosted by Pastors Pavel and Marina Savelyev, the faithful leaders of the dynamic "Dew" ("ROSA") Church.

During the terrifying communist regime, this unregistered church met "underground" to avoid persecution. Marina was a Jewish Christian who led worship during most of the evening services.

We had traveled to Russia with Pastor Moses Vegh, who was the keynote speaker at a previous conference. Sitting on the platform, it was so exciting to witness enthusiastic young adults packing out the auditorium each night of the five-day conference. Two thousand high school and college students jammed into the expansive but dimly lit auditorium that offered only a center aisle. Each row was about fifty-seats wide.

Dozens of colorful flags were displayed on wooden poles lining the back of the platform. Throughout the services, enthusiastic students rushed on stage to wave a flag. The responsive roar from thousands of young Christians reminded the enemy that Jesus Christ rules every nation, and the victories are already won! Each time a country was high and lifted up for Jesus, my heart soared.

During the evening praise services, I competed for a lone, dilapidated tambourine with missing cymbals. Kostya, one of the few church leaders who spoke English, was frequently pulled off the platform to interpret. Whenever Kostya set down his beat-up tambourine, I snatched it up to play. I looked forward to his frequent departures since I hadn't brought my tambourine from home. He'd return moments later and make me give it back. This amusing tambourine tug-of-war went on every night. In the former communist rule and reign, the auditorium was almost always filled with atheists. Playing a tambourine for Jesus on a platform where the Communist Party once stood was unimaginable.

I declared, "Kostya, when I return, I'm bringing you twelve white tambourines with colorful ribbons dangling down on each side!"

In his husky voice with a heavy Russian accent and a twinkle in his eye, he replied, "And don't forget the ribbons!" He was a spunky member of the Dew church, and ribbons matched his personality.

Every afternoon, at a nearby hotel, Pastor Pavik and Pastor Daryl water baptized hundreds of young people. They used a large sauna tub for the baptism pool. What made it interesting is that Pavik spoke no English and Daryl spoke no Russian. What a team!

Hundreds of young adults from all over Russia were packed in the pool area like American teenagers lined up to buy rock star concert tickets. However, these youths were lined up to identify with the death, burial, and resurrection of Jesus Christ, their Savior. It was a sobering sight.

My brother died today (July 28, 2019) after a courageous battle with cancer. For the past two weeks, I've been doing final edits on this book. I picked up this chapter today. How typical of the Lord for me to remember David's special place in my journey. My brother is now with Jesus, and that brings me comforting peace.

Again I will build you and you will be rebuilt, O virgin of Israel! Again you will take up your tambourines, And go forth to the dances of the merrymakers.

Jeremiah 31:4

Rejoice in the Lord always. I will say it again: Rejoice!

Philippians 4:4, NIV

Chapter Thirty-One

Russian's March for Jesus and Dancing in the Streets to Dispel the Darkness over Moscow

Daryl scheduled a second trip to Russia with Pastor Moses Vegh in March 1992. This time they were going without me. However, the Lord had use for me on that upcoming trip, even though I was unaware of His ultimate plan.

After returning home from Moscow, it seemed as if I was running into Russians living in Columbus every time I turned around! During this season in my life, I produced a live radio talk show as the hostess. I invited a young Russian fellow to be on the show to interview the representative who helped him get out of the country because of religious persecution. The morning of the interview, I slipped in the bathroom, breaking my leg and spraining my ankle. I did the show and went to lunch with a girlfriend afterward. I have a high pain tolerance. At three o'clock that afternoon, an X-ray of only my ankle missed the fracture in my leg. Two weeks later, after an additional X-ray, the doctor issued a cane because the bone had started to heal.

A few weeks before Pastor Daryl's trip back to Moscow, I was limping around in a fabric store with my cane, minding my own business. I had a designated church check to buy fabric to make an extra-long tablecloth to serve the deaconesses dinner the night before our next ladies' retreat. Even though I walked with a cane, I still planned to cook and honor our women in service with an elegant sit-down dinner in spite of the fact that I was hobbling around on a broken leg using a cane. For the ladies' sit-down dinner, I planned to spend about $35.00 on white fabric to make a twenty-foot-long tablecloth to cover two eight-foot utility tables end to-end.

While I was in the fabric store, the Holy Spirit spoke to my heart. "Buy enough white fabric to make six dance garments to send with your husband." Having sewn beautiful garments for our church dance team, I knew exactly what to purchase. I spent $238.00 on double circle skirt fabric, angel blouses, elastic, and pins. While hobbling to my car, loaded down with two heavy bags, the Lord said, "They don't own sewing machines, so I need *you* to sew these dance dresses." I froze in my tracks. *You tricked me, Lord!* Daryl was departing for Moscow in ten days.

I was tossing and turning all night—I had spent way too much money, and sewing all those dresses in time for the upcoming trip was impossible! The next morning the Lord reassured me. *"Do not fret, my daughter, you did the right thing. The Russian dancers will dance in the streets of Moscow to dispel the vast darkness over that city."*

That Sunday morning, I made an impromptu announcement without looking at my husband's face. Thankfully, several dedicated church ladies came to the rescue for this enormous sewing project. However, on Monday, as I was cutting out the first skirt pattern, the devil whispered in my ear. "You're going to make a *fool* out of your husband when he arrives with *dance attire*. That church doesn't even believe in dancing!" At the first conference, I had not seen any dancers, so I froze with doubt and fear. Therefore, that afternoon I called Moscow for confirmation. I dialed the number and got right through to Marina.

"Marina, will you have dancers at your conference next week?" I held my breath. It felt like my salvation hinged on her answer.

"Yes, yes. I will have some dancers at the conference."

When I mentioned this phone call to Marina, my husband exclaimed, "How on earth did you get through to Russia on one try? The church office has been trying to call Moscow for two weeks! All we get is a busy signal."

The Lord knew I needed the truth. Marina's response became like the fray check I was applying to the ends of the cut ribbon for the twelve white tambourines. Kostya was going to be thrilled to see those ribbons!

However, my husband was *not* thrilled about taking a huge suitcase stuffed with dance attire, yards of satin fabrics, and colored sequins to make banners also. During the final moments of packing, I tugged Lora Allison's *Celebration* book out of the clutched hands of my dear friend Marion to squeeze in a bulging suitcase. This instructional book featured beautiful pictures of Lora's banners.

When Pastor Daryl returned home, he brought back a thank you note from the dance team. In the letter, the lead dancer explained that she had been agonizing for months, praying for "dresses" for the dance team. Finally, the Lord rebuked her, nagging, "You of little faith, I already have your dresses on the way." According to the dates mentioned in her gracious thank-you letter, her answer from the Lord coincided with my divine moment of inspiration at the fabric store. Thank you, Jesus!

Daryl and I returned to another Moscow conference in September 1992. During an afternoon praise service, I was seated next to Marina, enjoying the six beautiful ballerinas as they ministered (all part Jewish) to Russian praise music in their new dance garments. Leaning toward my ear, Marina said, "We had a *March for Jesus* this past summer…the dancers were in front, leading about 2,000 people marching in the streets." She hesitated before continuing, "Umm, how to say this in English? The dancers were the 'hit of the parade.'"

Grabbing her arm, I gushed, "Marina! How did you know about *March for Jesus*?"

"I read about it in *Charisma Magazine*, so I organized one here. We also made seven beautiful banners from all the nice satin fabrics you sent us."

The Lord was true to His word about the dancers in the streets to *dispel darkness over Moscow*. My heart was overwhelmed by the Lord's faithfulness to perform His prophetic word.

In an upcoming month, the *March for Jesus* organizers sent out a documentary highlighting film clips of the participating cities worldwide. Daryl was at an organization meeting with several local pastors, planning the second Jesus march in Columbus. The video was moving along, showing brightly dressed Christians marching in Hong Kong, Japan, Korea, Australia, Great Britain, Switzerland, France, Italy, and Germany… then the colorful moving images stopped abruptly with a jarring black and white snapshot from Moscow. Pastor Daryl yelled out, "Wait! Stop the video, rewind to that picture from Moscow again." When the black and white reappeared on the screen, the still frame featured six triumphant dancers leading their Moscow Jesus march. My husband exclaimed, "My wife sewed the dresses all those dancers are wearing!"

Hearing about my husband's gush was solace for all the grief I took when it was time for him to lug that huge orange vinyl suitcase to those dancers in Russia!

A few years later, author/evangelist Lora Allison was ministering at a citywide Christian conference in Moscow. Lora told me that Marina quickly recognized her as the author of *Celebration* and introduced herself. Lora returned to Marina's church to view all the magnificent banners made from the fabric we had sent and from Lora's book that we'd also included.

Prior to his third return to Russia, Daryl had a prophetic dream of a large seaport filled with massive ships. The vision turned out to be Odessa, Ukraine, a beautiful seaport located on the Black

Sea. Odessa is considered the "Riviera of the Black Sea" with its crossroads of cultures, languages, trade, and the Black Sea's largest port. Many Russians come to Odessa to vacation because of its major cultural hub with an opera and ballet theatre, philharmonic orchestra, and museums.

During that return trip to Moscow, two male students were commissioned to Odessa "to scout out the land." We wouldn't have allowed them to go if we'd known how far they had to travel. Sending them from Moscow to Odessa was like a trip from Maine to Oregon by train.

We learned of "a new start-up Charismatic church," so our nine-member American team embarked to Odessa in faith. We traveled two days by train with Alexander, our reserved but mature high school student interpreter from Estonia. He called his parents to gain permission to travel with us for an extra six days. On the long train ride, whenever Alexander heard a new word from us, he jotted it down in his handy pocket notebook. By the end of the train ride, Alexander had more than 150 American slang terms on his list! Expressions such as *hang on a minute, let's roll*, or *catch ya later.*

On Sunday morning, our ministry team visited the Odessa congregation unannounced. The former Pentecostal-turned-Charismatic pastor was astonished to have nine Americans arrive, and he honored us accordingly. Many of his church leaders were mature Christians and serious college students from Africa. The University of Odessa offered an affordable education for them. I fell in love with Africa through these devoted Christians representing six or seven different nations. I bequeathed my lone tambourine to a somber-faced West African on the praise team. With a coy smile, she accepted my gift, knowing why I had picked her from all the rest.

In Odessa that Sunday morning, our team was asked to greet the friendly congregation. Pastor Ike from Lagos, Nigeria, interpreted our words. When I was invited to take the microphone, I could barely speak to the wide-eyed congregation because the spirit of the Lord overwhelmed me. It seemed more natural to close my eyes, lift up my arms, and sing in my heavenly prayer language. Spontaneously, the fresh-faced, young congregation joined in one accord, singing sweetly in various unknown tongues.

Years later, when I ministered in Nigeria, I reunited with our dear friend "Pastor Ike," whom we had first met in Odessa. I emptied my pockets and gave him every American dollar I brought intended for souvenirs. He had been without a job for several months, so his brief reunion with me was a divine connection. It is in times like that when I wish I had millions of dollars to give to young ministers attempting to build the church of Christ in third-world countries.

During our first Sunday morning in Odessa, Daryl and I encouraged the church "musicians and singers" to come forward to be released in worship. Our team prayed for about twenty-five students who responded to the call.

The Lord gave me a prophetic word for this church, which I read from my journal. "I am showing the world Odessa by putting it 'on the map.' First the natural, now the spiritual—Christians in Odessa will become a light to the world as a result of this sign."

Olympic figure skater Viktor Petrenko had already won the gold medal that previous February. A worldwide television network highlighted Viktor's hometown of Odessa, Ukraine, Four years later, sixteen-year-old Oksana Baiul, also from Odessa, won another gold medal. This certainly put Odessa on the map for the entire world to see.

However, God was painting a much bigger picture yet to be revealed.

During that weeklong visit, Pastor Daryl was graciously introduced to other Odessa city leaders, including the number-two bishop of the United Pentecostal Church district in Ukraine, Bishop Peter Serdichenko. Through this divine connection, Daryl was eventually linked to the entire UPC network of leaders throughout Ukraine in the next few years.

CHAPTER THIRTY-TWO

Missionaries
Edward & Linda McPherson
Birthing Praise and Worship
freedom in Odessa, Ukraine

The following summer, we returned to Odessa with another evangelistic team from our church. We were wide-eyed with wonder at all the Lord was doing in our midst. But it was not without moments of frustration. One Sunday afternoon, our five-member team walked about three miles from the church service. We arrived at our hotel, hot, dusty, thirsty, and tired. We piled onto the elevator to be lifted up to the fourth floor. However, the elevator stopped short on the second floor, and the door would not open. We were trapped.

Thankfully, Alexander was able to shout for help in Russian. The lady at the desk shouted back in Russian. Alexander had recently moved to America with a host family from our church. He returned as our official interpreter. I nervously joked that we might be trapped for hours before a maintenance man was summoned via the public transport system. My husband barked at me. He did not consider this a laughing matter. A temperamental team member became offended. She left the church over "the tiff" my husband and I had while being trapped in an elevator. The team toughed it out for a few more suffocating moments and the doors miraculously opened on their own. The Lord has ways of weeding out the weak-kneed or those not mature enough to handle ministry mishaps in the lives of pastors expressing frustration trapped in an elevator.

One morning I marveled at the oversized, orange-yoked eggs on my breakfast plate. Marion, whose hands I had pried open to gain Lora Allison's book bound for Russia, was eating across the room with other team members. Marion chuckled, "I don't have the heart to tell Barbara that she's eating duck eggs for breakfast."

The following year from our generous, mission-minded local church, the Lord planted Edward and Linda McPherson and their three-year-old son, Ryan, in Odessa as full-time missionaries. Linda is a prophetic and gifted musician, originally from Hope Temple, with Pastor Moses Vegh in Findlay, Ohio.

After learning the Russian language, Linda trained key musicians and numerous choir members from the Charismatic church and several citywide United Pentecostal churches. Although most of the older UPC choir members frowned on Linda's short hair, earrings, and slacks, her music was well received. The prophetic anointing on Linda's life was vivid. Those humble Christians were dry sponges soaking up a fresh Holy Spirit spring of refreshment from the Lord. The youth especially gravitated to Linda's glorious music.

During a subsequent trip to Ukraine, Edward and Linda organized a nationwide Worship Conference in Odessa. From America, we brought a dance troupe and other anointed musicians.

Marion and I personally constructed three beautiful banners with words in Russian. Linda had a praise team ready with several singers and musicians from Odessa. During the conference, some of the Pentecostal men pointed at my tambourine and snickered. But the Lord had the last laugh. In the years to come, numerous white tambourines were being played in countless Pentecostal meetings throughout Odessa. The Lord provided and multiplied!

For the Odessa Worship Conference, I arrived with another large suitcase bulging with donated dance garments, tights, ballet slippers, and white, long-sleeved leotards to give away. I prayerfully sought the Lord for direction to the "right person" to bestow this extravagant gift upon. Later a church deacon informed my husband that I picked the perfect recipient—a mother and her fifteen-year-old daughter, who traveled *five days* by train to attend our Worship Conference! Their hometown was the *only communist-ruled city left in all of Ukraine!* Months later, I received a thank-you letter and photographs from this mother-and-daughter dance team. The black and white pictures featured dancers twirling among several worshippers in a "March for Jesus" processional, which demonstrated the light of Christ in a very dark, atheist-governed city.

During the communist rule and reign, Christians prayed in hushed tones for fear of being deported to remote places like Siberia.

One evening our ministry team dined at Bishop Peter Serdichenko's lovely home.

"Who is that pretty woman?" I asked Peter's wife, pointing to the faded photograph on top of the piano.

"That's my sister. The communists arrested her because she is a Christian. I haven't seen her in eighteen years," said Kateanna quietly, with regret forever etched in her crystal blue eyes. "We still keep a suitcase packed…just in case they come to arrest us in the middle of the night."

For several years Linda and Edward continued to work tirelessly within the UPC network. Our generous local church supported them. Their young son, Ryan, also spoke fluent Russian.

One afternoon in Odessa, Daryl and I entered a smelly, urine-stained elevator with little Ryan, who was then about four years old. A man also stepped on, not realizing we were Americans. The burly man nodded, then gruffly spoke Russian to us with a tone of disgust. Ryan said something in Russian to the man. Little Ryan looked up at us to explain, "He says, 'It smells like a pig pen in here.'" The man looked stunned when he heard Ryan also speak to us in perfect English.

Songs of praise were birthed and sung in spite of deplorable living conditions—no running hot water during the summer and little or no heat in the winter. But worst of all, the McPherson's battled oppressive spiritual opposition during this challenging time period. Through intercessory prayer, the Lord gave Linda more than a hundred prophetic songs in the Russian language. The spiritual war waged on, but Jesus was the Victor! The Lord surrounded us with songs of deliverance, which are still being sung throughout Ukraine and in all the Russian-speaking churches in America.

Last Sunday, in our city of Columbus, I attended a contemporary Russian/Ukrainian church service with Linda and Edward. A delightful praise team of young men and women sang worshipful songs in Russian. At one point, Linda leaned over and whispered in my ear. "I wrote this song ten years ago," she said with a smile.

Those years in Ukraine were a blessing for everyone. God desired to loose the Holy Spirit on rigid congregations that had not entered the glorious courts of praise and worship.

Edward and Linda McPherson are currently residing as full-time missionaries in a Russian-speaking country in Central Asia.

Many nations will come and say, 'Come and let us go up to the mountain of the LORD And to the house of the God of Jacob, That He may teach us about His ways And that we may walk in His paths For from Zion will go forth the law, Even the word of the LORD from Jerusalem'

Micah 4:2, NKJV

CHAPTER THIRTY-THREE

Songwriter Mark Condon, Translating His Praise Music to the Russian Language

Two years after we first embarked to Odessa, that beautiful city on the Black Sea, Daryl was invited to be the keynote speaker at a national UPC leadership conference. Several thousand people, including bishops and pastors from throughout Ukraine, were in attendance those few days. Pastor Daryl taught on the subject of worship.

I sat next to Bishop Peter Serdichenko, his dear wife Kateanna, and their pretty, twenty-year-old daughter, Valencia, who loudly clapped and sang during the music service with exuberance. I didn't dare bring my tambourine that night! Educated in England, Valencia was eager to move away from the religious bondage of her Pentecostal forefathers.

Linda enthusiastically led the large choir of men and women onto the large platform. Our visiting musicians from America joined Russian orchestra members to enhance the large UPC choir with violins, flutes, and brass horns. By the end of the evening, Bishop Peter and Sister Kateanna were also clapping with joyous, newfound freedom!

The choir was filled with men and women of all ages. Depending on their age, the women were adorned with a "head-covering," which consisted of a lacey headscarf, a headband, or a drab babushka. The choir swayed and clapped to all of Linda's upbeat original songs. It was a dramatic departure from fear to freedom of spontaneous, heartfelt expression of praise.

Afterward, a UPC Bishop embraced my husband in tears. In broken English, he managed to say, "I lost my song ten years ago. Your message on worship returned singing to me…Thank you, and God bless you!"

Pastor Daryl traveled to Ukraine many more times in the years to follow. Alongside another UPC pastor, they water baptized countless Christians in the Black Sea during an outdoor summer ceremony with Bishop Peter. It was documented that more than 10,000 Russians/Ukrainians accepted Jesus Christ as Savior during those few years of revival. Many other Christian organizations began flooding in through this great open door during the time when it was very affordable to travel in this vast country.

About eight years ago, Edward and Linda came back to America on what seemed like a permanent furlough. In February 1998, Daryl and I resigned. It was a painful departure, but God was in it.

Unfortunately, the new church administration did not honor our commitment to our vast missionary support. Therefore, with heavy hearts, Linda, Edward, and Ryan were forced to return to Columbus. I love "the death of the vision." As painful as it is to experience, God always "raises *His plans* from the dead" for a greater worldwide impact and anointing than we could ever wish for or imagine.

Daryl and I were dining at a local restaurant and bumped into the McPhersons. I invited Linda to hear Evangelist Mark Condon minister in music at his United Pentecostal Church (UPC) in Columbus. We went on the following Sunday evening, which was Easter. Linda wept through the entire praise service.

Mark Condon has a unique style of music, and this gifted songwriter has produced eight very anointed praise and worship music CDs. His songs are heard around the world. Following that anointed praise service, we went out for pizza with Mark and Carol Condon. On the way home, I suggested that Linda consider translating Mark's music into a Russian CD to take back for "the Lord's unfinished missionary service in Ukraine."

The next morning, through previous church-related connections, I recruited a group of young UPC Russian musicians who embraced Linda with open arms. In fact, this group had been praying for Russian contemporary-style praise music.

Within a few weeks, Linda and I began meeting on a weekly basis. They were eager to learn new praise music. Linda also taught them prophetic singing. By the following Easter, Mark Condon's *House of Praise* was translated and recorded by Russian singers in a professional music studio.

With Mark's Russian CD in hand, Edward and Linda returned to Ukraine in 2003 to help with a new School of Worship and the

Arts in Kyiv, the capital of Ukraine.

Mark Condon's UPC church, along with Pastor Paul Cook, helped pave the McPhersons way back home. Back in Ukraine, Linda trained gifted Russian musicians to flow in the prophetic. She also was able to link up with several global outreach ministries located in Kyiv, including the Hillsong Church.

> *Let the word of Christ dwell in you richly in all wisdom, teaching and admonishing one another in psalms and hymns and spiritual songs, singing with grace in your hearts to the Lord.*

Colossians 3:16, NIV

CHAPTER THIRTY-FOUR

Pastor Daryl Sanders Evangelizing the Uttermost Parts of the Earth on the Artic Tundra

In 2005 Daryl was invited back to preach in Russia. This time he traveled to Vorkuta, located inside the Arctic Circle. He visited tents of the Komi tribe out on the Tundra at temperatures of fifty degrees below zero!

He had quite an adventure, too. While going on a mineshaft tour with fellow workers, the train went out of control and wrecked about a mile below the surface. Thankfully no one was seriously injured, but it was the most frightening experience of my husband's life. It was a true adventure while sharing Christ in a remote part of the earth. The scripture came to him, "Ask of me, and I will give you the heathen for an inheritance and the uttermost parts of the earth as a possession..." (Psalm 2:8).

The chorus verse, "Take Me to the Nations," was in my heart to sing all summer when the Lord first spoke to me about going to Russia. Our spiritual songs become tiny seedlings nurtured by fellow Christians in fertile foreign soil. Someday, we'll see the Lord in all His glory, and our worship will unite every tongue through love. We'll be planted together, singing for all eternity. We've seen glimmers of light among the nations to know that's true.

Daryl just returned from a Russian church conference in Seattle, WA. He was the keynote speaker as the guest of Senior Pastor Peter Cherbotov, who planned the event. Daryl met him in Ukraine many years ago and had a powerful prophecy for him that came true. Therefore, at the conference, Pastor Peter introduced him as "his father in the faith."

However, two weeks prior to this important Seattle leadership conference, Daryl underwent emergency knee surgery for a severe infection following knee replacement in his left knee last August. A week later, after a culture identified the exact bacteria invading his knee, the infectious disease doctor put him on an antibiotic I.V. drip to combat the infection, and he was transferred to a nursing home. Daryl was mandated to stay in the nursing home for another five weeks! Disappointed and feeling defeated, he canceled the Seattle trip and found a substitute preacher willing to take his place.

However, four days before the conference, the nursing staff came in and took out the I.V. drip from his arm. The doctor had changed his treatment to an oral antibiotic, and his surgeon released him to travel. Daryl instantly felt a surge of faith to make the trip to Seattle after all.

His longtime Christian friend, Bert Lindsay, accompanied Daryl as his nurse, pushing his wheelchair through the airport and helping him throughout the conference. Daryl was unable to bend his knee at that point in time, so Bert's assistance was certainly needed and appreciated.

The blessing of this testimony is that many years ago, Bert helped finance that first Ukraine worship conference without being able to attend. After learning of Daryl's physical dilemma, he volunteered to be his traveling companion. This host Russian-speaking church, which originated in Ukraine, has grown into a fruitful vine in America. Had it not been for the knee infection, Bert would have missed out on experiencing the fruit of the seeds he planted all those years ago. In addition, Lord used Bert at the Seattle conference to extend helpful wisdom to the church businessmen as a successful automobile dealer from Columbus.

Daryl later said, "I couldn't have gone to the conference without Bert's help. The miracle of my being released from the hospital in time became a testimony for increased trust. The devil meant it for evil, but the Lord was ultimately glorified in my secondary infection. My knee became the focal point of a bona fide miracle. Thus, my knee enhanced the atmosphere for an intensified anointing in each service. The Lord took all of us in the conference to a deeper level of faith each time we met throughout the three days.

Linda McPherson also attended the conference to work with the musicians. I asked her to recap some highlights of the conference since I was not able to attend.

With joy, she said, "Daryl was fantastic. His Bible teachings were rich and powerful, as usual. But I got the biggest charge watching Bert in action. Each time he got up to introduce Daryl, he'd give a timely exhortation to the church. He'd make a great preacher. You could tell he was loving every moment."

It's those kinds of unexpected blessings that make volunteer service so rewarding.

In fact, all our memories of traveling to Ukraine with teams of Christians are joyful. We have maintained wonderful friendships with our Russian and Ukrainian sisters and brothers in the Lord.

We're very grateful to the now-late Pastor Moses Vegh, who accompanied us on our first few trips to Russia and Ukraine. And in special memory of his beloved son, Marcus, who tragically passed away in October 2007 after a courageous battle with throat cancer.

I'm looking forward to a great and glorious reunion with Pastor Moses and Marcus Vegh in heaven someday. He was one of our dearest friends. Well done, my good friend and kingdom warrior!

"For Christ's love compels us, because we are convinced that one died for all, and therefore all died. And he died for all, that those who live should no longer live for themselves but for him who died for them and was raised again" (2 Corinthians 5:14–15, NIV).

CHAPTER THIRTY-FIVE

Dr. Billy Graham and Serving on The 1993 Greater Columbus Billy Graham Crusade

We were watching television one day, and while flipping channels, a Billy Graham Crusade came on the screen just as a young woman stepped up to the podium. The year was 1976. Daryl and I listened as this non-celebrity housewife addressed a huge stadium filled with people. Billy Graham was seated behind her a short distance away. She spoke with enthusiasm and encouraged the audience to make a difference in the world by giving generously to support the upcoming crusade in the near future. She only spoke for a few minutes, but her exhortation was compelling.

I turned to Daryl in awe. "That to me," I gushed, "would be *the* Greatest Blessing on earth to speak on behalf of a Billy Graham crusade!"

Seventeen years later, I followed Elizabeth Dole to the podium to speak at *The 1993 Greater Columbus Billy Graham Crusade.* Dr. and Mrs. Graham sat behind me as I addressed the 40,000 people that filled Cooper Stadium on Friday evening. The Lord places a desire in our hearts to fulfill it.

Daryl and I had served on the executive committee for eighteen months, and I was also the co-chair of the women's committee. My co-chair and I recruited four women from each of the thousand churches on board with the crusade. Leading up to the four-day crusade, we organized weekly prayer meetings and conducted special events with the 4,000 volunteer women.

The crusade program allowed me five minutes to speak and pray over the offering that evening. The days leading up to my moment were slightly nerve-wracking. Naturally, I prayed and prayed.

Billy Graham has often said, "There are three things that make a successful crusade; prayer, prayer, and more prayer." He is so right.

The Holy Spirit directed me to make an oversized door key out of cardboard and cover it with aluminum foil. The key had a jagged edge and looked exactly like a house key, except it was about two feet long and one foot wide. I had to make sure everyone in the stadium could see the large key as I held it up. Imagine speaking for five full minutes while holding a key in the air with an audience of 40,000 people looking at you! I wasn't sure I could do it, but since the Holy Spirit gave me the idea, the Lord would give me the grace to pull it off without shaking like a leaf.

I also prayed that I would not cry when I shared the story of seeing the lady on television and how I thought of no greater blessing than speaking at a Billy Graham Crusade.

When I stepped up to the pulpit, I pulled the tissue paper off my key and held it up in the air with my right arm. I didn't shake, stammer, or feel afraid. I choked back a tear when sharing the story about having the blessing of speaking for Dr. Graham. It was an honor and surely the biggest blessing that I've ever experienced and shall never forget.

I explained that the key I held represented us. We were the key to the next crusade because it was a huge expense to conduct a crusade where thousands of people would get saved. I felt the key served a purpose, and it worked. Weeks later, I was informed by the finance committee that the offering taken that Friday evening was the largest of all offerings taken during the crusade.

Delight yourself in the Lord; And He will give you the desires of your heart.

Psalm 37:4, NASB

CHAPTER THIRTY-SIX

Evangelist Dorothy Thomas Shackelford and the Visible Holy Ghost Encounter

There are outstanding Christians who will surely receive eternal rewards for their powerful impact on the lives of so many people. Dorothy Thomas Shackelford is one of those precious souls going down in history as a chosen vessel worthy of such honor.

When I served as the co-chair of the women's committee for the Billy Graham crusade, there were 1,000 churches involved from every county in Ohio. Each pastor selected four women volunteers from his congregation. Dorothy was selected from her church, and that's how we met.

As I pulled out of the garage that morning, the Holy Spirit said, "Take your boots," but I ignored the unction since it was not snowing.

Following the Billy Graham prayer rally held at her church, we drove to Wendy's for a bite to eat just as a snowstorm started. We were so caught up in sharing Jesus that six inches of snow had fallen before we knew it. Should have listened to the Holy Spirit about wearing boots!

At that time in my spiritual journey, I began reading Leanne Payne's books on inner healing and planned to attend one of her seminars coming up in Pittsburgh within weeks. As we stood in line to order food, I mentioned that Leanne had a national ministry to the LGBT community to free them. I'll never forget Dorothy's response. This tiny, petite woman began jumping up and down in glee!

"Barbara, I minister at the Franklin Country prison for women once a week, and the lesbian women are always asking for prayer, but I don't know how to minister to them."

Dorothy had taught school in Pittsburgh, and her son, a physician, still lived there. Before I knew it, we were driving to Pittsburgh in her navy blue BMW on a ministry adventure! She stayed with her son and each morning picked me up from my hotel.

The seminar was held at a beautiful stained-glass historic church, the original Covenant Church, founded by Sr. Pastor Joseph Garlington.

Since we were usually running late, we ended up sitting on the balcony because the main floor was packed. On the first day of the three-day conference, I encountered an athletic black woman who reminded me of Angela Davis of the Black Panther movement in the 1970s. This tough-looking young woman was dressed in combat fatigues worn by the military. Her hair was cropped in a short Afro. The first time she passed by, I said, "Hi," and smiled kindly. She snarled at me and continued walking past me. I noticed this scary girl sat in the very last row of the balcony, all alone. On the second day, I asked Dorothy to approach her since it might have been a racial thing. I took a seat on the edge of the balcony and hoped for the best. Dorothy invited the girl to sit next to her about five rows behind me. I glanced back a few times while quietly praying for "a breakthrough."

Dorothy was a very anointed woman, so I knew she was speaking life to this lost and hurting soul. The last time I snuck a peek, I could hardly believe my eyes. Dorothy was cradling this grown woman like a newborn baby and rocking her back and forth as if holding her in a rocking chair. It was profound. It brought tears to my eyes.

The next afternoon Dorothy and I walked down a paved alleyway towards her car parked on a side street. Coming toward us was the Angela Davis look-a-like, and I almost didn't recognize her. She was grinning from ear to ear, and I did a double-take to make sure it was the same gal. When we caught up to her, we heard an amazing testimony. She could hardly speak because her joy was bubbling over like soap suds. She kept saying, "You won't believe it, you just won't believe it." She finally explained that her pastor had assigned her to attend this seminar. In her mind, it was the last-ditch effort to find peace. She planned to commit suicide if she didn't find answers. Dorothy's expression of love was the hand of God reaching down from heaven. She realized that God truly loved her, and He really had a plan for her life after all. And, of course, Leanne Payne and her team were anointed to share testimony after testimony of the delivering power of God. It all came together for this girl. To God be the glory!

My friendship with Dorothy continued, and she became our special guest at all our church events.

An upcoming women's retreat was scheduled for St. Mary of the Springs, located near the Columbus airport. The cost was $38.00 a night to include all meals in the cafeteria with the elderly Dominican nuns since it was a retirement home that featured a conference center. I booked our ladies' retreat for Friday and Saturday night. After thinking it through, I decided to cancel the last night because dinner was served at 5 p.m., and we could have testimony time in the chapel and still be home by 9 p.m. We'd be saving the cost of an additional night's stay if I canceled.

When I picked up the phone to cancel, the Holy Spirit spoke urgently. "Don't ever put a price tag on My time of ministry. I will do my deepest work among the women from seven to ten on Saturday night." As if holding a hot potato, I flung the phone back into the cradle. I pondered those words in my heart and told no one.

At the retreat, Dorothy went missing during lunch on Saturday. "Where's Dorothy?" I asked my friend Sandy Hlasten seated at our table. "Oh, she's out at the flagpole baptizing one of our visitors in the Holy Spirit." We both chuckled because that was so like evangelist Dorothy.

When Dorothy finally caught up to our table for her meal, she whispered that there was a bridal shower to attend at 2 p.m. and she wouldn't be back.

"Oh, you have to come back!" I gushed without anyone else overhearing our conversation. "The Lord told me He was showing up between seven and ten to do His deepest work!"

Her eyes lit up with glee. "Really?" She was smiling brightly. "Oh, I will definitely come back then!"

After the 5 o'clock meal, we reconvened in the small chapel. The room had purple carpeting, a few rows of pews, and an organ on a small platform, a fireplace centered in the room with a Crucifix adorning the mantle. We placed a golden-crusted loaf of bread under the Crucifix with a silver goblet next to the symbolic Bread of Life. Dorothy and I sat on the edge of the organ platform facing the women seated in pews. The clock on the back wall was in full view. It was 6:15 p.m., and the women were excited to share their hearts. At 6:59, the room calmed to an uncomfortable silence because no one had anything else to share. Suddenly the feisty, red-headed Susan Rhodes jumped up from a front pew. "Dorothy, pray for me before we leave!"

Dorothy stood to pray over her, and down Susan went in the spirit. Pentecostals and the Charismatics refer to that as being "slain in the spirit."

"I'm next," I called out while rushing over for prayer. I went out in the spirit, too.

The rest of our dear church ladies began lining up for prayer with Dorothy. But one gal, "a diamond in the rough," felt frightened about all the women getting "slain in the spirit." Sandy

Hlasten escorted Jackie out into the hallway to privately calm her down. Later, when Sandy led the gal back into the chapel, Dorothy and I quickly met them in the center aisle to continue ministering.

Jackie was leaning over from the waist, so Dorothy and I bent down to pray with her. All of a sudden, Dorothy looked at me with bright eyes. She whispered, "He's here; He's here right now."

My head jerked up to "see" what Dorothy had whispered in my ear. From behind the stooped-over Jackie, Sandy stood toward us and also faced the Crucifix mantel located about six feet behind us. By her stunned expression, I knew Sandy also witnessed a manifestation of the Holy Spirit. Later, she told me that the glowing mist started from the communion elements resting on the mantel. This supernatural demonstration of God's Glory had already floated past us before I spotted the glittering formation that resembled a small cloud of gold dust floating toward the rear wall.

The three of us trembled in awe as we watched this shimmering form continue along each connecting wall before circling back behind us to the large Crucifix above the communion elements.

When the glorious presence arrived back at the mantel, it hovered over the loaf of bread, which rested alongside the silver goblet containing grape juice we had used for communion hours earlier.

The ladies were still laid out on the deep purple carpeting while soaking up His presence in the holiest atmosphere anyone had ever experienced. I looked at the clock, and it was exactly 10 p.m.

The Holy Spirit is *real*.

CHAPTER THIRTY-SEVEN

Mrs. Coretta Scott King
Helping to Heal Race Relations

My mother once told me that as a little girl, my favorite play-mate was a "colored" dolly. My dad was born and reared in the Deep South, but thankfully, he was not a racist. Before super high-ways were built, every summer, our Michigan family of five trav-eled two days by car through the vast Blue Ridge and Smokey Mountains finally to reach South Carolina for a visit with Grand-mother and other family members. On one such family vacation, I experienced my first uneasy feeling over the differences in skin tone. I was five years old. We had stopped for a fill-up at a com-bined gas station and grocery. Skipping alongside my dad across the weathered wooden planks, a little bell over the doorway tin-kled as we passed through. The clerk behind the counter was just about to accept money from a black man checking out with only one or two items sitting on the counter. But as soon as we entered the store, the clerk harshly rebuked the colored man to "wait." His harsh and demeaning tone caught my attention.

My dad and I moseyed around the store, selecting snacks. The same dark-skinned man was patiently waiting at the counter when we returned to pay for our purchases. It was obvious that the gen-tleman was forced to wait until we checked out. After my father was finished, the fellow was finally allowed to pay his money.

Feeling a twinge of guilt for this injustice, I asked my dad to explain. My father got down on his knees to face me. He simply said, "It's the South, and colored people are considered less important than white people." He added, "But it is very wrong." I still remember the incident as if it happened yesterday.

I grew up in Dearborn, Michigan. Believe it or not, the deed to my parents' house still reads: "No colored people allowed to buy this home." Orville Hubbard was the mayor of Dearborn, Michigan, for thirty-six years, from 1942 to 1978. Sometimes referred to as the "Dictator of Dearborn," Hubbard was the most outspoken segregationist north of the Mason-Dixon line. During his administration, non-whites were aggressively discouraged from residing in Dearborn, and Hubbard's longstanding campaign to "Keep Dearborn Clean" was widely understood to mean: "Keep Dearborn White." The civil rights movement was going on during my years at Dearborn High, but my teachers never mentioned it as a worthy cause to consider. Therefore, my initial cross-culture encounters happened during college. I never saw an African-American my age until I entered college.

On the other hand, my husband grew up in the inner city as a minority white child. My husband Daryl was bussed out of the inner-city school system to suburban schools because teachers recognized his high IQ. He developed as an athlete at the downtown Cleveland Y.M.C.A. Daryl's disabled father supported the family on a small pension. As a result, Daryl experienced poverty at an early age. By high school, his family had moved to a suburb with better opportunities; therefore, Daryl excelled in academics and sports.

At age 18, Daryl married a pretty but troubled girl right out of high school. She was his very first love, and being responsible, he married his pregnant sixteen-year-old girlfriend. By the time Daryl finished college, he had two babies to support. He also worked a third job to pay for his wife's private psychiatric sessions. After ten years of a tumultuous marriage, life had become an emotional mess. Divorce was imminent. Daryl gained custody of his two children and moved on. We met two years later through a mutual friend.

When we eventually married, Daryl was a successful businessman. I did not know him when he played for the NFL. Having those extremely contrasting experiences in life gave Daryl a balanced sense of values, especially regarding healing race relationships. As a leader in Columbus, Daryl set out to make social changes for the betterment of society. Sharing his ideals, I supported every effort to strengthen racial reform. In 1990, Daryl started "The Churches...One Foundation." The title of this non-profit organization came from the famous hymn "The Church's One Foundation," which, of course, is Christ Jesus, our Lord. The board represented black, mainline, and white suburban churches.

These twelve honorable pastors worked in harmony for the goal of the One Foundation mission statement: "Supporting Churches and Organizations That Help the Poor, the Disadvantaged, or the Homeless in Central Ohio." The board adopted several inner-city ministries to assist financially through donations from their suburban church support.

In 1992, a One Foundation dinner was held at the King Arts Complex. Bank One sponsored this formal event for one hundred couples. As Daryl and I walked through the expansive King Arts Complex lobby, the Lord spoke to my heart. I heard the Holy Spirit say, "Stop. I want you to remember this moment." I stopped dead in my tracks. I looked down at the marble floor and waited for the Lord to speak further. But I heard nothing more from the Lord. It certainly was puzzling, so I hurried on to catch up to my husband. Daryl patiently waited for me in the elevator to reach the ballroom for the One Foundation gala event.

One year later, I crossed that same marble floor, personally accompanying Mrs. Coretta Scott King on a tour of a building dedicated to her late husband. It was April 3, 1993, the 25th anniversary of the death of Dr. Martin Luther King, Jr. Earlier that year, I organized ongoing "race reconciliation" luncheons at the King Center. My goal was to bring black and white churches together for racial unity. During the planning stage, the Lord spoke to my heart again. He said, "Invite Mrs. King as your first guest speaker."

I offered her three dates, one each in March, April, and May. I was not connecting the sacred April date to Dr. King's death. I said to my husband, "Watch, she's probably going to pick the month of April because I have that Billy Graham women's event at World Harvest Church the night before."

It was a busy and productive time in our lives. Daryl and I both served on the executive and administrative committees for *The 1993 Greater Columbus Billy Graham Crusade.* I also served as co-chair of the women's committee.

By working with the 1,000 churches involved with the crusade, I helped recruit 4,000 women volunteers. The women's rally was on Friday, April 2. That night I returned home exhilarated but exhausted. I had to get up early the next morning. As I pulled the covers up around my chin, the Lord said, "Go anoint that hanky for Mrs. King." I said, "Oh, Lord, I'll do it in the morning." But He said, "Do it now." So, I pulled myself out of bed and went down to the kitchen at about 1 a.m. My alarm was set for 6 a.m. The hanky came from Bishop Timothy Clarke's Martin Luther King, Jr. rally in January. For sale in the church lobby was an array of tee shirts, plaques, hankies, posters, and artwork in honor of Dr. King. The soft cotton handkerchief had blue pansies embroidered on it with a Scripture verse from the Psalms. I planned to give it to Mrs. King. I retrieved the white handkerchief from my Bible. In obedience, I anointed it with a few drops of holy oil while dedicating the hanky to the Lord. I prayed that it would have special meaning to her. I tucked it back inside the cover of my Bible, which was sitting next to my camera and purse—lined up for my early morning dash.

Our good friend, Kevin Miles, was kind enough to donate a driver and Cadillac limousine from the company he owned and operated in Columbus. Kevin is also the executive director of Crime Stoppers in Columbus. Pastor Daryl and Pastor LaFayette

Scales collected Mrs. King and her traveling companion at the airport in grand style. Along with a private reception in her honor, I waited with anticipation for her arrival at the King Arts Complex center. When Daryl introduced me to Mrs. King, the local news media stood close behind me, with several cameras focused on her face. I leaned over to embrace her and noticed a red lipstick smear on her beautiful white teeth. It has happened to every woman at least one time in life. I whispered in her ear, "Mrs. King, you have lipstick on your teeth." As a typical female response, we both grabbed at the sides of our empty pockets for Kleenex and came up empty-handed. Then I remembered the hanky in my Bible at a nearby table. I slipped away and quickly returned with the hanky as the cameras were still rolling. I slipped it into her hand, and she quickly took care of the matter in one swipe. God anointed her mouth in a unique way because she was a voice to the nations. Her speech was eloquent. Many times, she departed from her printed notes and shared poignant things from her heart regarding her faith. It was a tribute I will never forget. The late Mrs. King was a gracious lady, and her passionate speech touched every heart that gathered in her honor that day.

She sat next to me during our lunch, and we privately shared a candid conversation. We chuckled about the lipstick smear. She took out the gift hanky and told me the scripture was her favorite Psalm. Unfortunately, I don't remember the exact Psalm imprinted on that hanky. It remains my one regret about that day.

Mrs. King loved the idea of *One Foundation*. As we traveled back to the airport, she said to my husband, "I am going to tell my pastor all about this wonderful program!" After I kissed her goodbye at the airport gate, she lovingly smiled. She looked into my eyes and spoke some final words to me. "Thank you for doing something important for race relations in your city. Please keep this program going. I am very honored that you asked me to be a part of it."

"Finally, all of you, live in harmony with one another; be sympathetic, love as brothers, be compassionate and humble. Do not repay evil with evil or insult with insult, but with blessing, because to this you were called so that you may inherit a blessing."

1 Peter 3:8–9, NIV

"Truly the signs of an apostle were wrought among you in all patience, in signs, and wonders, and mighty deeds."

2 Corinthians 12:12, NKJV

Chapter Thirty-Eight

Evangelist Rodney Howard-Browne and Unusual Manifestations of the Holy Spirit

We were enjoying a quiet seaside vacation in Sarasota, Florida, when a phone call came through from Pastor Moses Vegh. He urged us to meet him at a large church in Lakeland to hear Rodney Howard Browne preach at a weeklong leadership conference. The year was 1993.

The previous year, Pastor Vegh prophesied to Senior Pastor Karl Strader that his church would soon see record crowds because the Lord was bringing revival. The dwindling Carpenters Home Church had seen better days.

We invited our Christian friends, Doc and Susan Furci, to make the trip. Dr. Don Furci had a thriving family medical practice in Sarasota after they did mission work in India.

When we arrived at the church, Pastor Vegh ushered the four of us to a ringside pew close to the front so we wouldn't miss a thing. We were more curious than anything because this "laughing phenomenon" was nothing we embraced. The sanctuary held several thousand people, and it was packed to capacity. I noticed Marilyn Hickey sitting on the front row and other notable Christian leaders who had come to the conference.

After the lively praise session, Pastor Rodney Howard-Browne took the microphone and began what might be considered a comedy hour. However, the brunt of all his jokes was the unenlightened sitting in the pews—most specifically, the legalistic strongholds governing Christian leaders and their stiff ministries. He began his shtick, poking fun at the religious doctrine prevalent in modern-day churches. He quipped, "Some of you pastors are 'deacon-possessed,' and you need deliverance!"

Jesus attacked that same religious spirit with a vengeance condemning the religious rulers as a "brood of vipers." Nothing plugs up the flow of the Holy Spirit more than the bondage of rigid religious rules and regulations.

Pastor Karl Strader's son, Stephen, and his attractive wife, Janice, were also seated up close and personal. We were seated in the next section on a curve, so I was able to easily observe all the important people sitting in the front row, middle section.

At one point during his delivery, Rodney Howard-Brown walked over to Janice, a lovely blond dressed to the nines in a bright blue chiffon dress best suited for a wedding party. She put up her hands in mimic protest and yelped, "No, no, no…please don't!" Rodney laughed and touched her forehead. She collapsed in a drunken slump and never moved for another forty-five minutes. Trust me, I remained glued to the situation, waiting for her to move or "wake up," but she was completely knocked out and didn't move an eyelash that entire time frame.

Rodney continued his non-stop delivery exposing churches steeped in tradition. "It's time to have the abnormal in our services. It's time we started having something supernatural. People today talk a great deal about the Spirit of God, but if Jesus were here, they'd run away from Him! I don't want to be so full of pride, tradition, and bondage that I won't allow the Spirit of God to move. Don't have a church service with three hymns and preaching out of *Encyclopedia* and *Reader's Digest*."

As Rodney was winding down, he walked over to Janice and pulled her up off the pew. The woman was so inebriated she could hardly stand. He carefully guided the staggering woman across the front section towards the far right of the sanctuary. She staggered like a drunken sailor. I had never witnessed anyone drunk in the spirit, so I remained bug-eyed as the scene unfolded.

When Rodney and Janice finally reached the far side of the sanctuary, he called out an entire delegation of Canadian church leaders to stand and come down front. About twelve to fifteen well-dressed pastors in expensive silk suits and gold watches quickly gathered. Janice remained staggering, unable to focus on the formal-looking group of men who each looked like a centerfold for GQ magazine.

Once the stylish men were properly assembled in a line, Rodney gently shoved Janice to face them. In a blink of an eye, the entire group was flung backward in unison and lay on the floor, laughing their heads off. I'd never seen anything so astounding.

After the service ended, we all lined up to receive a personal prayer from Rodney Howard-Browne. We each fell out under the power of the Holy Spirit after he prayed for each individual. I'm grateful for the impartation through the laying on of hands.

Revival with Rodney Howard-Browne went for another sixteen weeks in that Lakeland church with three to four thousand people in meetings twice a day. No one was more thrilled than Pastor Vegh, whose prophetic word had come to pass.

Driving back to Sarasota, our group discussed the amazing meeting we had just attended. Don confessed that during the praise service, his eyelids were stuck shut for several minutes. An unexplainable supernatural sign from God to a Christian physician who remains one of the most spiritual and godly men I know.

What was interesting about this meeting is that my husband never attended church without wearing "proper attire." In all the years leading up to that church service, whenever he preached the Gospel, he wore a suit or sports jacket with a shirt and tie. Since we were on vacation, Pastor Daryl only brought one tie, and earlier, he could not locate it in our rush to drive up to Lakeland. Throughout the service, he felt conspicuous not having his proper tie on and kept pulling closed his shirt collar.

Later, the Lord chastised Pastor for being so self-conscious over his outward appearance and challenged him to break free from tradition by preaching without his customary tie after we returned home. Sure enough, that following Sunday, there were some traditionalists who became "unglued" at the sight of their pastor not wearing a tie! It was rather funny since it proved Rodney Howard-Browne's point. Daryl actually wanted to wear Bermuda shorts and a golf shirt to provoke a reaction from the traditionalists, but I thought that shorts would be carrying the point a bit too far. Not wearing a tie was all that was needed.

God does have a sense of humor, and obviously, He uses laughter to break the mold to deliver us from religious barriers and traditions.

"The Lord does not look at the things people look at. People look at the outward appearance, but the Lord looks at the heart"

1 Samuel 16:7

"Not everyone who says to me, 'Lord, Lord,' will enter the kingdom of heaven, but the one who does the will of my Father who is in heaven."

Matthew 7:21

CHAPTER THIRTY-NINE

Evangelist Randy Clark, Pastors John and Carol Arnott, and the Toronto and Brownsville Revivals

Our dear ministry friends Pastors Paul and Eleanor Stern enthusiastically testified of "The Toronto Blessing" and urged Daryl and I to make a trip to Canada to receive a blessing. That urging came to us sometime in 1994.

All five of their children were born on African soil. Mom Beall also prophesied that later in life, Eleanor would have an orphanage in Africa, and that also came true fifty-five years later. All five children serve in ministry. Jon and Molly Stern have served in Kenya for over thirty-five years. Pastor Paul Stern died a few years ago, leaving a lasting legacy to all who adored him. He was one of the apostles ordaining Daryl as Senior Pastor to launch Zion Christian Fellowship in 1985.

In 1995, Daryl made a journey with a group of leaders from the Capital City Association of Ministers (C-CAM). As a busy Mom of three children and doing church work, I didn't pay much attention to their praise report, so I had no interest in going until a few years later.

The Toronto revival began with faith and expectancy. Vineyard Airport Church Pastors John and Carol Arnott invited Pastor Randy Clark to minister for a series of meetings in Toronto. At the time, Pastor Randy was Senior Pastor of Vineyard Christian Fellowship in St. Louis. He was experiencing powerful manifestations of the Holy Spirit as people were powerfully touched by God each time he took the pulpit.

After Pastor Randy arrived at the Toronto Vineyard Airport Church, his anointed ministry was launched into a global magnitude. On January 20, 1994, the power of the Holy Spirit fell upon 120 people gathered at the Thursday night meeting. The spark of revival began with immediate fruit measurable by the end of 1995. It has been documented that over 900 first-time conversions took place in the renewal the first year.

Over 600,000 people from all over the globe visited Toronto by the end of 1995.

Sometime in 1996, during a church fellowship in our home, Linda McPherson shared how visiting Toronto the year before had helped her cope with the religious spirits in Odessa and intense spiritual warfare. She began to gush about the experience. "I saw a thirty-foot angel in the spirit. That spot in the sanctuary was especially anointed when anyone passed by…Holy laughter and people falling out under the power of the Holy Spirit." My curiosity was piqued to know more about the Toronto Blessing, so I organized a trip with our minister of music, Beth Emery, Linda McPherson, and my spiritual daughter, Tina (Smith) Powell. Toronto offered special conferences throughout the year, so it became one of those side trips that we managed to "squeeze in" between events at our church.

The Sunday night before our departure on Monday morning, Beth and I were at church running off copies and tying up loose ends for the Women's Retreat the following weekend. We finished at about 3 a.m. and came back to my house to get a few hours' sleep. We departed at 7 a.m. and drove to Toronto, stopping for gas, bathroom needs, and lunch. We arrived just in the nick of time for Monday night's service at an airport hangar that had been converted into a church building. Needless to say, we looked and felt haggard, as well as extremely tired and hungry. My mind was on eating the pizza we planned to eat but didn't because we ran out of time. I had done all the driving with the car keys in my purse, so as I was nodding off, fighting sleep, I was tempted to slip out to the pillow in the back seat. My heart was longing for the pillow and eating pizza after the meeting.

The only thing keeping me from slipping out was that the speaker was teaching about "Abba Father," and this was the message Mike Evans taught when I got "zapped" at the *JESUS* outdoor rally years earlier. The man at the podium also mentioned, "All our church leaders are at their weekly home group meetings." That made me nervous and wonder if the "second shift" had a valid anointing to minister? Were we being gypped out of a spectacular Toronto Blessing that Linda raved about?

At about 9 p.m., about 150 people were ushered into a large vacant room with about ten lines of silver duct tape on the tiled floor, forming lines spaced ten feet apart. Each silver line had about ten or twelve people standing in wait. It was very organized, and we rushed to the "top of the line," closest to the side where pairs of prayer warriors stood so that we would get prayed over "first." My heart sank when the man and woman walked passed us to the far end of our line. *Great,* I grumbled. *We'll be here another half-hour.*

The short, athletic-looking gal was getting closer to my friends to my right. They all "went out in the spirit" with strong arms behind them to catch them fall out. When she got to me, I was not having any of it. I was tired, hungry, and my heart felt stony and unreceptive. Paul said, "My spirit is willing, but my flesh is weak," but in this case, even my spirit was weak.

"Oh," she began in a soothing, sweet voice. "The Father loves you so much…" My mind responded with, *You're just saying that to get me to cry…nice try.* She kept praying, but I knew it was useless. I felt sorry for her because there was no way she was getting through to me. When I felt a man behind me ready to catch me, I gave her a "courtesy drop" to get rid of her.

Once I safely landed on my back, I pulled my crumpled nylon ski jacket back in place and rested my hands on my stomach. My fingers were overlapping each other just at the tips, and I glanced at the clock. It was 9:45 p.m. I thought, *Well, Lord, I didn't get anything; maybe tomorrow will be different.*

This is what the Holy Spirit spoke back. "Oh yeah? Try moving."

At first, I thought I was imagining everything. But I could not disconnect my fingertips. Then I realized my head could not move to look down at my toes. I could turn my head to the right or left as if motioning the word "no," but there was a brick under my chin. Then I inquired of the Lord. "How long will this last?" He said, "Several hours."

As I rested there, completely paralyzed from my chin down, I listened to the sounds of those around me. I heard laughter, quiet crying, and short snorting noises, but nothing out of the ordinary. I felt completely normal other than having a spiritual "saddle block" like I did when birthing my son.

Beth, Tina, and Linda were now sitting up and talking near my feet, but I couldn't see them. "Come closer so I can see you. I can't move."

When they stood to check my condition, Linda kicked my foot as if to test me. It flopped over. A man in charge of closing-up shop began flicking the lights on and off because it was the time to depart. It was close to 11 p.m. We were the only group left in the room. He came over and directed me to get up. I said, "Sir, I cannot move." He fetched a computer chair with wheels. Linda got the keys to bring the car around to the front of the building. When this man, Tina, and Beth lifted my arms to hoist me up to the chair, I began laughing hysterically. I was dead weight, so it was extremely difficult for them to maneuver my body onto the chair. The more they manhandled me, the harder I laughed. They rolled the chair, holding my limp body, across the long room, down the dark corridor, and out to the curb where Linda was waiting with the car.

The passenger door was wide open, and I feared my face was going to fall on the sharp door corner's edge. I had absolutely no control over my body. My hands resembled a paraplegic's limp hands. Beth slid in next to me on the front seat and held me up as Linda drove. Tina rode in the back seat.

The hotel was not far away, so the employees were accustomed to the crazy charismatics arriving "drunk" and laughing. The bellman was dressed in a red uniform with brass buttons. He opened the door to help me out. "Ma'am, you're going to have to stop laughing if I am to help out of the car." As he attempted to lift my heavy, dead weight, I fell on the sidewalk. The three of them managed to get me into a wheelchair that someone produced.

I was wheeled to the front desk, but I was too zoned-out to function. Tina said I resembled someone stoned on heroin because my eyes were completely dilated, and my body had gone limp. I had become too weak to laugh anymore. I felt completely drained and remained paralyzed.

We were ushered to our room which contained two queen beds and a large side-sofa bed. I was somehow placed on the sofa bed while the bellman, Beth, and Linda left to retrieve our suitcases from the car parked in the hotel's garage. When the door closed, a white, twinkle mist permeated the room, creating a holy atmosphere. I asked Tina to pull a chair beside me as the prophetic began to quicken me. I prayed over her life and prophesied over all her children. When the luggage arrived, the bellman stared at me with a scared look on his face. When asked, he told me his name was Philip. I said, "Come over here, Philip. God wants to speak into your life." I prophesied over him, but he looked scared to death and couldn't get out of there fast enough.

The girls were sound asleep by the time I came "undone." It was close to 2 a.m. The thaw started at my feet and flowed up through my body as if coming out of anesthesia. I managed to get to the restroom but in slow motion. The next morning, we took an elevator down to the main floor dining room to eat breakfast. I'm a fast walker, usually five-feet ahead of everyone else, but I could not keep up with them. If a fire had broken out, I could not have run or moved quickly. I kept yelling, "Wait up, I can't walk that fast."

After breakfast, we planned to drive to Niagara Falls on our day off from scheduled church meetings. The next session was Tuesday evening. The daytime seminar was scheduled from Wednesday through Friday.

We continued moving toward the attached hotel garage, and as soon as I entered the towered parking lodge, my legs buckled, and I fell to my knees, unable to move. Thankfully, no cars were rounding the corner because I would have been run over. That had never happened before, but I knew it was part of the "Oh yeah? Try moving" bit the Lord was putting on me.

We arrived at the magnificent Niagara Falls on the Canadian side, which featured picnic tables, log cabin restaurants, lovely flowering gardens, and breathtaking views. I sat on a bench, unable to partake in much. I felt foggy but didn't realize that I was in a drunken state that remained on me the entire week. Since I had never experienced being "drunk in the spirit," I was unaware of what was going on within my spirit.

When Philip, the bellman, saw me the next evening, he looked very relieved. He said, "You were dead weight, so I knew you were paralyzed, and it scared me."

Throughout the meetings that week, I experienced "carpet time," and each time, I was paralyzed, unable to move an inch. Everyone in our group was also experiencing unusual manifestations except Tina. She remained our "designated driver" since we three were always too drunk to drive.

One night after getting prayed over, Beth was unable to talk. All she could do was whistle. Beth has a beautiful singing voice with a college degree in music. Her whistling was pure and a pleasure to hear. She chirped like a bird for over an hour, amazing everyone around her in the crowded duct-tape prayer room.

A young woman from England scooted over to Beth with an open Bible. Kneeling next to her with a beautiful British accent, she began reading from Isaiah 5:26. "He lifts up a banner for the distant nations, he whistles for those at the ends of the earth. Here they come, swiftly and speedily!" Beth began to frantically whistle with fast short chirps since she could not express her joy in any other way. She was unable to speak words, just whistle!

When we got into the car with Tina behind the wheel, Linda, also a gifted musician, was seated next to the whistling bird in the back seat. Suddenly, the whistling turned into a recognizable song. Linda, sounding like a drunken sailor, slurred, "You can't whistle that; it's not a Christian song!" But Beth kept whistling the tune "Around the World in 80-Days."

I was in the passenger seat and asked if anyone wanted to stop and eat. Beth began frantically kicking the back of my seat as if to say, "Yes, Yes! I am starving!" That took us to a new level of laughter.

A few months later, I traveled to Lagos, Nigeria, with Beth with a team of women from our church. While ministering to a classroom of Nigerian church members, Beth began to share the Toronto experience. On a previous ministry journey, she had traveled from Hawaii to Singapore and on to Ukraine with our church, and then to Africa. *She had traveled around the world in 80 days!*

Tina was becoming upset that she was not receiving anything from the Lord all week long. She held back, feeling like Cinderella, the slighted stepsister missing out on the upcoming ball. The fairy princess arrived when Carol Arnott prayed over Tina. Nothing manifested until a youth group from Minneapolis came around receiving prayer from Carol. There were a couple of teens looking out of place. Tina sat on the steps of an open stairway, observing some of the kids getting a touch from the Lord and others getting nothing, like her. All of a sudden, Tina shot off her seat to pray over the few dejected teens. They went out in the spirit. She thus entered into a Holy Ghost anointing that surpassed anything we had experienced!

When any of us were "winding down," Tina would touch our arm, and we'd instantly begin to laugh and become drunk all over again.

Carol brought Deth and me up to the platform one night to testify of our experiences. Afterward, we were slain in the spirit, lying side-by-side with each other. The spirit would come and "electrocute" us, and our bodies would rise up under this amazing power as if we were actually being electrocuted.

On the long way home, we took turns driving, just sober long enough to take the wheel a few hours at a time. At one rest stop, we entered the bathroom laughing and carrying on. I called Daryl from a pay phone and started laughing so hard I slid down the wall, unable to stand. There was an American Veteran food trailer at the curb, raising money by selling coffee and snacks. The Am-Vet lady inside the open booth glared at us in disgust because she probably thought we were inebriated from alcohol. We were drunk on the New Wine of Heaven!

We had a women's retreat that Friday evening back in Columbus. When we pulled into the parking lot, I remember trying to park in a straight line, but it took several attempts while hitting the curb each time. Victoria, a church member, observed us and scratched her head at my pathetic driving ability.

Evangelist Cereda Rispress was our guest speaker. She got a

kick out of our goofiness when we greeted her. We were not sober.

The lodge offered sleeping rooms off the main meeting room, along with additional nearby cabins. In the main lodge, several hallways connected, and each time I intersected with Tina in the distance, we were both knocked down by the spirit, even though we were fifty feet from each other! It was a true zap off our feet.

Cereda and Daniel Rispress were highly respected community leaders from West Virginia. Cereda carried herself in a very dignified manner. She always dressed in classy clothing and carried an executive briefcase to all her staff meetings. They moved to Columbus and were part of a church start-up at that time period. They now have a powerful prophetic church and School of the Prophets on the Eastside of Columbus. In one of her teaching sessions, she mentioned "never falling out in the spirit to land on the floor wearing nice clothing."

Cereda got the biggest kick out of the four of us experiencing unusual manifestations. She chuckled whenever we remained drunk during praise and worship sessions that weekend.

Sunday morning, we all left for home in time for church. When Cereda entered the hallway leading to her church office, the Holy Spirit hit her like lightning. Her briefcase went flying up and down, and it was a genuine Toronto experience.

A month later, Cereda and Daniel attended a Rodney Howard Browne meeting in their hometown of West Virginia. Dressed in the nines, the stunning couple was ushered to their usual ringside

VIP seats. However, they needed to depart early, so all eyes were on them leaving. When Cereda neared the exit door, Rodney called out to her through the microphone. "Hey, lady in the white dress! Don't leave yet!" At the sound of his voice, she fell out in the spirit—her first time "on the carpet." Rodney began chuckling and continued talking to her through the loudspeakers. She responded in a drunken-sailor voice, barely able to move. Everyone in the room laughed with joy at the power of the Holy Spirit. God has a great sense of humor!

Jesus wants to pull us out of our religiosity into a place of complete surrender to His Grace and Lightning Power.

The Holy Spirit is so *real*!

"The law of the Lord is perfect, reviving the soul; the testimony of the Lord is sure, making wise the simple" (Psalm 19:7).

CHAPTER FORTY

Dr. Chris Tunde Joda, M.D. and the Lagos, Nigeria Ministry Trip

It was to be just a routine physical exam with a new physician a friend had highly recommended. It was the spring of 1994.

I was sitting on the exam table about to meet this female doctor when a young man knocked on the door before walking in to greet me.

"Hello, I am a resident doctor," he said. "Dr. Tallo will be coming in to continue after I do an initial exam if that's okay with you."

He knocked my knees with a rubber hammer, checking my reflexes. Next, he had me cough while listening to my chest with a stethoscope. He felt my neck for enlarged lymph nodes and inspected my ears and throat with his battery-operated exam light. He turned every now and then to jot down notes on my clean white medical chart. Suddenly the door burst open, and he respectfully stepped back as Diane Tallo whirled in to take over. Her magnetic presence filled the room as she took command, greeting me in an efficient and friendly manner.

The physical exam continued as Dr. Tallo, an endocrinologist, began probing my neck with the perceptive fingers of a gland specialist. She stood behind me, reaching around to the front of my throat, pressing here and there with tender pokes from her fingertips. She knew exactly how to explore for problems. I was a perfectly healthy human specimen coming in for a routine physical exam with a friendly new doctor.

Suddenly Dr. Tallo quickly filled a Dixie cup with water. "Here, drink this," she said with a strange tone. As I swallowed, she pressed into my throat with those amazing fingers. Looking at the young intern, she pronounced with sternness, "She has a lump!" Ever the teacher, she instructed the young man to feel the place at the base of my neck, which he had missed in his initial exam.

My body stiffened. Within a split second, she was directly in front of me, about two inches from my face.

"Now, don't be alarmed," she cautioned while peering intently into my frightened eyes. "I'm going to have this lump on your thyroid biopsied under ultrasound. So, even if it is cancerous, there is a 90-percent success rate for this kind. You can live a perfectly normal life on synthetic thyroid medicine in the event and..." I didn't remember a thing from that point on because I was in mild shock. *Cancer* is all I heard.

I don't remember driving home that day. I regretted changing doctors, but that was a form of denial. I dreaded the thought of becoming a thyroid-disease victim like my husband, who, for the last thirty-eight years, has been a virtual prisoner to thyroid medication three times a day. *No, thanks...*I thought, also having trepidation about the aspect of another surgery in my life. I did not want to live out my remaining years dependent on drugs because I was highly sensitive to medication. Aspirin made my ears ring. When I had gall-bladder surgery, I stopped breathing on the operating table. I was not looking forward to having my throat slit open to remove a cancerous growth.

The unknown is always more stressful than having to deal with the plain, simple facts spelled out. Uncertainty produces anxious and dreadful thoughts. I had been blessed with a vivid imagination, but the downside of a creative mind is the tendency to jump to wrong conclusions or imagine the worst possible scenario.

My faith wavered. I was afraid. Fear struck hard and left me motionless. This was not going to be easy. *I had a lump.*

Fear is tormenting. The scripture verse "Fear hath torment, but perfect love casts out fear" had not become a reality in my heart. At that point in time, perfect love was not in the main frame of my thinking while worrying about cancer.

After discovering a lump on my thyroid, I realized that God knew if I had cancer or not. However, I was afraid to ask Him. After two days of fretting, I sought Him in earnest prayer. I prostrated myself across the bed with my face buried in the comforter. I listened intently for the fateful answer. What I actually heard changed my life forever.

This has nothing to do with your thyroid, but it has everything to do with your ministry. You do not have cancer. This lump is nothing but tissue. You are afraid of success. You are afraid of failure. You are afraid of moving forward with Me because you are afraid of jealousy. You are afraid of rejection. When you find out that what I said to you is true, you will have the faith to confront all your fears.

Naturally, I shared this exhortation from the Lord with my husband. Afterward, I also told an elder of the church and his wife.

It was a week before I could get in for an appointment at Riverside Hospital for the biopsy exam. Daryl was at my side. It was a somber situation, so neither of us said much in the waiting room.

On the stainless-steel exam table, the young technician couldn't locate the infamous lump. Her ultra-sound wand was hooked up to a television monitor. She said, "I need to locate the physician who will be doing your biopsy." They returned moments later. The doctor poked and pushed my neck. He probed for several minutes. "How did Dr. Tallo locate this lump? I can't seem to find it…"

I explained how she stood behind me and wrapped her arm around my neck. So, the doctor had me sit up to perform the same exam as Dr. Tallo.

Looking very relieved, he said, "Oh, here it is; I found the lump." Looking at the technician, he said, "Put the wand right where my finger is on her neck." I froze with anticipation.

He looked at the monitor to examine the lump. "Oh, that's just *tissue*. I don't need to put you through the pain of a biopsy. You can get dressed and go home."

The Scripture verse where Peter and John went "walking and leaping and praising God" had new meaning. Fueled faith to move forward with God was ignited. With invigorated faith, my next missionary destination was West Africa. I traveled to Lagos, Nigeria, with an evangelistic team from our music department. Our church's music minister, Beth Emery, had frequently traveled to Nigeria as a guest of Dr. Chris Tunde Joda, M.D. Our team of women felt confident traveling with Beth, who is a trouper. It was another mission trip that had a great impact on my life. I returned home with a soaring heart from being with so many dedicated and loving Christians in Nigeria. The quality of their lives is so inferior compared to the standards in America, but these precious Nigerians are very rich in faith. This trip caused me to become more determined to meet the needs of the poor and disadvantaged in my own sphere of influence.

The faithful men in our church were not idle during these years. Daryl organized and sponsored numerous teams to attend Promise Keepers, founded by Coach Bill McCartney, a long-time friend of his. Promise Keepers has had a powerful impact on millions of men around the world by strengthening core Christian values and establishing greater integrity in marriages.

Thankfully, in Christ Jesus, there's always room to grow and improve relationships. We develop deeper compassion for the less fortunate through enrichment seminars and missionary journeys.

"In God, whose word I praise, in the LORD, *whose word I praise- in God I trust; I will not be afraid. What can man do to me?"*

Psalm 56:10–11, NIV

"The LORD *is my light and my salvation—whom shall I fear? The* LORD *is the stronghold of my life—of whom shall I be afraid?"*

Psalm 27:1, NKJV

CHAPTER FORTY-ONE

John F. Kennedy, Jr. prophecy in the London Nigerian Church in Route to Lagos, Nigeria

Our mission trip to Lagos, Nigeria, included a three-day stay in London to minister at the thriving Nigerian church located in East Leyton. It was in October 1996. Our five-member evangelistic team consisted of female singers and dancers from Zion Christian Fellowship. We also brought beautiful gift banners that had been constructed by my hands. As the token spare dancer, I tagged along because one of our dancers had bowed out.

Our praise and worship team leader was Rev. Beth Emery, Minister of Music at ZCF. Before coming on staff at Zion, Beth had been hand-selected by Pastor Judson Cornwall to introduce prophetic praise and worship at Bishop Harry Jackson's church in Washington, D.C., where she calls home. During her seven years at Hope Christian Church, Beth met Dr. Chris Tunde Joda, MD, the founder and apostle of over sixty-two Nigerian churches in Lagos called Christ Chapel International.

This was Beth's tenth trip to Nigeria, but our first. Dr. Joda always rolled out the red carpet for Beth because she worked hard and supported his vision to birth prophetic vision through anointed music, dancers, and pageantry in all of his glorious church conventions. She hand-selected her team based on anointing and willingness to work hard, not complain and go the distance.

Our gracious London host church put all of us up in a quaint hotel across the street from the church office complex. During the day, the girls went sightseeing and shopping. Evenings consisted of lively church meetings with the local Nigerian church with other guest speakers who had come to celebrate this annual fall conference.

My roommate was Cheryl, a young married woman with no children. She was a gifted dancer and looked forward to ministering on her first overseas trip. As the pastor's wife, I granted her the double bed and slept on a comfy side cot against the wall and window. We were very contented occupying three rooms in this modest hotel.

On Saturday morning, I awakened, dreaming about the graveside memorial service for Jacqueline Kennedy held at Arlington National Cemetery. My husband and son, Bo, had watched the televised service together in our family room a few years earlier, on May 23, 1994.

In the actual service for his mother, John Kennedy Jr. stepped up to the podium he read a passage from 1 Thessalonians 4:13–17.

"But I would not have you to be ignorant, brethren, concerning them which are asleep, that ye sorrow not, even as others which have no hope. For if we believe that Jesus died and rose again, even so them also which sleep in Jesus will God bring with him. For this we say unto you by the word of the Lord, that we, which

are alive and remain unto the coming of the Lord shall not prevent them which are asleep. For the Lord himself shall descend from heaven with a shout, with the voice of the archangel, and with the trump of God: and the dead in Christ shall rise first: Then we which are alive and remain shall be caught up together with them in the clouds, to meet the Lord in the air: and so, shall we ever be with the Lord. Wherefore comfort one another with these words. This is the word of the Lord."

I glanced at my nineteen-year-old son sitting next to his father across from me on the sectional in our family room, both gazing at the TV screen as John read the Scripture passage. I choked up by wondering what Bo would say at my memorial service. It was an emotional moment at the time, and now I was dreaming about it on my way to Nigeria. I wondered why I would dream about something that had already happened years earlier.

The next night, I awakened at about 2 a.m. after tossing and turning. I lay on my bed, wondering what was troubling my spirit. Then the Holy Spirit spoke these words, "I have three things to say to John Kennedy, Junior, and if you don't write him, I will trouble your sleep like this until you do." Since I had dreamed about John the night before, I knew the Holy Spirit was up to something important.

I turned on the bedside lamp and quietly slipped out of bed to find my notebook and pen. Thankfully, Cheryl remained sound asleep and undisturbed by the light.

This is what the Holy Spirit gave me to send to John F. Kennedy, Jr. on Sunday morning, October 20, 1996.

"Count and number your days and apply them toward finding Wisdom. Learn my ways, says God, a higher way of thinking and reasoning. Truth to dispel darkness. Reckon with Me, make your peace with Me and find rest for your soul. Doubt is troubling your, and sleep is escaping your soul. Find rest in Me, weariness will flee, and the weight you carry upon your shoulders will be lifted by Me. I am the Way, the Truth, and the Light…no man can come to the Father but by Me. The mysteries of life will be solved, your understanding will be enlightened, and our soul shall escape the fire of early death. Fear has gripped your heart and laid seize upon your soul. Be free young man, for I am the Author and Finisher of your faith. Search Me out while I may be found. Do not let your heart grow cold, for I am calling you. I have tender words to comfort you with; I need your surrender of arms. The swords in your heart are drawn, ready to fight, but I am not your enemy. My love for you is unconditional, so lay down your guard and allow Me to speak to you. I have words of Wisdom and words of Life."

The next day I requested permission to use a computer in the church office to type up a cover letter of introduction to accompany the prophetic word. I asked John to read chapters 4, 5, and 6 in the book of John. I told him he'd be comforted by the last words of Jesus to his beloved disciples the night before His crucifixion.

On Monday, using my credit card at a pay phone, I called George Magazine in Manhattan and spoke to the person who answered the phone. I asked for the address and inquired whether John Kennedy would get a personal letter addressed to the address the man gave me. He said John was in town and would certainly receive all mail addressed to him.

Years earlier, JFK Jr. had founded George Magazine. When I returned home a month later, I discovered the November publication had Billy Graham on the cover of George Magazine. That previous summer, John had cut his honeymoon short with his bride Caroline Bessette to spend a few days in Asheville, NC, to interview Dr. Graham in his mountain home. I remember thinking, *No wonder the hounds of heaven were after John Jr. with Billy Graham praying for him!*

The three things God had to say to John in this prophecy were the following:

1. "Count and number your days and apply them toward finding Wisdom."

2. "The mysteries of life will be solved."

3. "Your understanding will be enlightened."

4. "Your soul shall escape the fire of an early death."

I dismissed the mention of early death as only the "fear of death because of the Kennedy curse," sadly, I didn't realize God actually meant physical death.

About two and a half years later, Daryl and I accompanied our friends on a private plane to attend a prophet's seminar in Saginaw, Michigan. We were their special guests on this trip. We boarded the eight-passenger private aircraft in Columbus on the morning of July 17, 1999. John's plane had gone down over Martha's Vineyard on Friday night, but we were unaware of the tragedy since we left so early on Saturday morning.

The church conference was inspiring, with a private lunch with a small group accompanying the keynote prophet and later returned to afternoon teaching sessions. We dined at a lakeside restaurant before returning to the small airport around 6 p.m. Our two pilots were watching the news on the wall-mounted television, reporting the accident with aerial shots of the ocean where John's plane had crashed.

I became numb. On the two-hour flight back to Ohio, I envisioned that the plane that went down was similar to the one we were in, and I had little trouble envisioning how it must have felt going down the night before. I can't remember feeling so sad and helpless for this young man who was a national treasure. Later I learned that his wife and her sister were also killed in the terrible plane crash.

I felt distraught and questioned whether or not John actually received my letter since I gave the stamped envelope containing the prophecy to a young Nigerian man in the church to mail. Did I have enough stamps on it? Why didn't I go to the post office and mail it by registered mail to make sure it was received? If I had only known it was an early death God was warning of…and if he did receive my letter, did he laugh at it? I should have called John DeLorean to speak on my behalf and deliver the letter in person since he lived in New York at the time.

Larry King interviewed Billy Graham a few days later as all of America was mourning the loss of another Kennedy. I felt a sense of relief to know that Dr. Graham spent a meaningful time with John talking about spiritual matters during the interview for George Magazine. He said, "John Jr. had a deeper relationship with Jesus Christ than his father did…"

Later that summer, sometime in August, I was journaling and writing out my prayers as part of my quiet time with the Lord. The Holy Spirit knew how grieved I was and broke into the flow of my own personal prophecy to give me a personal message concerning John's tragic death.

An excerpt from my prayer journal in August 1999:

"Call forth that which is not seen. Call forth My heavenly resources. Use your talents and giftings in a disciplined way to gather the outcasts and to set the captives free. I shall ordain you and anoint you with greater authority. Power to do My will. Power to overcome the enemy's devices. JFK did not laugh at your letter; he took it to heart and pondered the meaning in great depth. His flesh dominated his life. His spirit man did not relate because he was steeped in religion and misunderstanding of who I am. He followed his own instincts and was not able to relate to following

the Holy Spirit. He is with Me, learning what he could not comprehend on earth. He is in peace with his wife, a better place. He now knows his life was in vain, but in death, many have sought Me, and for that reason, he did not die an early death in vain. Seek Me, My dear Barbara..."

And isn't that what hinders so many Christians from leaning and relying upon the Holy Spirit? Following our own instincts?

Each time I thought of John and Caroline during those months of mourning, the same song rose up from my spirit from the musical Westside Story. And anytime I hear the song, I still think of John and Caroline, another romantic *tragedy.*

SOMEWHERE

There's a place for us,
Somewhere a place for us.
Peace and quiet and open air
Wait for us
Somewhere.
There's a time for us,
Someday, a time for us,
Time together with time spare,
Time to learn, time to care,
Some day!
Somewhere.
We'll find a new way of living,
We'll find a way of forgiving

John F. Kennedy, Jr . . .

Somewhere…

There's a place for us,

A time and place for us.

Hold my hand and we're halfway there.

Hold my hand and I'll take you there

Somehow,

Someday,

Somewhere!

Music by Leonard Bernstein, lyrics by Stephen Sondheim. Copyright 1956.

May the God of hope fill you with all joy and peace in believing, so that by the power of the Holy Spirit you may abound in hope.

Romans 15:13, NIV

And who of you by being worried can add a single hour to his life? And why are you worried about clothing? Observe how the lilies of the field grow; they do not toil nor do they spin, yet I say to you that not even Solomon in all his glory clothed himself like one of these...

Matthew 6:27–29, NIV

CHAPTER FORTY-TWO

The Kenneth E. Hagin Camp Meeting, Dr. Joda Encounters Holy Laughter

For over twenty years, Dr. Joda attended Kenneth Hagen's Camp Meeting every July. Following an inspiring week in the powerful Holy Spirit-led camp meeting, he traveled throughout America, ministering at the various churches in his vast network. Zion Christian Fellowship made every effort to accommodate his schedule whenever he showed up like a migrant bird.

Due to international time-zone differences, Dr. Joda became a night owl by default. Evangelist Beth (Emery) Bryant, our minister of music, introduced us to him years earlier. Being fellow night owls by nature, Beth and I loved late-night excursions with him. Beth and I affectionately called him the Joda-Bird—flitting from place to place and stirring up craziness. We dearly love him. He became ecstatic discovering an open-all-night Walmart because his international schedule always had him awake at odd hours of the night. And typically, he'd fall asleep on you while transporting him from the airport.

Joda could outshop any shopaholic I ever met, and the phrase "shop-till-you-drop" was so true of him. He always bought recognition gifts for his church leaders and, of course, a myriad of things not obtained in Nigeria.

One time, Beth asked her husband Vincent to accompany Joda to Schottensteins, the original, massive "buy-out" store of designer-name brand merchandise sold at huge discount prices. This was Dr. Joda's first experience. Six hours later, Beth called me very worried. Vince eventually surfaced. He was in the check-out line with Dr. Joda and his four shopping carts full of rare discounted "finds."

One late evening, at about 2 a.m., I was quietly reading my Bible while the rest of my household was sound asleep. When the kitchen wall phone rang, I quickly rose from the couch, thinking, *It's either Beth or Bo.* My son is another nocturnal being who was attending an audio-engineering school in Manhattan. Bo usually never called Mom before the midnight hour.

In the middle of the second ring, I answered, "Hello?" with a cheerful, wide-awake voice, sounding as if it was mid-afternoon instead of the middle of the night.

Dr. Joda was chuckling, "I knew you'd be awake, Barbara!" All alone in a hotel room in Tulsa, he was all buzzed up from another action-packed Kenneth Hagin Camp Meeting session. His clock was two hours earlier than mine in Ohio, and his cup was overflowing with the joy of the Lord. "Now, who can I call to share all that the Lord has done at the camp meeting?" There were very few people in his phone book who could have taken that call, and I was the first one he thought of. "Listen to this anointed praise song I just learned!" He sang it to me before sharing other exciting camp meeting miracle highlights.

True to form, Dr. Joda loves lavish and extravagant church conferences. Therefore, his own annual camp meeting with his 62 Lagos churches is illuminated with as much bling as one can muster up in Lagos, which is not a whole lot. Beth has been his praise and worship leader in countless conventions throughout the decades, bringing various artistic praise teams who flow in prophetic dance, banners, flags, and mime.

About twenty-five years ago, during Easter break, Comrade Tina Smith and I took four of our pre-teens to Pensacola to spend time on the beach by day and attend the Brownsville Revival each night. The route from our motel back to church took us past a string of automobile dealerships. Each high-lighted car lot was strung with bright-colored metallic streamers that glittered in the sun. It was several miles of dazzling metallic that nearly blinded you.

"Oh, wouldn't Dr. Joda just love to hang those shiny streamers at his church conventions!" I exclaimed. So, during his next visit to Zion Christian Fellowship, our congregation presented him with over a hundred yards of silver, blue, and red metallic streamers. Pictures from his next event showed the glorious streamers glistening in the wind outside the seafood packing company, his main outdoor church location with a seating capacity of several thousand.

That same year, on a typical summer visit, he traveled with his sweet wife, Victoria, and their two school-age children. They were staying in our home, so I planned a backyard weenie-roast following our Sunday evening service. My husband was in Odessa ministering. Dr. Joda was our popular guest minister as well when Pastor Daryl was not away. We welcomed our dear Nigerian friend anytime he passed through Ohio.

Whenever the Joda-Bird was on the loose in a church office, he'd find some unsuspecting saint to spring into action before causing them to become slightly stir-crazy. I made myself available on that Sunday visit, faxing countless papers to his London church and Nigerian churches. He was preaching that night. The praise and worship had long begun by the time I slipped into a front-row pew next to Sister Tina, my fellow Toronto and Brownsville revival Comrade.

Now, Dr. Joda wasn't quite sure about the wild testimonies from these two revivals. Beth and I were flying high during a previous visit to Lagos immediately following our trip to Toronto. In fact, he especially pooh-poohed the laughing mania that happened to so many under a super-natural gush of the Holy Ghost.

When I finally entered the sanctuary for service, the music minister, Michael, was on the grand piano, playing soft chord progressions. It was odd to see a married couple standing on the platform, facing us, their heads bowed down in an attitude of prayer. A holy hush had fallen on the entire congregation. Something was up.

Wearing my secretary/administration hat, I remained slightly out-of-breath from being in a dither trying to deliver Dr. Joda out to the pulpit on schedule. Needless to say, I felt completely void of anything spiritual to contribute to the meeting. However, what happened next was as if I had just come out of an intensive prayer vigil instead of fax-machine chaos.

"What's going on?" I whispered to Tina.

"I don't know," she whispered back, shrugging her shoulders. "Michael suddenly called Susan and Kerry up and asked us to pray for them. And I have a *word* for them."

"Okay, let me set it up," I said before heading to the platform for a microphone.

"Good evening, folks," I said, smiling. "Before Dr. Joda comes to bring us a *word* from the Lord, Sister Tina has something for this couple. Come on up, Tina."

Moments later, I handed off the microphone to Tina and stepped aside. She stood in front of this couple with her back to the congregation. I was stationed next to Susan as Tina began to speak a prophetic word over them. Suddenly, Susan, under the power of the Holy Spirit, began teetering back and forth, about to fall out in the spirit. I quickly extended my arm to steady her. As soon as my hand touched her back, I was jolted up by an invisible electrical bolt, landing flat on my back. My entire body literally flew up and off several inches from the floor!

Since my first experience being paralyzed happened a few times in Toronto, I was not afraid of becoming immobile for the next few hours. But this frozen state was more unusual since I couldn't open my eyes, move my eyebrows, or utter a sound.

Meanwhile, as if nothing unusual had just happened, Dr. Joda preached his heart out; all the while, I remained glued to the floor about five feet from where he stood.

Robyn, one of our prophetic dancers, was concerned. She leaned over to the person next to her and whispered, "I'm worried about Pastor Barbara; she hasn't moved an inch for over an hour and a half."

When the service ended, Steve, a strong former Marine captain, and another man attempted with all their manly might to lift me up. Steve whispered in my ear with a chuckle, "Barbara, you are embarrassing us; we can't budge you." I heard him, but I still could not speak or open my eyes.

Since Steve had just previously clutched my arm and shoulder when attempting to help me up, the next person to receive a transference jolt of the Holy Spirit occurred when Steve, a conduit, reached out to shake Dr. Joda's hand. After taking hold of Steve's hand, Dr. Joda immediately went into a wild, uncontrollable Holy Ghost laughter!

Meanwhile, while that was happening somewhere in the crowded sanctuary, I sluggishly came undone. I slowly unraveled enough to roll over on my side, then, minutes later, I regained enough muscle strength to roll onto my stomach to crawl to a nearby platform bench. After I managed to pull myself up, I remained slumped in a drunken stupor, unable to talk or stand up.

After some friends helped me step off the platform and steady me out to my car, I sobered up enough to drive our guests while listening to a laughing hyena all the way home.

The backyard bonfire with the two Joda kids, my three, and Tina's four was a complete blast. It became a particular blessing when we learned that the Nigerian children had never experienced roasting a hotdog over an open fire. Later, I was told that's all they ever wanted to eat again!

Dr. Joda quietly sat on a nearby bench-swing, laughing and mumbling to himself like a drunken sailor through the festive outdoor celebration and later into the night. It was so amusing because the great Toronto-revival skeptic got completely zapped. Our Lord has the greatest sense of humor, and God surely had the last laugh!

"Then our mouth was filled with laughter, and our tongue with shouts of joy; then they said among the nations, "The Lord has done great things for them" (Psalm 126:2).

All Scripture is breathed out by God and profitable for teaching, for reproof, for correction, and for training in righteousness.

2 Timothy 3:16

How God anointed Jesus of Nazareth with the Holy Spirit and with power. He went about doing good and healing all who were oppressed by the devil, for God was with him.

Acts 10:38

CHAPTER FORTY-THREE

Dean Demos and Janet Shell Ministering at Hope Temple Birthing Prophetic Worship

We first met Senior Pastor Moses Vegh and his Minister of Music, Dean Demos from Hope Temple, in 1980. We were at Bun's Family Restaurant in downtown Delaware, Ohio. Daryl and I were also part of the Ohio planning delegation for the upcoming "Washington For Jesus" rally. It was planned for August 1, 1980, where over a million Christians planned to gather on the Mall for worship, prayer, and a cry for repentance for our nation.

After the business meeting, we sat privately with Moses and Dean for fellowship over a bite to eat. Dean was hyped up at the thought of tens of thousands of Christians worshiping in an open-air gathering on the Washington D.C. Mall. He spoke excitedly. "There's a unique *sound* that comes from that many voices raised in one accord singing in the Holy Spirit. That's the *sound* Satan hates because he can't confound it. That *sound* becomes a weapon of warfare against him."

I stared at Dean for an extended moment because I bore witness to his declaration. This was revelation truth from a minister of music that, during the 1970s, helped birth corporate worship as we know it in the 21st-century church. But, of course, I did not know anything about this anointed man with a rich baritone singing voice. Nor had I experienced the heavenly worship birthed at Hope Temple in Findlay, Ohio.

At that time, Daryl and I were teaching our annual "Understanding God" classes in a rented space; therefore, we needed a church to water baptize our students. Since Hope Temple was intimately affiliated with Bethesda Missionary Temple in Detroit, it was a perfect fit to take our students to Findlay to experience the "death, burial, and resurrection of Christ" through water baptism.

Our students often protested, "Well, I was sprinkled as a baby, doesn't that count?" We taught "circumcision of the heart" that happens when, through water baptism, God performs supernatural surgery to cut away the enmity toward God to gain a new heart to love Him.

One evening, I was in the back of the classroom grading homework papers, listening to the annual debate regarding water baptism on whether or not it was really necessary to get fully immersed in water. It happened in every new class of students.

Daryl was teaching his classroom of students, so I was partially in tune while checking the answers of their homework papers. Suddenly, the Holy Spirit rose up within me to speak revelation truth to those wondering about "going to heaven" if they weren't water baptized. Those probing seemed to be missing the point of water baptism. There were always a few knuckleheads in every class.

I raised my hand to speak revelation that the Holy Spirit dropped in my heart regarding the big debate. "Becoming a Christian is like marriage. You enter into marriage with a legal contract between man and wife. You are legally married whether or not you consummate the marriage. Thus so, you are legally a Christian and will have all the benefits of the Cross whether or not you submit to water baptism. You will go to heaven without being water baptized. However, water baptism is like consummating the marriage. You enter into an intimacy with the Lord because you will receive a new heart to love God with all your heart."

We cannot worship God without a circumcised heart. The Bible says we are born in sin under the Adam and Eve curse. Our natural-born heart contains "enmity towards God."

No, a person is a Jew who is one inwardly; and circumcision is circumcision of the heart, by the Spirit, not by the written code. Such a person's praise is not from other people, but from God. (Romans 2:29, NIV)

The first time we attended Hope Temple for a Sunday morning service, it was truly the worship experience of a lifetime. If there was ever a model to follow, this was it for sure!

Hope Temple offered a sixty-piece orchestra accompanied by Lois Teetsorth on the organ and another saint playing a keyboard. Rev. Janet Shell helped her father lead the orchestra, which was comprised of about twenty of her best violin students ranging from five to about eighty-five years of age. Ralph Shell was the lead trumpet player. Also featured was Linda McPherson on flute and a wide range of brass instruments fully in tune. Teenager Marcus

Vegh was occasionally on the drums, always grinning like his dad.

The church held about 900 members, and the song service was lively, upbeat, with simple but anointed choruses based on Scripture verses. As one song ended in a certain key, the same key segued into the next song arrangement that was easily followed by the congregation and the orchestra. There was no sheet music. At one point, the congregation usually broke out in spontaneous "singing in the spirit," like we had also experienced at Bethesda Missionary Temple.

As the congregation entered His gates with rejoicing, progression to enter the Holiest of Holies was the ultimate goal. This place in worship is where the sacrifice of our lips becomes consumed on the altar of the Lord.

As the music slowed in tempo, there was a lull when a tangible "holy hush" fell upon the congregation of saints. Whatever chord ended on a song, the organist and keyboard player continued softly playing the chord progression until heaven produced a *new song* in our midst. Waiting on the Lord with expectancy always produced something supernatural.

The first time in a Hope Temple service, after a holy hush fell upon the congregation, a little girl began playing a new melody on her violin. She couldn't have been more than five years of age. Soon, the rest of the orchestra followed her, "playing by ear" to this sacred sound, quickly picked up this simple violin tune. After going through the melody and coming into one accord, a person in the congregation birthed the "words" to accompany the prophetic song.

Dean Demos quickly wrote the words down on transparency and flipped the new song on the overhead screen for the entire congregation to join in. Within just a few breathtaking minutes, a new song was birthed. It was usually a "keeper" to be sung the next time the congregation gathered to praise the Lord.

In another inspiring and uplifting Hope Temple Sunday morning service, an individual choir member might prophetically sing out words with a distinct melody. The orchestra quickly picked up the tune to enhance the song for the congregation to sing within minutes of hearing it.

All in all, it was mind-boggling to experience such a worship phenomenon.

A few years later, Zion Christian Fellowship was birthed with the ministry help of Pastor Moses and Bette Vegh, their son Marcus Vegh, Pastors Dean and Patty Demos, Rev. Janet Shell, and Music Minister Lois Teetsorth.

Anointed violinist and Evangelist Janet Shell frequently traveled with us to Ukraine with her team of singers and dancers to conduct worship seminars and conduct prophetic orchestra workshops. We are forever grateful to such gifted servants the Lord sent our way.

Thirty years later, I served as a board member of the Ohio

Holy Spirit For Real

Prayer Summit led by Pastor LaFayette Scales and Pastor Paul Hoy. There were several other Columbus leaders who also served. We planned for months in advance, and each prayer summit was held downtown at the Vet's Memorial facility. The year was 2009.

The Seven Mountains of influence were prayed for throughout the day, with music breaks performed by various community churches between each prayer vigil.

In 1975, Bill Bright, founder of Campus Crusade, and Loren Cunningham, founder of Youth with a Mission, had lunch together in Colorado. God simultaneously gave each of these change agents a message to give to the other.

During that same time frame, Dr. Francis Schaeffer was given a similar message. That message was that if we are to impact any nation for Jesus Christ, then we would have to affect the seven major spheres of influence or mountains of society that are the pillars of any society. These seven mountains are:

1. Business
2. Government
3. Media
4. Arts and Entertainment
5. Education
6. Family
7. Religion

There are many subgroups under these main categories. About a month later, the Lord showed Francis Schaeffer the same thing.

354

In essence, God was telling these three change agents where the battlefield was. It was here where culture would be won or lost. Their assignment was to raise up change agents to scale the mountains and to help a new generation of change agents understand the larger story.[2]

In 1977, Daryl and I had the privilege of spending two days with Francis Schaeffer in his mountain chalet community, L'Abri, when we were in Switzerland.

So, on this particular all-day prayer summit, Linda McPherson came over to inform me that Mary Baker, wife of Pastor Jim Baker at Zion Christian Fellowship, would be leading a set of music that morning. As a board member, I knew the music line-up, but I was unaware that Mary was the worship leader.

Afterward, I was personally introduced to the young couple since they were fairly new to ZCF. They were very cordial to me, and we discovered that Jim and I both grew up in Dearborn, Michigan. We weren't able to talk long because they had a babysitter watching their small children.

Before they dashed off, I thanked Mary for her excellent music contribution and commented on a certain song she sang. It was especially beautiful.

Pastor Jim beamed. "Mary wrote that song!"

I lit up with genuine joy. "Well, I really loved that song; it was very anointed."

---

2 Bright, Bill, founder of Campus Crusade for Christ

"Yes, I wrote that song." She remained intent as if speaking prophetic revelation to me. "But I believe a day is coming when songs will actually get birthed right within the midst of our church services by congregation members."

I smiled lovingly, feeling like her grandmother. I said nothing but hugged them goodbye as they dashed off.

Mary obviously did not know that prophetic worship and birthing "new songs" was Zion Christian Fellowship's legacy. Under our thirteen-year leadership, there were prophetic dancers, pageantry with banners, and new melodies birthed from a full orchestra nearly every Sunday—anointed musicians playing a new melody from a flute, violin, or piano prophetically trained by many gifted ministers like Dean Demos, Janet Shell, Terri Terry, Lois Teatsorth, Beth Emery, Sam Sasser, Francis Frangipane, Linda McPherson, Ray Hughes, David and Kathie Walters, Vallery Henry, Marc Dupont, Lora Allison, Daniel Cason, Justin Cornwall, Robert Cornwall, Rachel Titus, Larry and Devi Titus, Patricia Beall Gruits, Paul and Eleanor Stern, Phil Stern, Jon and Molly Stern, Charles Green, Mel Davis, Moses Vegh, LaFayette Scales, Ern Baxter, James Robison, Pat Roberts, Evelyn Christenson, Chris Tunde Joda, and Rod Parsley, who either served on staff, were special-guest ministers or participants in the city-wide conferences and events that Zion Christian Fellowship co-hosted. These anointed men and women imparted lasting spiritual gifts, and we were truly blessed.

In addition, we traveled to China, Nigeria, and Ukraine, teaching the principles of praise and worship with demonstration of power through anointed messages and evangelistic teams of anointed dancers and musicians. While living as missionaries in Odessa, Ukraine, with her husband Edward and their young son, Linda McPherson birthed—Holy Spirit-inspired—over *800 songs in the Russian language.*

On Sunday, Linda and I sat together in a service at a Ukrainian/ Russian Charismatic on the Westside of Columbus, Ohio. The service was spoken only in Russian, as was the worship service. As the praise team segued into another song, Linda whispered, "I wrote this song." They were still singing her music eight years after she returned from Ukraine the first time!

In addition, Linda and I coordinated a Russian-music project with our ministry friend, Mark Condon, using his Brentwood-Benson Music CD, *House of Praise.* We recruited a few young musicians to translate each song into Russian language. Afterward, we debuted the music at Mark's church with a concert and a Russian and Ukraine member choir. Within a year, Linda and Edward returned to Ukraine with a Russian version of *House of Praise* by Mark Condon.

Edward and Linda are full-time missionaries living in Kazakhstan, a country in Central Asia, using their fluency in the Russian language in a Muslim-dominated country. Linda continues to birth prophetic praise and worship in the nations.

I thank the Lord that Zion Christian Fellowship still has anointed ministers of music who carry our original vision for worship. A glorious revelation I carry deep within my heart for every church in the world.

Thank you, Lord, for this precious young couple, Pastor Jim and Mary Baker, who value the firm foundation we laid. May the world continue singing the *new songs* birthed through all the gifted musicians and music composers who were an important part of Zion Christian Fellowship over the past thirty years. May Your Light continue shining in the N.W. Columbus community. May the Holy Spirit continue birthing New Songs within every New Testament Church in the world as believers worship You, dear Lord, in Spirit and in Truth.

Yet a time is coming and has now come when the true worshipers will worship the Father in the Spirit and in truth, for they are the kind of worshipers the Father seeks (John 4:23, NIV).

Many nations will come and say, "Come, let us go up to the mountain of the LORD, to the temple of the God of Jacob. He will teach us his ways, so that we may walk in his paths." The law will go out from Zion, the word of the LORD from Jerusalem (Micah 4:2, NIV).

CHAPTER FORTY-FOUR

Vickie Jamison, Billye Brim, Miss America Cheryl Ann Prewitt, and End-Time Handmaiden, Gwen Shaw, with a Tangible Touch from the Holy Spirit

I'm always in awe of any Christian who has felt the tangible presence of God during his or her sacred prayer time. Throughout my life with Jesus, I have had supernatural encounters with His divine presence but none quite so extraordinary as the one I am about to share now.

Sometime in 1982, I was privileged to hear the late Vicki Jamison sing and share the Gospel on the four-day Caribbean out of Miami. Billye Brim, Vickie Jamison, and Cheryl Ann Prewett (Miss America 1980) were the ministry-team presenters. Vicki Jamison had a national Christian television program entitled *Vicki Live*.

From Columbus, five church ladies, Lu Parry, Anita Shaw, Barbara Molly, Bonnie Slight, and I, traveled in two separate cars, driving two days to reach Miami in great anticipation of an action-packed cruise with Jesus.

On our return trip, we stopped somewhere in Florida for an End Time Handmaiden's conference with the founder, Missionary Gwen Shaw. Anita was ordained as an official handmaiden after her forty-day fast, a requirement for membership.

I also had a special connection with Gwen because, during a Sunday afternoon nap, I had a dream that I placed my cherished gold bracelet on the collection plate. My husband presented me with this gift on our wedding day. A few minutes after I awakened, Anita called to admonish me to come back to church that night to hear the guest speaker, Gwen Shaw, a missionary to the nations. That evening I was back in church, listening to Gwen talk about her mission work in China and the need for printed Bibles to smuggle in…The Holy Spirit spoke to my heart, "Give her your bracelet." I began to agonize because I planned to present this bracelet to my son's bride on Bo's wedding day. It was, to date, my most sacred possession. I battled with the Lord in my heart… *This is just a test, isn't it, Lord? You really don't expect me to give this bracelet up because it means so much to me… Please, Lord, don't make me do this…* I have tears in my eyes remembering, even now.

After service that evening, I cried while placing the bracelet in Gwen's hands. She assured me that she would get the best price for it in Hong Kong on her way back to Mainland China the next week. Years earlier, I gladly, without hesitation, sold my engagement ring and other valuable jewelry to contribute to the financial needs of others. However, that bracelet had remained untouchable for sentimental reasons.

So, with that gift, I planted seeds in China. After pioneering Zion Christian Fellowship, Pastor Daryl and our church evangelistic team smuggled Bibles into China through American Dennis

Balcombe, a true legend in China because he speaks both Mandarin and Cantonese! For decades, Dennis has been preaching the Gospel in the most remote places in Mainland China. We faithfully supported his ministry while in leadership at ZCF. Dennis, his wife Kathy, and their young son and daughter stayed in our home often.

Getting back to the cruise ship headed to Nassau—what impressed me most about this ministry team was the emphasis on the Word of God and bringing the participants into His healing presence through praise and worship. Billye Brimm quoted scriptures from memory faster than any human being I'd ever heard. Her prayers were powerful as she declared and decreed the Word of God to challenge us to follow her lead.

Each time Vicki Jamison sang, she brought tears to my eyes because the presence of the Lord was so real. She also testified how the spirit of Jesus often "sat at the end of her bed" to speak to her in visions and dreams. She caused me to long for this same tangible experience! So, when I arrived back home, I prayed diligently to experience Jesus up close and personal. I prayed or actually *begged* God to show up on my bed, too. For several weeks, before retiring for the night, I sat on my bedroom floor with knees locked to my chest, rocking back and forth, pleading, "Please, God, I want to experience your physical touch; please, Lord, I am begging you." All I can say is, be careful what you beg for…

Before we entered full-time ministry, for about a decade, Daryl taught a men's Bible study every Friday morning from 7 a.m.

to 8 a.m. The thirty or so men assembled in a banquet room at a Worthington restaurant that was a thirty-minute drive from our country home.

Each Friday morning, he awakened at 5:30 a.m. while I remained sleeping. Before leaving, he'd sit on the edge of the bed, and I'd feel his gentle hand on my shoulder as he silently prayed for me. On the morning of my "visitation from Jesus," I opened my eyes long enough to see the bathroom light as Daryl shaved. It was a typical Friday morning routine. After turning over to my opposite side, my back to rest of the bedroom area, I heard Daryl speaking softly as he walked around quoting Philippians 4:8, which had become a significant scripture to me, so I knew the verse by heart.

"Finally, brothers and sisters, whatever is true, whatever is noble, whatever is right, whatever is pure, whatever is lovely, whatever is admirable—if anything is excellent or praiseworthy—think about such things."

While listening to Daryl quietly quote this Scripture verse, I also heard the faucet water running from the kitchen sink while making his coffee. Daryl could not be in two places at the same time! I became instantly alert because it was obviously an answer to my fervent prayer, begging God for a physical touch from Him. At that moment, "Daryl" stopped talking, and I felt a gentle hand on my shoulder. Too terrified to open my eyes, I shook in terror, causing bedsprings to creak. *This is really Jesus. What is He going to say to me?*

As His hand rested on my shoulder, time stood still. He spoke to my spirit.

Daughter, I have a high call on your life. Your anointing is very powerful. But many will come against you, and women will speak evil of you. The stronghold of jealousy has followed you all your life...this is your cross to bear, it is your thorn in the flesh to keep you humble and dependent upon me. Remember to think on what is pure, lovely, admirable, excellent, and praiseworthy, and you will never falter or become afraid... His hand lifted off my left shoulder, but the bedsprings continued to creak as I trembled in holy fear.

In the next moment, Daryl opened the closet door to dress, and I jerked up in bed to drill him. "Were you just in here quoting Philippians 4:8 out loud?"

"No." He looked at me in a peculiar way.

"You weren't just in here speaking that verse in a hushed tone like you were trying to memorize it?"

"No, why do you think that?"

"Did you just come over here and rest your hand on my shoulder like you always do before leaving?'

"No. I just walked in here to get dressed."

Thankfully, this profound encounter with the Lord prepared me for the challenging years of full-time ministry that followed

His physical touch and precious admonition to rely on Him in times of trouble.

If an enemy were insulting me, I could endure it, if a foe were rising against me, I could hide. But it is you, a man like myself, my companion, my close friend, with whom I once enjoyed sweet fellowship at the house of God, as we walked about among the worshipers.

Psalm 55:12–14, NIV

CHAPTER FORTY-FIVE

Evangelist Marc DuPont Brings "Catch the Fire" to Columbus, Ohio

Willard Jarvis, the Senior Pastor of Redeemers East Church in Columbus, was the spiritual patriot of our city. Our beloved spiritual father passed away in June 2001 after leaving a profound legacy of divine significance that impacted my life and countless others.

After escaping from his rigid, anti-Holy Spirit doctrine church, Brother Jarvis became a prominent figure in the charismatic movement and all things supernatural. He was loved and respected by all community church leaders who prayerfully desired to see revival break out all over the land.

Thirty-five years ago, Pastor Jarvis formed an organization called *Capital City Association of Ministers* that became the sponsoring backbone of every citywide event. C-CAM held monthly meetings with important guest speakers. These luncheons were hosted by the various churches involved. That seemed to diminish all turf-guarding by an all-on-board attitude among respected city leaders.

You could always count on Pastor Jarvis to lead the crusade for a potential revival. For decades, the pastor was a gracious host to distinguished world leaders moving in the Holy Spirit.

One evening Pastor Jarvis called me on the telephone to personally hear about my experience in Toronto the previous year. Before ending our conversation about the amazing power of God, he invited me to be on the *Catch the Fire* steering committee to host guest speaker Marc DuPont, who was on staff at the Toronto Airport Christian Fellowship from 1992 to 1996. Later, it was re-named *Catch the Fire Toronto.*

The three-day Catch the Fire conference was scheduled for the spring of 1997 at Christ the King church. Senior Pastor Rey Dempsey and his wife Miriam would be hosting the three-day event.

The first steering committee meeting was held in the office of Pastor Scott Kelso. His church was hosting the monthly C-CAM luncheon following our morning meeting.

Six committee members sat in a semi-circle around Pastor Scott's desk. There were three area pastors seated to my right and two pastors to my left. We all had experienced the Toronto Bless-ing at least once. What wild thing that happened next was a com-mon occurrence at the Toronto revival; therefore, it did not shock any of them when the Holy Spirit made His presence known.

Realizing that these dear, dedicated Columbus pastors had been praying for "revival" for many years, it occurred to me that it might just happen with this upcoming event. Perhaps we should prepare ourselves for a "suddenly."

"What happens if revival really does break out?" I asked, look-ing around at the six men. "Are we prepared to go beyond just three days?" The host church would need to be available to serve indefinitely.

All eyes turned to Pastor Rey Dempsey, seated at the far end of my row.

When he answered, "Yes," a Holy Ghost lightning bolt struck me mute. I yelped as an electrical jolt lifted me from my seat a few inches. Supercharged by this invisible force, I slumped like a limp rag doll in my chair. Pastor Rey jumped up to make sure I was okay. I was so drunk I could not utter a single syllable.

The meeting ended on that note. About thirty minutes later, I became sober enough to make it to the dining hall. Still in a stupor, I sat down at a dining table. Millie McCarty came up behind me, leaning over my shoulder to greet me. Milly is a dedicated counselor who opened Light House Counseling Services in 1982. She's been a crusader for mental health and emotional healing through Christian counselors who support her vision. Her ministry, "Pathways of Hope and Healing," has touched thousands of lives.

Instead of returning her friendly greeting, I pointed to her face. With slurred words, "You are going to write a book."

She grinned. "Yes, I just started a book!"

Months later, Marc DuPont launched the Catch the Fire event that was supported by leadership all over the city. It was a scheduled three-day conference. But God had other plans for Columbus.

Catch the Fire lasted five months!

We gathered every night because the glory of God produced miracles, salvations, and deliverances, with nearly a thousand in attendance. John and Carol Arnott came through with words of encouragement. I was asked to share my Toronto testimony. Carol said what happened to me was extraordinary, even by Toronto revival phenomena. Francis Frangipane was another guest speaker.

Even though Catch the Fire lit many hearts, it set our church on fire, nearly burning it to the ground. In fact, Daryl and I were nearly torched to death in the months that followed.

I remember one particular night of the anointed Catch the Fire conference, two of our elders came by, standing on the side line, observing. With folded arms, their facial expressions were of disdain. There were no other of our church leaders in attendance. We were naïve to think our congregation was all on board for the next move of God. My husband calls it the "older brother syndrome" that is prevalent in every church.

Prophetic leadership needs established Apostolic covering to protect the office and its purpose. Rumblings started. A pipeline of dissension began through phone calls undermining our qualifications for leadership. Bedlam broke loose.

False accusations began, and soon the plot thickened with disturbing character assassination. A letter was distributed intimating church funds were misused. After we were forced to resign, a forensic audit was done by attorneys from the Author Anderson Accounting firm. We were cleared of any financial fraud, but that official legal report was not made public. Those few in leadership who organized the coup duped the congregation by withholding the truth of this audit.

One day during the grieving period of death, the Lord spoke to my heart. He said, "This is not about who is right or who is wrong. This is… (I gasped) This is all about dying. You are not to defend your character or write any letters."

We were condemned without a trial, and our ministry was shattered by the lies of a few who wanted us burned at the stake.

Pastor Jarvis was getting ready to retire from being president of C-CAM. A city-wide event honored him at a large banquet held at Der Dutchman Restaurant in an Amish country community near where we resided.

Our ministry friends, Scott and Linda Kelso, picked us up and we "doubled dated" to the event. It was a lovely affair, paying tribute to a man who had served Columbus for nearly four decades. During a formal ceremony, Pastor Willard Jarvis confidently passed his leadership baton on to Scott Kelso as the new president of the Capital City Association of Ministers.

On the way home, Linda and I chatted together in the back seat. Scott was driving. Halfway home, I overheard Scott ask my husband about a certain businessman who was causing havoc at our local Christian radio station as the newly appointed president. A few of Pastor Kelso's congregation members had been faithful station volunteers, but they were immediately fired by this new tyrant taking command of the station.

Daryl intently looked at Scott for a few seconds before responding. "That man was at the helm of what happened to us, and that's all I want to say."

A year earlier, when the sparks of dissension started, the Lord spoke to Daryl in a dream. "For the sake of the baby, do not fight them." So, we both were silenced as lambs before the slaughter.

Ten years earlier, Vision Bible College was a ministry my husband helped pioneer with the team support of C-CAM. Gifted Bible teachers from the community taught a Thursday night class for an entire month. Students came from all over the city for excellent teaching. I was getting my theology degree at the time, and Scott Kelso happened to be instructing my class that particular month.

Upon returning home from the banquet, I spent some quiet time with the Lord. While praying, the Holy Spirit said, "Write a letter to Scott and Willard. Tell them everything you know about the man Scott asked about…"

I quickly dismissed the notion since the Lord had admonished me to "die" and not defend myself.

My red-letter edition Bible was open on my lap while I prayed. When I looked down, the two pages were passages from the Book of Acts in all black letters except for one short scripture in red ink.

My eye went right to the red passage: "Do not be afraid; keep on speaking, do not be silent. For I am with you, and no one is going to attack and harm you, because I have many in this city" (Acts 18:9–11, NIV).

I burst into tears and cried my heart out. Feeling this was my release, I spent the next few hours writing a letter that would take courage to present to our two leaders of C-CAM.

The next morning, Daryl read the long letter and agreed it was sanctioned by the Lord. The following Thursday night, I waited till class time ended before privately approaching Pastor Scott. I began to get emotional. "This is the hardest thing I've ever had to do," I said, choking back tears before extending him two copies of the exact letter.

As a result of my letter, a week later, Pastor Jarvis and Pastor Scott Kelso met in a church board room with Pastor Rey Dempsey residing. The meeting went on for nearly four hours to pour over our financial records. At that point in time, we had no idea that the week-long forensic audit had already been performed by Arthur Anderson Accounting firm, initiated by the devious businessman and his cohort, master-minding our dismissal.

At this meeting, Pastor Lee Ault and Pastor Ron Hopkins were in attendance to lend support to us.

Pastor Scott and Willard sat directly across from us, pouring over detailed financial statements. They had been told we carelessly governed the church like a Ma and Pa organization with absolutely no accountability to anyone.

Their eyes were opened to the truth. We were indeed accountable, and the proof was in the countless stacks of spreadsheets and IBM financial reports containing line-item budget numbers that our two outside accounting firms managed for our church.

A lady named Dorothy was our church accountant and office manager. She was on staff with the Billy Graham Evangelistic Crusade in Oregon and was brought in as office manager of the 1993 Greater Columbus Billy Graham Crusade. Daryl and I both served on the executive and advisory boards. After the crusade ended, Dorothy decided to stay in Ohio and needed a job. So, we hired her expertise in managing money with global ministry affairs.

We accepted the death of the vision and moved on with our lives with dignity and grace from the Lord. Thankfully, the C-CAM leadership expressed kindness with pledged continued support that helped ease the regret of loss.

As we departed from that long meeting led by Pastor Jarvis and Pastor Kelso, the four of us formed a group hug. Pastor Jarvis looked at my husband. "Daryl, I have always considered you to be a strong Christian leader in Columbus. I still believe in your leadership, and I plan to make that known." Then Pastor looked at me with the same admiration. "Barbara, you are a writer! Why aren't you getting paid to write for a living?"

Those were dear Willard's last words to me before his death. He never knew that I was later hired by Pastor Rod Parsley to be his executive research writer.

CHAPTER FORTY-SIX

Pastor Rod Parsley Discovering the Lost Song

It was my birthday and the first day on my job as a writer for Breakthrough, an international evangelistic television ministry through World Harvest Church. The year was 2001.

That day, I was invited to eat lunch in the A-wing conference room and ended up sitting with Mr. Haynes and Rowlan Hairston. I enjoyed their company, and they made me feel very welcome. While we were still talking at the table, from behind the wall, a small child was singing unabashed and straight from the heart. It was a moment from my childhood. "Who is that singing?" I inquired. Rowlan explained, "Oh, that's Austin. You can hear him singing like that around here all the time."

Not knowing that seven-year-old Austin had autism, I thought it precious for a child to feel the Holy Spirit freedom to sing with such heartfelt expression. When I was four years old, I used to sing like that, too. After closing the lid, I'd often climb up on the back of the toilet seat to an open screen with a wide windowsill that resembled a window seat. That special place became my sanctuary. Towering trees shadowed the back of the quiet alleyway behind our little house. In the summertime, with the birds chirping, I sang to God in my enchanted haven. Tears rolled down my cheeks while I seemed to reach the heavens with my singing. I didn't care who heard me. In a previous chapter, I shared why I had stopped singing when my great-grandmother asked my mother who sang the best of her children.

During the nine months my teenage mother carried me, she desired to have a boy. After the doctor delivered me, he announced, "*Oh, it's a beautiful girl.*" In stunned denial and disappointment, Mother cried out, "*He is not!*" Therefore, rejection from her womb and from her spirit was strong at an early age. Tragically, I never bonded with my mother. God called me from the womb because He knew me and loved me.

One afternoon I was praying in my husband's Lazy Boy recliner chair, feeling relaxed in the sweet presence of the Lord. I was home alone when the doorbell rang. The sad, lonely girl standing on my front porch was my son's acquaintance from Young Life, a Christian program for high school kids. Emily and Bo attended two different private high schools located about a half-hour drive from our country home.

"Is Bo home?" Emily asked without smiling.

"No, I'm sorry, he's not home from school yet. Can I give him a message, Emily?" I smiled brightly, but she never responded to my friendliness anytime she stopped by.

Emily was fifteen years old and had lost her mother the year before. She had an older brother and sister who were twins. I thought it tragic to lose a mother at that age.

When I returned to my prayer position on the Lazy Boy, I asked the Lord to heal her heart for the loss of her mother. I also prayed for her siblings to heal as well.

Then the Holy Spirit spoke to my heart. "Now we're going to pray for your mother."

My eyes remained closed as I "tuned in" to what might happen next since I thought I had dealt with all my mother issues throughout my Christian life.

I remained quiet for a few moments before hearing a male voice tenderly calling me by name within my spirit.

"Barbara, wake up. Barbara, wake up."

More silence.

"Barbara, wake up. Barbara, wake up."

Finally, my own voice responded.

"But she doesn't want me," I said with sadness.

"I want you, please wake up. I have need of your life."

My heart could hardly contain the anguish I felt, knowing that it was my Lord Jesus who called me from the womb. Most likely, I would have been stillborn if He had not urged me to awaken.

My father fought a few bloody battles in the South Pacific during World War II as a young marine. However, Dad never spoke to us about the war. He had a photo album that we often looked through as curious kids but without details. But a few years ago, my cousin Tommy heard some war stories after he and my dad drank a few beers while painting the walls in our living room. Years later, Tommy repeated these stories to me. I learned that my late father survived a foxhole air raid from Japanese forces. After the spray of bullets stopped, my dad discovered that all three of his buddies were dead. Years later, I sought the Lord about this story while grieving the loss of my dad. The Holy Spirit spoke to my heart. The Lord said, "I saved him because you were in his loins…" God has revealed that to me because I needed to know that He has plans for my life.

"Before I formed you in the womb I knew you, before you were born I set you apart; I appointed you as a prophet to the nations" (Jeremiah 1:5, NIV).

So, on that particular birthday of mine, listening to Austin sing with such a sweet expression was another meaningful blessing to me from the Lord. I'll never forget hearing him sing because it was just like the way I used to sing—with all my heart.

During the difficult time of losing a church and our pristine reputation, I lost my song.

One late evening I watched a Christian program featuring a summer Camp Meeting with Pastor T.D. Jakes. Pastor Parsley was the keynote speaker to what looked like 20,000 men in the outdoor audience. I watched with extreme curiosity what this white man "from the cornfields of Columbus" (as he often describes his church location) would have to say to an audience of predominately black men. I entered in as Pastor Parsley had us lifting our hands to the north, south, east, and west. By the end of that anointed and timely message, I was completely at peace and set free. When I sat down to read my Bible, a new, lovely spiritual song arose in my heart. God's presence was very sweet, with the evidence of spiritual melody from heaven.

Pastor Parsley preaches every New Year's Eve for a few hours. That first year on staff, Daryl and I attended the service bringing in a new song and a new year. Throughout the dynamic message, the pastor did not stop to call anyone out with a word of knowledge. After two hours of preaching his heart out, he walked up the aisle and looked at me. He reached over Daryl to pull me into the aisle. My legs buckled because the anointing was so strong. He proclaimed that I was set in place at World Harvest. As the only one who received a *word* from the Lord that night, I felt extremely honored and blessed. The Holy Spirit is *real*.

"He put a new song in my mouth, a song of praise to our God. Many will see and fear, and put their trust in the LORD" (Psalm 40:3, ESV).

"Is this not the fast that I have chosen: To loose the bonds of wickedness, To undo the heavy burdens, To let the oppressed go free, And that you break every yoke? Is it not to share your bread with the hungry, And that you bring to your house the poor who are cast out; When you see the naked, that you cover him, And not hide yourself from your own flesh? Then your light shall

*break forth like the morning, Your healing shall spring forth speedily, And your righteousness shall go before you; The glory of the L*ORD *shall be your rear guard. Then you shall call, and the L*ORD *will answer; You shall cry, and He will say, 'Here I am. If you take away the yoke from your midst, The pointing of the finger, and speaking wickedness,*

> *If you extend your soul to the hungry And satisfy the afflicted soul,Then your light shall dawn in the darkness, And your darkness shall be as the noon-day. The L*ORD *will guide you continually, And satis-fy your soul in drought, And strengthen your bones; You shall be like a watered garden, And like a spring of water, whose waters do not fail. Those from among you Shall build the old waste places; You shall raise up the foundations of many generations; And you shall be called the Repairer of the Breach, The Restorer of Streets to Dwell In."*

Isaiah 58:6–12 (NIV)

CHAPTER FORTY-SEVEN

World Harvest Church with Benny Hinn, Mother Ellen Parsley, Henrietta Albright, Donald Trump, and Perry Stone

If you've never experienced an annual Dominion Camp Meeting at World Harvest Church, you're missing an opportunity to see God's glory manifest in supernatural ways beyond comprehension. World Harvest also hosts other amazing conventions throughout the year.

In 1977, with humble beginnings, the Parsley family began their outstanding ministry at a backyard picnic table with seventeen people. It is now a global network. Daryl and I have traveled all over the world—Africa, Europe, Ukraine, Russia, and China. No matter what country we're in, whenever we say, "We're from Columbus, Ohio," the response has always been, "Oh, do you go to Rod Parsley's church?" It's truly amazing.

Pastor Rod and Joni Parsley have been faithful to the call upon their lives through many trials and tribulations that have purified their faith. They lead extraordinary lives with humility and compassion.

On January 30, 2018, the pastor's beloved mother, Ellen Parsley, experienced her homecoming with the Lord. His father, Clyde, the bulwark of the family, passed away a few years ago.

Daryl and I were members of World Harvest for over ten years. We also served on staff during part of that tenure. We are grateful for the opportunity to experience a truly prophetic church impact the nations.

Mother Parsley, as she was affectionately called by church members and Bible College students, was a passionate teacher of the Holy Scriptures with an intense anointing that manifested in unusual supernatural ways.

My friend, Barbara Thompson, told me that one time after Mother Parsley prayed for her during Bible College chapel, she fell out, landing on her side with both ankles lifted off the floor by a few inches. Her legs began moving back and forth as if she were swimming. She laughed, "I stayed like that for about a half-hour because I could not lower my feet or budge an inch!"

Pastor Parsley promoted *The Center for Moral Clarity* on the steps of our Statehouse, downtown Columbus in October 2006, with thousands in attendance. It was a weekend convention, so hundreds of out-of-state ministers participated, too.

At that time, Daryl was the executive director of the ministerial fellowship. After accepting the position, Pastor Parsley had asked him to "double" the membership from 600 to 1,200 pastors. Daryl doubted this was possible, but when Pastor Parsley entered the staff meeting on his first day, the Holy Spirit quickened my husband's spirit. At the sight of Pastor Parsley, faith arose in his heart, and he heard the Holy Spirit say, "You can do this." Daryl shortened the application, and by the next year, the membership grew to over 1,800, thus tripling the membership!

Several hundred visiting ministers attended this *Center for Moral Clarity* weekend convention. During the praise service, the Holy Spirit said to me, "Mother Parsley is supposed to pray for Daryl." Throughout the service, I became more and more inebriated and ended up far on the south side of the sanctuary, too drunk to stand. Daryl disappeared somewhere on the crowded platform with Pastor Parsley, helping direct several hundred guest ministers to receive recognition and prayer.

When it was time to return to our seats, I staggered toward my pew. I stopped in front of Mother Parsley, teetering, barely able to stand. With the slurred tongue of a drunken sailor, "You're supposed to pray for my husband."

She exclaimed, *"Daryl?"* When she spoke his name, we both turned our heads in the same direction, and there was Daryl walking toward us. At that exact moment, I flew backward as if I'd been shot out of a cannon. My feet moved so fast that I was literally air-born or on the back wheels of invisible roller skates. I landed on my back at the base of the platform. Then, the sensation of several heavy winter coats was piled on top of me. I could not hear a sound.

When I came to, there was my husband, curled up in a fetal

position at the feet of Mother Parsley. He later told me that she had prayed for him three times, and each time he was slammed down. I love it. This elderly, petite woman knocking down a former NFL offensive tackle with the sound of her voice and the power of Jesus!

There is never a dull moment around World Harvest. Our infamous friend, Henrietta Albright, can attest to that statement. She passed away last year, but she's left a lasting legacy. Years ago, when she and hubby Gilbert "Gib" first began attending World Harvest, after service, Pastor Parsley would rush over the backs of pews to greet her as royalty. Henrietta had been a radio personality for decades, and her southern Ohio twang was synonymous with Christian radio.

I'd pick Henrietta up for Sunday evening service, and the two of us were like two lightning rods together. Going out to eat after church, we'd engage waitresses, busboys, people at Walmart and end up ministering the Gospel to whoever crossed our path. We'd also flock to prophetic meetings in and out of town.

"Do you act like this around your family?" I asked her once. "Oh, heavens no! They'd think I was crazy." Attending Sunday night World Harvest services together, Henrietta called me her "drinking buddy" because we were often so drunk under the power of the Holy Spirit, laughing and acting silly. There is no high comparable to that of the Holy Spirit!

One Sunday evening, during an exuberant praise service, I began shouting Hallelujah at the top of my lungs. I loved to shout, and World Harvest Church is the perfect atmosphere to feel free in the spirit. I felt Henrietta cringe, but then she tried it out for size. After she shouted, she turned to me with a word from the Lord. She began saying, "When I see my doctor tomorrow for test results before he tells anything, I am to shout 'Praise the Lord' and speak in tongues." It was my turn to cringe.

The next day, her Egyptian doctor waltzed into the exam room, smiling from ear to ear. In a broken accent, "Mrs. Albright, how are you!"

When she began speaking in tongues, he answered back in his native tongue! The doctor kept marveling, "Authentic, so authentic!" He rushed out to get the nurses to hear her because it was so profound. Of course, crazy Henrietta had no clue what she was speaking!

Fifteen years, long before President Donald Trump was in office, Henrietta shared a dream about him. I responded, "Pastor Parsley was in New York City as the personal guest of Donald Trump a few weeks ago! I was in service when he briefly mentioned it from the pulpit." Of course, the entire congregation was on pins and needles to hear details, but Pastor remained coy about his personal visit with Donald Trump and did not share any further details.

In her dream, Henrietta was seated next to Donald Trump at a large board meeting table with several other people. He turned to her and smiled. He said, "I don't know you, but I like you, and I trust you." *End of dream.*

Daryl and I are big supporters of Trump, and throughout the primaries, we watched nearly every televised rally. One afternoon, I thought, *Donald Trump needs to get his message out on the radio, too.* With that thought, I immediately had the interpretation of Henrietta's dream.

When I called her, she was in a nursing home recovering from surgery. Gib intercepted the call. "Tell Henrietta that I have the interpretation of her Donald Trump dream." She called me right back with all ears because that dream had haunted both of us for many years.

Since Henrietta was synonymous with radio, Donald Trump was saying, "I like radio, but I don't know radio, but I trust radio." My dear Henrietta died a few months later, surely a grand homecoming when she met Jesus face-to-face. Pastor Parsley spoke at her funeral. Thankfully, she didn't go to her grave without the interpretation of that Donald Trump dream. I miss her so much.

Visiting guest ministers always brought blessings to World Harvest Church. Pastor Benny Hinn never ceases to amaze, and I will never forget one particular glory moment. The entire congregation was standing when Pastor Benny gently blew toward us. Daryl fell backward in the spirit, with about twenty people behind him going down like a domino effect. I dropped like a rag doll on the pew in front of me and remained drunk for hours.

After Perry Stone preached at a camp meeting service, I remember thinking he was a more powerful preacher than a teacher, and we all know he's a profound Bible scholar. He let loose at World Harvest and was spinning around like a top and getting back to his Pentecostal roots, that was for sure!

My twin daughters were with me during that teaching session with Perry. Afterward, I was so drunk I couldn't drive. We went to Bob Evans for a meal before evening service. The girls were laughing at me because I was too tipsy to hold my fork and get food to my mouth. I stained my blouse with spill, so we had to stop at Walmart to buy a new shell for under my jacket.

Most pastors around America have prayed for "revival," and I have seen it firsthand at World Harvest Church for years. Anytime Pastor Parsley has an altar call, hundreds of people surrender their lives to Christ Jesus. That alone is quite remarkable, and if 200 or 300 people getting saved isn't revival, I don't know what is.

The Holy Spirit is *real* at World Harvest Church!

After the private Bible study in Trump Tower, Pastor Parsley is spiritually connected to President Trump; I feel this is the perfect place to share this prophecy and how it came forth.

On May 31, 2017, I received the following prophetic word for President Trump as I was ending my personal letter to him, sharing Henrietta's dream and getting on the radio.

God bless you, President Trump. May the Lord speak to you in dreams and visions to continue carrying the righteous torch for America! The following prophetic utterance came right after I wrote that last sentence.

Yes, says the Lord your God. I have you as the apple of My eye in this very hour of darkness that prevails over the nations. Do not doubt that this is My hour to bring glory in the midst of evil and cunningness. Do not listen to voices of human reason, rather tune into My Holy Spirit on a daily basis. I have words of wisdom to impart to you and to give you clear direction to go forward with My agenda.

Seek My face, says the Lord your God. I have given you the keys of heaven to unlock prison doors...many will repent and call forth My name in this hour.

This hour will unfold many hidden treasures from above...I have many warriors and spiritual powers in step with you to keep you safe and free from the debris that is often fall-out from the lies of the enemy.

Keep your faith, do no sway to the left or right, but keep your eye on the prize...Heaven is real, and many are dying from not knowing the truth. Keep free from voices that are not from Me... surround yourself with heavenly-minded men and women who may not always speak forth...but I have wisdom to impart through them...learn to listen to those who have remained silent, but have great power in Me. Seek them out and ask of Me...I will send you men and women who hear from Me and know My voice of reason. Seek Me daily.

My Word will renew and refresh as nothing else can...be still... quiet your heart, and you will know that it is I, the Lord your God, who can calm the storm and settle the heartbeat of those who are bringing fear and intimidation to those around you.

Stop and seek Me, pray and let those around you know that you are hearing from Me and will follow the course of action set out to bring forth fruit of righteousness in this hour of need. Many are counting on you to bring forth answers...seek Me daily, I will not leave you empty-handed, you will have worth to bring forth that will amaze and shock those who have had nothing good to speak on your behalf.

Ignore the voices as Nehemiah did...set forth to build the wall and bring forth an economy that will change the nation and bring Me glory. Do not be afraid to step into the waters, I will part the waters to lead you to dry land and comfort in My presence. You will be a voice for Me....count it all joy when persecution comes to reform those who have little faith...but remember, it is the faith of a mustard seed that will move mountains of oppression and mountains that hide the Light of My Son, Jesus Christ, who has come to set the captives free.

Walk in freedom, walk in love and compassion for those who do not have a voice.

Become My Voice, says the Lord your God. I am very pleased with you.

Like a brave soldier, you will conquer many things in your lifetime. I will anoint you to break the bands of wickedness and yokes of bondage. Be free to love Me in spirit and truth. You are the man I have called to bring forth revival to this country. Watch and see what I will do with one yielded man of importance. I will use you in mighty ways.

Watch and see says your God.

You can be sure the Holy Spirit is for *real* in the life of President Trump!

CHAPTER FORTY-EIGHT

The Poor Among Us, a Challenge to Help

Helping the poor is a privilege. In the process, valuable life lessons gained certainly outweigh any hardship endured. That might sound trite, but it's true. Christians have numerous opportunities to help others because desperate needs surround us like the air we breathe. When the heart is ready, God sends someone with troubles your way. If it's a test of merit, how will you score on Judgment Day?

Aiding the less fortunate will accomplish several things in your character. You will also become incredibly grateful for the privileged life you enjoy in America. Generosity will deliver you from boredom, depression, self-pity, self-hatred, and criticalness. Best of all, your newfound joy will inspire missions of goodwill in others. Needless personal spending will halt if you sincerely desire extra money to give to the less fortunate.

However, getting involved with the poor and disadvantaged is daunting because fear stops most Christians in their tracks. Vain imaginations and lofty thoughts often hinder an attempt to fulfill Christ's command:

"Religion that God our Father accepts as pure and faultless

is this: to look after orphans and widows in their distress and to keep oneself from being polluted by the world" (James 1:27, NIV).

Trepidation prevents personal involvement because the underprivileged usually live in unsafe neighborhoods. Don't attempt any inner-city ministry without the prayer support of your spouse and/or your pastor.

Many Christians like to preach, counsel or dish out advice to the downtrodden, but talk is cheap. Genuine Christian ministry will touch you where it hurts, in the wallet.

World Harvest Church, through Pastor Rod Parsley and the Bridge of Hope ministry, helps free Sudan slaves at the cost of $38.00 per human rescue. To support this ministry, I stopped having my acrylic nails and pedicures done. That $2,000 a year sets many fellow Christian captives free, and in doing so, something in me gains liberty, too. Recently, a former Sudan slave came to thank our church. In a tearful expression of gratitude, the Sudan Christian man presented our dear Pastor with a heavy set of metal shackles that were on his ankles before his release.

It used to cost me $140.00 for a color touch-up and a haircut at an upscale salon. In another salon with less ambiance, I receive the same quality hair product and service. My sweet, young hair stylist Misty is from a broken home. She has opened up to me, and I've had many opportunities to shine my light for Jesus. These savings enable me to keep giving to the needs of others. I stopped buying upscale clothes, shoes, and purses for the same reason.

Clipping out store coupons certainly helps because every dollar saved adds up. Watching out for discounts on disposable diapers, toilet paper, laundry soap, and shampoo is another blessing because government food stamps do not cover non-food items. It is not beneath me to purchase my own clothing at consignment shops, even though I can afford designer clothes. I've learned to be content with less.

My husband tithes at least 10 percent of our gross income to our church, so my personal giving comes from my weekly household allowance. I wish I had more to provide, but shopping at resale stores and thrift shops is another way I am able to give to the needy. What a joy to find gently used baby clothing, toys, and furniture for young single mothers who might sleep with their children on a bare mattress on the floor.

Most single mothers appreciate having an advocate to sign up for food stamps, housing, and other public assistance because it's a humiliating process. Sitting long hours in welfare agencies and accompanying a gal to speak to her assigned caseworker is something I've frequently done in the past. Gathering her necessary documents—sending off birth certificates and collecting other identification—is tedious but an essential step to gaining available government assistance.

When a single mother has rats in her basement or sewage backing up, there is a legal course of action to force the landlord to take care of the problem. My volunteer work at the Legal Aid Society helps with these situations.

Eleven years ago, we sponsored a spiritual daughter, Katrina Brown, to attend cosmetology school. Through Katrina, I met her thirty-three-year-old friend Tamika, a struggling mother of four young children. Many times, the Holy Spirit prompted me to help Tamika with her monthly school-loan payments for her to remain in cosmetology school.

Tamika had very little furniture for the three-bedroom home she was renting with a government subsidy. After scanning the newspaper's classified section, I located a well-made walnut dining room table, a hutch, and six chairs for $300.00. Tamika had never owned a formal dining room set. The lady with the furniture also sold us a complete set of china (dishes) for an additional $25.00. With my van and Tamika's van, we loaded all the furniture in only one trip. Because Tamika is such a conscientious mother and a hard-working student, the Lord put it upon my heart to help her.

During a luncheon for professional fundraisers, I shared this joyful experience with an executive director of the *Governor's Aids Task Force.* "I was happier giving that dining room set to Tamika than if my husband had given me a beautiful diamond ring." My friend Sally smiled back at me. "I know exactly what you mean; I've given in the same way. It's very rewarding, isn't it?"

For the next six months, I found additional used furniture. When Tamika's eleven-year-old daughter learned that she was getting some bedroom furniture, Brooklyn immediately disassembled the two beat-up bunk-bed frames to carry out to the street. Brooklyn and her eight-year-old sister, Kira, were thrilled with their matching "new" lacquer-white, high-tech desk, three dressers, and a hutch to display their nearly-new Barbie Dolls, games, and books; I also discovered at a consignment shop.

The coordinating headboard was for a double bed, which the four of us girls set up with my drill and screws. We also hauled all the remaining pieces of furniture up the stairs. For an added touch to match their new purple bedspread, I spray-painted the ten pairs of drawer-pulls purple, too. For very little money, their room was transformed into a lavender haven fit for two happy princesses. Tamika said, "My girls never invited their friends over, but now they want to have sleepovers every weekend because they're so proud of their new room!"

Two years ago, when Tamika was nearly beaten to death by her brother, I tearfully prayed for her as she was wheeled into the hospital trauma unit. Her eyes were swollen shut like a bludgeoned prizefighter, with bloody tears trickling down her cheeks. Before the first hospital transferred her to the trauma unit downtown, Tamika called me to contact Katrina to take care of her children.

Three weeks after the assault, for moral support, I accompanied Tamika when the Grand Jury documented her testimony. She hobbled through the impressive paneled doors on crutches, and the white of her eye was still blood red. More importantly, I witnessed a conscientious social worker counsel Tamika through her severe post-trauma.

Through Tamika's prayers, her brother Kyle was given probation with court-appointed, mandated anger-management counseling. Their broken relationship was eventually restored. However, last month, while viewing *Charlotte's Web* at a movie theatre with Tamika and Laura, she received an urgent cell phone call. Tamika's only brother was shot and killed hours earlier. She was crying so hard it took Laura and I about half an hour to coax Tamika back to my car. I wrote Kyle's obituary.

Many times, a woman has life experiences that translate into viable working skills. Many resumes have been spiffed up to gain better employment, something that is time-consuming but very rewarding to me. Tamika mentioned that she organized a "block watch" for children in her neighborhood. That task requires leadership and administrative skills—qualifications an employer seeks.

Recognizing talents and skills in people is a special gift of mine. When runaway Katrina lived with an inner-city family that had adopted her, a twenty-two-year-old male family member was artistic, so I presented art supplies to "DW." Taking it a step further, the Holy Spirit inspired me to enroll DW in a summer painting class at the *Columbus College of Art and Design* near his home. He was able to ride a bike to class. When I tracked down his ninth-grade art teacher to solicit a letter of recommendation for a CCAD scholarship, she remembered that "Donnie" was gifted but informed me that her former student "could not read." With that information, I met with the Executive Director of the literacy council, which happened to be across the street from the art school.

DW was soon receiving private tutoring to learn to read. Through my encouragement, Laura was eventually reconciled to her mother, who had need heard from her for over five years. Needless to say, that was a tearful reunion.

Over the past thirty-five years, I've involved myself with young women, beginning as a volunteer in a *State of Ohio Correctional Institute,* three miles from our previous home. These teenagers committed serious felons, from grand theft to murder, but they were too young for adult prison.

Every Sunday morning, my faithful friend, Shar, picked up eight or nine teens in her large van. She'd drive them to her home for breakfast. The girls had their own special closet full of dresses and shoes to change into before attending church. Afterward, they spent the entire day with Shar, eating lunch and dinner before returning,

With permission from the Correctional Institute Superintendent and the help of generous donations from friends, Shar and I converted a large two-room kitchenette into a fully furnished volunteer center. Together, we held Bible studies and led song services with the groups of girls who signed up. Shar also served cupcakes with motherly hugs.

For the past twenty-five years, Shar has also run a "safe house" for victims of domestic violence. Shar once owned a Christian bookstore in a college town. One morning Shar came to her bookstore to discover a bicycle and a traumatized, totally mute woman sitting on the doorstep. After work that day, Shar took the stranger home and cared for her every need. It was several months before "Elizabeth" started to talk again. Shar discovered that the thirty-five-year-old woman had biked all the way from upstate New York to Delaware, Ohio. Our unconditional love for Elizabeth helped her to trust again. Elizabeth eventually received professional counseling and was restored back to mental health.

From my active involvement at the correctional institute, a lively, freckle-faced, honey-blonde, sixteen-year-old named Michelle came to live with our family after completing a sixty-day rehab. Her concerned drug counselor interviewed me, and she enabled Michelle to be released to our care as a ward of the court. My husband and I agreed to take Michelle to "ninety consecutive Alcoholic Anonymous (AA) meetings in ninety days." While she lived with us for eighteen months, Michelle accepted Christ as her Savior and attended a private Christian school with my son, who was in grade school at the time. We love Michelle dearly and consider her a daughter.

Thirty years ago, an overweight young woman entered our church with a newborn baby and a toddler in tow. Tina was the first near-homeless person ever gracing our suburban doorway. When the Lord asked me to "mentor her," I challenged the Lord because Tina was so desperate. But thankfully, I obeyed. After befriending Tina and helping her gain child support through the courts, public housing, food stamps, a used vehicle, and schooling, she is a well-paid nurse and off welfare. In addition, Tina lost 150 lbs. and she is now an ordained minister. She recently received an invitation to preach in South Africa! God sees the beginning and the end of our lives.

Since my "boot camp" with feisty Tina, precious diamonds in the rough continued to come my way to chisel and refine. In this two-way process, God works on my character, as well. God never does anything one-sided! Each dear woman is unique, and the tough lessons learned have been important to me. Wisdom received through first-hand experience is extremely valuable.

Knowing Tina's lifelong dream to become a nurse, I located an affordable nursing program for her. In addition, I accompanied her to the ninety-minute orientation with the Public Industry Council (PIC), which paid her complete tuition from a federal grant.

Tina passed the Ohio State nursing exam to become a Licensed Practical Nurse (LPN). When Tina called me with the good news, she was crying so hard I thought she had failed.

After being on welfare for many years, Tina's first job interview was at a large hospital. The night before, I shortened the sleeves of a consignment shop trench coat so she could have something fashionable to wear for added confidence. When I dropped her off for the interview, I quickly slipped my Rolex on her wrist, on loan, for a final touch of class. Tina got her first nursing job at this hospital, and we rejoiced at the goodness of God.

Last summer, when a twenty-year-old woman was raped, I spent the night in the emergency room witnessing every careful procedure done for the victim, including an AIDS blood test. The police detective spoke to me at length, as did the counselor, who wasted no time getting there to minister life to my young friend's traumatized spirit. Through DNA samples off her clothing, the rapist was identified because of previous rape charges. Thankfully, she did not contract a sexually transmitted disease.

As a former board member of *Teen Challenge*, I am painfully aware of the drug and alcohol abuse that is destroying a large population of our youth. Fortunately, help is available through numerous state agencies. Free drug assessments are conducted by qualified counselors with prevalent rehab programs in nearly every major city. Most family physicians have a list of drug and alcohol agencies to contact. *Teen Challenge* is a Christian residential program for men and women of all ages, with successful drug and alcohol treatment centers all over the globe.

If someone has a son or daughter struggling with these destructive forces, point them in the right direction. Some churches have support groups for sexual abuse, rape, and domestic violence victims, but most churches aren't usually staffed by licensed professionals. Non-profit agencies are federally funded by your taxes, so take advantage of the affordable professional help.

On a business trip a few years ago, my husband Daryl and I traveled to California. We stayed a few days longer to enjoy some sightseeing. On a whim, I called a former classmate living in San Francisco. Sigrid was also a bridesmaid at our wedding, but we had not seen each other in over twenty years, so it was a poignant reunion. During dinner with our husbands, Sigrid shared a high school story about me that I had completely forgotten about:

"Barbara was very popular in high school. She was a member of the 'A-group' in high school, and I must have been in the 'C-group,'" laughed Sigrid. "One Friday night, Barbara had a pajama party and informed all of us that she also invited some 'new girl' from her study hall to come over, too. Pat was from the 'wrong side of the tracks,' so Barbara warned us, 'Now if you're not nice to Pat, I won't be your friend anymore.'" After Sigrid jarred my memory, I did recall giving Pat some of my clothes so that she would feel better about herself.

Thirty years later, I used this same power of influence as a Christian community leader. During a private luncheon in our former suburban, lily-white church, I introduced our women leaders to my idea of linking up with an all-black church for "race reconciliation." This race reconciliation attempt would involve the two churches coming together, in *one accord*, for monthly luncheons somewhere near a bus route.

This fellow African-American church was similar in doctrine, and Sr. Pastor was a close associate of my husband, the Sr. Pastor of our church. The response was tremendous. In fact, five or six women came to the microphone to tearfully confess their fears in the form of repentance. We all wept as God examined our hearts for secret prejudice and racial hatred. A few months later, the Lord arranged for the late Coretta Scott King to be our first luncheon speaker!

God is pleased with our efforts to love and accept others who struggle "fitting in." The church should be a refuge for the down-trodden, and the body of Christ is required to sacrifice time and especially money to help those less fortunate. Every act of mercy is a jewel in the Crown of Glory that awaits us on Judgment Day. However, the earthly joy of giving is reward enough for me.

"For I am already being poured out as a drink offering, and the time of my departure has come. I have fought the good fight, I have finished the race, I have kept the faith. There is reserved from me in the future the crown of righteousness, which the Lord, the righteous Judge, will give me on that day, and not only to me, but to all those who have loved His appearing" (2 Timothy 4:8, NIV).

CHAPTER FORTY-NINE

The Miracle Save of Shem Josiah and His Mom Katrina Brown, through the Power of Intercession

After learning that the unborn baby was a boy, it was time to find a suitable name. My friend, Katrina Brown, wanted a "non-traditional" Bible name. I suggested consulting my husband since he is so knowledgeable of the Bible. The three of us were out to breakfast the morning she asked my husband for a name.

Sitting across the table from her, my husband said, "What about Shem, Noah's righteous son?"

Katrina said, "Oh, I love that name! I've never heard it before." So, it stuck.

Months later, while reading in the Old Testament, I came across Josiah, a righteous king who started his reign at age eight. Katrina loved both Hebrew names. *Shem* means "fame and renown," and *Josiah* means "the Lord saves."

She was in mild labor pain while taking her final exams that June. Our Shem Josiah was born on June 24, 2007. I coached Katrina through labor with many trips to the maternity ward before they finally let her stay. After that third trip, I think I would have checked in myself.

I had the joy of being at this precious child's delivery. Baby Shem let out a loud, healthy cry upon arrival into the world. Katrina touched him, and I captured it all with my digital camera clicking away. He was whisked to the warming unit for a clean-up by two attending nurses. Katrina was talking to the female OB/GYN, who was tending to her post-delivery needs. The atmosphere was electrifying because a new life had entered the world. With all the prayer that went up for this baby, I am certain the angels were rejoicing, too!

When Shem suddenly stopped crying, I observed urgent commotion across the room. One nurse placed an oxygen mask on the baby while the other attendant dashed to the wall telephone close by. A tall male physician arrived within seconds. I heard him say, "Why isn't he breathing?" Katrina was unaware her son was in danger because she was chatting it up with the female physician who was delivering the afterbirth.

I quietly but quickly went into action, too. I slipped over to the lounge sofa I had been sleeping on through the night hours of Katrina's labor. While sitting with my knees pulled up to my face, I began calling down heaven in fervent prayer. My heart pounded. After a few minutes of prayer, I felt the need to "do something," so I darted over to the baby as the two nurses and doctors stared at him, waiting for something to happen. I kept saying "Jesus, Jesus, Jesus" in reverence as I ran my hand lightly over his motionless little body. Then, Shem reached out and grasped my index finger with his left hand. His little hand wrapped around my entire finger, and it felt strong. It seemed like a desperate grasp. In fact, he communicated, "Don't ever quit praying for me, Nanna. I need your prayers in my life." He started to cry again, to our relief. It was the happiest sound I've ever heard in my life. From that moment on, I felt a spiritual connection with this child.

Then the baby was whisked away to the Neonatal Intensive Care Unit for a procedure to clear his lungs. He was diagnosed with pneumothorax, which is a condition that causes air leaks into the space between the chest wall and the outer tissues of the lungs. If undetected, it can be fatal. However, we did not know these facts until much later.

When Katrina was informed that her baby was in trouble, the nurse did not give us any details. She said, "I'm sorry, but you won't be able to see your baby until tomorrow. He is in the NICU for observation."

"Will my baby be okay?" she asked.

"I don't know," the nurse replied.

Katrina began to cry out, "Jesus, Jesus, save my baby." And the Lord did. An hour later, a very nice nurse "sneaked" us to see the baby. Although baby Shem was hooked up to scary-looking wires, seeing the tenderness in Katrina's face as she gazed upon her baby was precious. He seemed healthy and content as he slept. She had such a look of awe and wonderment to view the life she had created. It brings tears to my eyes, remembering those treasured few moments with her.

As a new parent and a single mom, she was conscientious and alert, as are all young mothers bringing such a tiny baby home for the first time. For the health of her baby, Katrina breastfed for several months.

Shem turned two years old on June 24, 2009. He loves church and attempts to sing Christian music whenever he hears it on the radio. He's been the joy of my life, and I adore this precious little boy with all my heart. He loves his nanna just as much. He is very attached to me and frequently spends the night with our family.

This past November, during church, our pastor announced that it was "baby dedication Sunday." Katrina was in the service that morning, sitting near the back with the baby. I nudged Daryl and whispered, "Oh, I wish we'd known. We could have had Shem dedicated this morning." It had been something on my heart to do for months.

About sixty couples began lining up on both sides of the platform with their infants. There were two lines. Pastor Parsley began praying for the babies on one side while his wife, Joni, began praying for the opposite side.

Suddenly, Katrina appeared at the end of a line holding Shem. I was delighted that she had gumption enough to dedicate her son without previous church instruction. Katrina walked up on the platform, but somehow, she and Shem got blocked from Pastor Parsley's view. All the parents holding babies were now off the platform, so Pastor Parsley and Ms. Joni turned to face the congregation. One of the ushers nudged the pastor to acknowledge Katrina. The pastor quickly turned around to face her. He said, "Well, you get the double blessing." He said that because *both* he and Ms. Joni placed their hands-on Shem for the prayer of dedication.

I was delighted that happened because the "double blessing" is truly an honor to bestow on a child, and Shem is a special child deserving of that tribute.

After church Daryl and I explained the biblical meaning of a double blessing to Katrina. She was also very pleased to know that Shem had been singled out for such a prayer.

My husband planned to drive out of town on business following church. Therefore, Katrina drove me home that Sunday afternoon. She desired to return to church that evening.

When we got to my house, I fixed a light meal for us and spent quality time with the baby. It's always a joy to visit with him since Katrina no longer lives nearby. She's now living on her own in low-income housing and is no longer financially dependent on her mother's monthly support.

When Katrina left my house to drive back to church, it was getting dark and raining hard. The baby was buckled in his car seat in the back. The peculiar thing about that day was that as I watched them drive away, I started to weep. I'm always sad to wave goodbye and somewhat choked up. However, when I closed the front door, I felt an overwhelming sense of grief, as if I was never going to see Shem again. It was the first time in my life that

I felt a sense of impending doom of a loved one. Naturally, I began to pray for protection with extreme emotional intensity. After being doubled over in agony for several minutes, the grief sensation lifted, and I experienced peace in my soul.

I inquired of the Lord because I thought maybe He was trying to teach me a Bible lesson on prayer. I pondered in my heart, "Lord, should I be praying with that kind of same intensity each time they leave my house?"

Within minutes, Katrina called my cell phone. She was hysterically screaming but unable to speak or tell me what was wrong! I could hear a lady trying to talk to her. The woman asked, "Where's the baby?" It was a car accident. Then the phone went dead. I thought that our sweet little boy had been killed. Everything in my body went numb. In fact, I could hardly move my legs.

I managed to call Daryl to inform him that Shem had probably been killed in a nearby car accident. He had already arrived in Michigan. He said, "Calm down. Don't drive by yourself; go get Bo."

When my son and I arrived at the accident scene, there were two fire trucks, three squad cars, and two medical cars with their lights blinking. It was on the interstate highway. It looked like the scene of a ten-car pile-up, and we still did not know the condition of the baby! I continued to cry and pray fervently with all my heart and soul.

Suddenly, through the rain, I saw Katrina with Shem in her

arms, climbing into a fire truck to fill out an accident report. I still could not move, so Bo jumped out of the car to assist Katrina.

Later, we learned that as Katrina was getting off the main highway to approach the interstate, out of nowhere, a drunken truck driver crossed her path and spun out of control in front of her. She couldn't avoid crashing into him. When Katrina's small 2007 silver KIA crashed, the baby started screaming. The fast-moving, oncoming cars almost hit her car several times. A lady in a van stopped to help. She also stood on the highway attempting to get the speeding traffic to slow down because Katrina's car and the red truck were blocking a lane of traffic.

What made it extremely dangerous was that Katrina was trapped in the car because the electrical power shut down. She couldn't open her doors or windows. In a panic, she crawled across the seat to see if the baby was hurt. There was just enough juice left to get a rear window halfway down. She was able to crawl out of the window and pull the baby through to safety as cars sped close by at high speeds.

The right front side of Katrina's car was severely damaged. The male truck driver was bleeding and taken to the hospital. He was also placed under arrest because he was so drunk. Later we prayed for his salvation and ultimate sobriety.

When Pastor Parsley heard about the near-fatal accident, he rejoiced with us because the Lord truly intervened in something that could have been tragic. In fact, this testimony on the miraculous power of prayer first appeared on April 17, 2009, on the Break-through network for the world to see.

Together, when Katrina and I watched the documentary about her accident on the television, we both cried. She looked at me with tears in her eyes. "God has really saved my life. I'm so thankful for all that He's done in my life."

My spiritual daughter, Katrina, continues to live for the Lord in spite of many trials and tribulations in her life. In 2015, she spent several hours a day copying the entire Bible, word-for-word, in perfect penmanship, filling-up many lined journals. I told her that amazing feat belongs in the Guinness Book of World Records!

Katrina Lee Brown became a 4.0 GPA and a Phi Theta Kappa National Honor Society recipient at Columbus State Community College before her son Shem Josiah was born on June 24, 2007. Actually, she was taking her final exams while in mild labor and graduated with perfect attendance! Through difficult circumstances, Katrina had dropped out of school going into the 9th grade and never attended high school. Through her diligent work in community college, she was awarded the five top financial scholarships. In the finance office to collect, the woman handing Katrina the prestigious awards exclaimed, "Who are you!"

Katrina is able to quote countless scripture from memory. She loves Jesus with all her heart. As a true evangelist, she carries a passion to see people set free through Salvation and delivered from all addictions by the power of Lord Jesus Christ. She knows that the Holy Spirit is real!

"Do not be anxious about anything, but in everything, by prayer and petition, with thanksgiving, present your requests to God. And the peace of God, which transcends all understanding, will guard your hearts and your minds in Christ Jesus" (Philippians 4:6–7, NIV).

But if you are led by the Spirit, you are not under the law.

Galatians 5:18

Gentleness, self-control; against such things there is no law.

Galatians 5:23

In the beginning was the Word, and the Word was with God, and the Word was God.

John 1:1

As he was talking with them, Goliath, the Philistine champion from Gath, stepped out from his lines and shouted his usual defiance, and David heard it. Whenever the Israelites saw the man, they all fled from him in great fear.

Now the Israelites had been saying, "Do you see how this man keeps coming out? He comes out to defy Israel. The king will give great wealth to the man who kills him. He will also give him his daughter in marriage and will exempt his family from taxes in Israel."

David asked the men standing near him, "What will be done for the man who kills this Philistine and removes this disgrace from Israel? Who is this uncircumcised Philistine that he should defy the armies of the living God?"

1 Samuel 17:23–26 (NIV)

CHAPTER FIFTY

Abraham, Our Father of Faith

"Do not be afraid, Abram. I am your shield, your very great reward." Genesis 15:1 (NIV)

The journey that changed the world began with a relationship between an obedient man named Abram and Jehovah, the self-existent, eternal God. Abram, whose name later became Abraham, was a man born a few generations after the great flood that destroyed an entire wicked civilization, except the family members of a righteous, blameless man named Noah. God told this obedient man to build an ark to save his family, even though it had never rained before!

Abraham, the patriarch of ancient Israel, intimately knew God; the Bible tells us that He listened and obeyed the voice of God. God talking to Abraham is the first recorded account of God speaking directly to man again since God made a covenant with Noah and his sons, directing them to "be fruitful and multiply, and fill the earth..." (Genesis 9:1, NKJV).

Going forward with God began with Abraham's step of faith—*a result of hearing the voice of God.* God had glorious plans for the future. The Lord needed an obedient servant to accomplish His ultimate goal, which was Jesus Christ, the Savior of mankind, and He found His man, Abraham, whose name means "exalted father of many."

God commanded Abraham to leave his father's house, his extended family, friends, and motherland to travel to an unknown country. The Lord said to Abraham, *"I will make you a great nation and bless you, and make your name great; and you shall be a blessing. I will bless those who bless you, and I will curse him who curses you, And in you all the families of the earth will be blessed"* (Genesis 12:1–3, NKJV).

Abraham was a righteous man. His faith in God qualified him to be considered a trustworthy servant to carry out this important assignment. God promised to make Abraham a great nation, yet I doubt that's the reason Abraham chose to follow God's commission. Abraham would have left everything to follow the Lord's commandments, not ever expecting a reward for his obedience.

Abraham obeyed because he was loved and accepted by God.

If we are ever to go anywhere with God, we must be in the right relationship with Him from the depths of our souls. He must be our Lord and the master over every area of our life.

We must know God's voice and allow Him to direct us through the power of the Holy Spirit.

God is looking for obedient hearts to accomplish His purposes in this generation. To go forward with God requires great courage and a willing heart to obey His every command. He needs to be the captain of the ship, the commander-in-chief of every move we make for a collision-free journey.

We cannot expect the Lord to take us to promised places with Him if we aren't ready for the journey. Our motives must be pure, expecting nothing in return for our willingness to follow the Lord.

The Lord is our reward, and if we are in a proper relationship, *His love for us is all we will ever desire in life.* Nothing satisfies our longings like Him, and as we sojourn through life, His love for us can be compared to nothing else. *It is this wondrous love that compels us to obey.*

When we accept His divine love for our lives, we will trust Him enough to expose our character flaws and magnify those unproductive places of the heart with the lens of the Holy Spirit. He has ways to bring correction and discipline into our lives as we submit to the process. *His ultimate goal is to prepare us for the journey.*

Abraham was *willing* to travel across desert plains in pitched tents, leading a caravan of people, including his wife Sarah, his nephew Lot, and many servants. It was an extreme hardship requiring sacrifice, but the Lord faithfully appeared along the way to encourage Abraham in his demonstration of obedience.

"To your descendants I will give this land" (Genesis 12:7). Abraham responded to this tremendous blessing with an act of worship by building an altar to the Lord who had appeared to him. He could not have understood the dynamics of that promise since Sarah was barren, and *he had no descendants.* This altar was a display of Abraham's genuine love and honor for God, a place of

total surrender. Not my will, Lord, but Yours—the ultimate act of obedience to God's plans for his life.

There is nothing mystical or magical about faith. It is very practical, and faith is measured by the amount we demonstrate through our acts of obedience to the clear or complex commands from God. It is that simple. Every act of obedience comes from our will; we must *choose to obey*. And when we do, obedience produces a portion of faith that *motivates us to keep on obeying God*.

I desire to please God, but I don't always obey His commands, thereby failing His expectations and standards of excellence for my life. I often fall short, but that does not affect the way the Lord feels about me. I may feel guilty for failing to obey, but I can freely ask for forgiveness, knowing that His mercy is extended to me. I learn from my mistakes. I, therefore, ask for the grace to obey more quickly the next time another opportunity for obedience comes my way.

My disobedience to God only delays His overall perfecting process for my life. He is perfecting all that concerns me. There is a master blueprint for my life, and the speed at which I obtain it depends upon my obedience. But God will love me *even if I never get there* or ever attain what it is that He wants for my life. That's the mystery about this walk of faith; God loves us even if we fail miserably. But because He is a loving God, *His ultimate desire is that we succeed and achieve our fullest potential.* He desires that we live in a productive fashion, developing all of our God-given talents to the fullest potential.

He wants us *to go forward in faith*. And for many of us, that requires *getting unstuck*. When we attempt to follow God in our own strength and natural abilities, we may become timid and reluctant to trust God completely. If we fail to understand and accept God's unconditional love, we will be afraid to let Him have complete control of our lives. Many of us remain stuck in neutral, playing it safe, enjoying all the benefits of God, and sensing peace about going to heaven. We may be leading godly lives, staying busy and quite active, but not busy about the Father's business. And there is nothing wrong with being neutral, but we will miss the joys of the journey. He has so much more for our lives if we will just trust Him and learn to obey without a moment's hesitation.

So, how do we *do* come to trust God completely? Is there a simple formula for faith? Do we have to cross the desert in pup tents to demonstrate genuine faith? What is the secret of great men and women of God who have done mighty exploits for God? How do we move mountains with faith the size of a mustard seed? It is God that moves the mountains, but faith must be present to do so. Jesus said, *"If you have faith as small as a mustard seed, you can say to this mountain move from here to there and it will move, and nothing will be impossible for you"* (Matthew 17:20–21, NKJV).

Jesus often responded with the "mustard seed illustration" and other parables whenever his disciples cried out in exasperation for *"more faith"* when they didn't measure up or couldn't make something happen. What they actually needed might have been *more obedience* to forgive, *more obedience* to fast and pray, *more obe-*

dience to repent of pride, or *more obedience* to express genuine love. The Lord wanted them ready for the journey, and it wasn't additional faith they needed. *It was obedience.*

And that is usually the case with us; we often bypass the elements of virtue and godly character development to demonstrate "faith through works." Nothing is more thrilling than casting out a demon of a tormented soul, but if it is done with an attitude of "Wow, look what I did! See how spiritual I am!" we completely miss the mark of Christianity. We can be zealous in doing good for others when our motive is to be seen by men. And what we end up with is *dead works,* a boost to our egos, and the possibility of a religious spirit.

Almost fifty years after God bid Abraham to follow Him, the Lord appeared to Abraham when he was ninety-nine years old, telling him the promised child would come into fulfillment by that time the next year. Sarah was listening nearby as the Lord spoke of this baby, and she laughed at the prospect of having sex, let alone conceiving a child at their age! *"I've grown old, shall I have pleasure, my lord being old also?"* (Genesis 18:12, KJV.) She had already demonstrated doubt and disbelief years earlier by offering her handmaiden, Hagar, to bear Abraham's promised child. A child name Ishmael was born; however, he was not the child of the promise.

Sarah and Abraham conceived a child and named this promised son Isaac, whose name means "laughter." Isaac was cherished by his parents and grew into a strong young lad. The Lord tested

Abraham once again, but this was the ultimate test of obedience, one that changed the face of history forever.

God was requiring Abraham to sacrifice his only son up as a burnt offering on a mountain in the land of Moriah. What sort of God would ask such a thing? What sort of God would test a man's faith with such a grave request? It seems incredible that God would tell Abraham to "*take...your son, your only son Isaac, whom you love,*" and offer him up as a sacrifice. Though the sacrifice seemed to go against God's promise of an heir, Abraham knew God would still fulfill His word, even if it required Him to raise Isaac from the dead (Romans 4:17). Isaac was in the hands of God, he was a gift from God, and he belonged to God.

Abraham and his son Isaac took a three-day journey to the place on the mountain as God directed. They gathered wood for the burnt offering, but Isaac did not know he was meant to be the sacrifice that day. Isaac said, "*Look, the fire and the wood, but where is the lamb for the burnt offering?*"

And Abraham said, "*My son, God will provide for Himself the lamb for the burnt offering.*" So, the two continued together.

They came to the place where God sent them. Abraham built an altar there and placed the wood down. He then bound Isaac, his son, and laid him on the altar upon the wood. Abraham stretched out his hand and took the knife to slay his son. Suddenly the Angel of the Lord appeared from heaven and said, "*Abraham, Abraham! Do not lay a hand on the lad, or do anything to him, for now I know that you fear God, since you have not withheld your son, your only son, from Me."*

Abraham lifted his eyes and looked, and there behind him was a ram caught in a thicket by its horns. So Abraham took the ram and offered it up for a burnt offering instead of his son. The Angel of the Lord called to Abraham a second time out of heaven and said, *"By myself I have sworn, says the Lord, because you have done this thing, and have not withheld your son, your only son—blessing I will bless you, and multiplying I will multiply your descendants as the stars of the heaven and as the sand which is on the seashore; and your descendants shall possess the gate of the enemies. In your seed all the nations of the earth shall be blessed, because you have obeyed My voice"* (Genesis 22:2–18).

Abraham's faithfulness paved the way for us to come into covenant with God through the promises made to him. Through Abraham's obedience came Jesus Christ, the Son of God, who died for our sins so that we may come into a loving and eternal relationship with God the Father. Abraham's journey opened the gate for us to follow, allowing us to partake of the blessings of God.

Genuine faith comes from a relationship to God the Father, through Jesus Christ, His Son, and the demonstration of heartfelt obedience to His will for our lives.

"But I will establish my covenant with you, and you will enter the ark—you and your sons and your wife and your sons' wives with you..." (Genesis 6:18, NIV).

"I will be with you and will bless you. For to you and your descendants I will give all these lands and will confirm the oath I swore to your father Abraham. I will make your descendants as numerous as the stars in the sky and will give them all these lands, and through your offspring all nations on the earth will be blessed, because Abraham obeyed me and kept my requirements, my commands, my decrees and my laws" (Genesis 263–5, NIV).

Jesus said, "If your brother sins, rebuke him, and if he repents, forgive him. If he sins against you seven times a day, and seven times comes back to you and says, 'I repent,' forgive him."

The apostles cried out to the Lord, "Increase our faith! This is an impossible task!"

Jesus replied, "If you have faith as small as a mustard seed, you can say to this mulberry tree, 'Be uprooted and planted in the sea, and it will obey you.' Suppose one of you had a servant plowing or looking after the sheep. Would he say to the servant when he comes in from the field, 'Come along now and sit down to eat?' Would he not rather say, 'Prepare my supper, get yourself ready and wait on me while I eat and drink; after that, you may eat and drink?' Would he thank the servant because he did what he was told to do? So you also, when have done everything you were told do, should say, 'We are unworthy servants; we have only done our duty.'" *It's simple obedience you need as a servant of God* (Luke 17:4–10, NIV).

The Holy Spirit guides us into all truth. We never have to fear going in the wrong direction. He is truly for real.

That according to the riches of his glory he may grant you to be strengthened with power through his Spirit in your inner being.

Ephesians 3:16

And do not get drunk with wine, for that is debauchery, but be filled with the Spirit.

Ephesians 5:18

And because you are sons, God has sent the Spirit of his Son into our hearts, crying, "Abba! Father!"

Galatians 4:6

CHAPTER FIFTY-ONE

Singer Stevie Wonder, Beth Bryant, Steven Furtick, and Jacqueline Ayemperourmal and a Divine Connection with Motown Music at World Harvest Camp Meeting

This testimony goes down in history as one of the most unusual "divine connections" I have ever encountered so far in life. But oh, what a wonderful ending chapter to such a beautiful, Holy Ghost journey!

My longtime friend, Evangelist Beth (Emery) Bryant, is an anointed vessel who continues to share her gift of music and teaching with the world. She serves small, inner-city churches, mega-churches in her community, and congregations among the nations.

Beth and her husband, Vincent, live right outside of Washington, D.C., and she has spent the last forty-five years traveling the globe as a singing evangelist. They are active in full-time ministry and her gift for training up prophetic worship teams is in great demand. Thirty years ago, Judson Cornwall personally placed her in a D.C. mega church to "keep the prophetic flowing." That's quite an endorsement given to Dr. Harry Jackson, the senior pastor.

A few years back, Beth was working with a small, inner-city

church, one night a week, all year long. When Easter Sunday was fast approaching, naturally, Pastor Max expected her to "shine" at the keyboard with the now polished praise team. Imagine his disappointment when Beth explained she was committed to ministering at another congregation in her network. It had been on her schedule for nearly a year.

"But, Pastor Max, it will be okay!" she pleaded, trying to cheer him up to no avail. "I recorded a backup soundtrack to accompany the singers!"

The Monday morning after Easter Sunday, she dialed up Pastor Max to inquire how the service went in her absence.

"Well, you won't believe who showed up to take your place!" His voice was brimming with joy. "When I apologized for not having anyone at the keyboard, Stevie Wonder stood up to volunteer!" Dear God.

Stevie was in D.C. visiting his cousin who attended that church. I laughed with joy, telling Beth she got upstaged by Stevie Wonder. Being from Detroit during the wonder years of Motown music, I am one of his biggest fans.

Two summers ago, in mid-June, I stood in line at an Ft. Myers T.J. Maxx department store with a single purchase in my hand. I glanced back at the tall, pretty African-American woman behind me. Stevie Wonder was singing "Cherie Amour" over the store's loudspeakers. The Holy Spirit gave me a sentence to say to her, but I resisted because it was such an odd way to strike up a conversation with a stranger. After three nudges, I turned to face her.

"This is Stevie Wonder singing. I am from Detroit, and I saw him perform when he was only twelve years old. I was sixteen."

She smiled back at me and commented with a distinct New York accent.

"Oh, your accent. You must be from New York," I responded, keeping the conversation alive since I knew the Lord was up to something.

"I'm from Columbus, Ohio, and I am so excited about going back in a few weeks to attend Camp Meeting with Pastor Rod Parsley!"

"Oh, I love his ministry," she said enthusiastically. "I'm an evangelist."

"Well, so am I!"

"My husband was just in Columbus last week. He is a traveling consultant with a large furniture company."

We continued to chat, and I asked her to remain around to exchange email and phone numbers. When we gathered in the lobby, I met Jacqueline's friendly husband, Selva Ayemperoumal, a handsome gentleman from India. Later, I learned that they met in Paris when she was there as a visiting high school student. They have been married for over thirty-five years with six gifted and nice-looking young adults.

Our close, spiritual friendship has been truly divine, orchestrated by the Lord. We have spent many meaningful hours together praying, singing, laughing, and sharing the goodness of God. I love her with all my heart. She's been a true gift from the Lord. To think that I could have missed it by not speaking up when the Holy Spirit was using Stevie Wonder as a reason to talk to her. Since I easily talk to any stranger, it was very odd that the Lord specifically used this Motown icon to start up a conversation.

A few decades ago, Jacque was pregnant with her oldest daughter, Sarah, when choir director, Joann Mcfatter, called Jacque forward by a Word of Knowledge when they were fellow church members in N.C. Since that powerful impartation came from prophetic singer Joann, Jacque has received over 5,000 prophetic songs! Never have I met anyone more grounded in the Word and intercessory prayer. Jacque is a true prayer warrior of deep faith. I've been the blessed recipient of her gift of exhortation through Words of knowledge received from being in the presence of the Lord. Together, we are attending Janet Shell's "Fire by Night" prophetic conference in a few weeks. Glory be!

That summer that I met Jacqueline, I traveled to Columbus to attend World Harvest Dominion Camp Meeting. This story about Stevie Wonder is not over yet.

Sunday morning of the 2015 camp meeting, Pastor Steve Furtick from Elevation Church in Charlotte, North Carolina, was the guest minister. During his opening remarks, he sincerely thanked Pastor Parsley for being such an inspiration to him. As a teenager, he listened to *all* of the pastor's classic sermons and began naming them as he leafed through his collection of CDs transferred from old cassette tapes. It was such an honor to hear those titles that the pastor preached in days gone by.

Then Pastor Steve began talking about music and how his mother was a big Motown fan. When she was pregnant with him, she listened to all the old classic Motown music. "It is in my DNA as a result," he chuckled. He said that it was important for his kids to know about the greatness of Michael Jackson's music and other gifted recording stars. I am actually listening to Motown music as I type this. Since I was born in Detroit, I am also a big Motown music fan!

Pastor Steve looked at Pastor Parsley as if he was about to give him a most sacred treasure. I think there were tears forming. "My mother gave me a special gift when I turned thirty, and, Pastor Parsley, I want to present it to you."

Pastor Furtick reached down and picked up a vintage vinyl record album that was over forty years old. On the cover was Stevie Wonder! I felt absolutely spiritually faint. I might have been the only one in the room that got the significance of that gift.

I shared this story with Pastor Parsley and suggested he invite Stevie Wonder to Camp Meeting some year! Now wouldn't that be something?

The Holy Spirit is so real!

But the fruit of the Spirit is love, joy, peace, patience, kindness, goodness, faithfulness.

Galatians 5:22

Whoever keeps his commandments abides in God, and God in him. And by this we know that he abides in us, by the Spirit whom he has given us.

1 John 3:24

Therefore I want you to understand that no one speaking in the Spirit of God ever says "Jesus is accursed!" and no one can say "Jesus is Lord" except in the Holy Spirit.

1 Corinthians 12:3

CHAPTER FIFTY-TWO

Three Different Holy Spirit Gifts Identified

My stories have revealed the Holy Spirit's gifts in action. There is often great confusion and controversy among believers because there are three categories of God-given gifts given to the body of Christ.

While there are different kinds of gifts (1 Corinthians 12:4), spiritual gifts are God-given graces (special abilities, offices, or manifestations) meant for works of service to benefit and build up the body of Christ as a healthy congregation.

Although disagreement exists between denominations, most Bible scholars classify spiritual gifts into three categories: 1) ministry gifts, 2) manifestation gifts, and 3) motivational gifts.

Sadly, the misuse and misunderstanding of these three spiritual gifts often bring division in the church. It's understandable because many mainline denominations reject the operation of supernatural manifestation gifts that only happened in the Book of Acts and ended there.

First Corinthians 12 states that spiritual gifts are given to God's people by the Holy Spirit for "the common good." Verse 11 says the gifts are given according to God's sovereign will, "as he determines." Ephesians 4:12 tells us these gifts are given to prepare God's people for service and for building up the body of Christ.

The term "spiritual gifts" comes from the Greek words *charismata* (gifts) and *pneumatika* (spirits). They are the plural forms of *charisma*, meaning "expression of grace," and *pneumatikon*, meaning "expression of Spirit."

The Ministry Gifts

The ministry gifts serve to reveal the ultimate purpose of God for every church to function with excellence. This category is to identify those anointed for a full-time office or calling rather than a gift that can function in and through any church member. A simple way to remember the ministry gifts is through the five-finger analogy:

Apostle: An apostle establishes and builds churches; he's a church planter. An apostle may function in many or all of the ministry gifts. He is the "**thumb**," the strongest of all of the fingers, able to touch every finger.

Prophet: Prophet in Greek means to "forthtell" in the sense of speaking for another. A prophet functions as God's mouthpiece, speaking forth God's Word. The prophet is the "**index finger**," or pointer finger. He points to the future and points out sin.

Evangelist: An evangelist is called to be a witness for Jesus Christ. He works for the local church to bring people into the body of Christ where they can be discipled. He may evangelize through music, drama, preaching, and other creative ways. He is the "**mid-**

dle finger," the tallest one who stands out in the crowd. Evangelists draw a lot of attention, but they are called to serve the local body.

Pastor: The pastor is the shepherd of the people. A true shepherd lays down his life for the sheep. The pastor is the "**ring finger**." He is married to the church; called to stay, oversee, nurture, and guide.

Teacher: The teacher and the pastor are often a shared office, but not always. The teacher lays the foundation and is concerned with detail and accuracy. He delights in research to validate truth. The teacher is the "**pinky finger**." Though seemingly small and insignificant, he is designed specifically for digging into tight, dark places, shining a light, and picking apart the Word of truth.

The Manifestation Gifts

The manifestation gifts serve to reveal the power of God. These gifts are supernatural or spiritual in nature. They can be further subdivided into three groups: utterance, power, and revelation.

Utterance: These gifts say **something.**

Power: These gifts do **something.**

Revelation: These gifts reveal **something.**

Utterance Gifts

Prophecy: This is the "forth-telling" of the inspired Word of God primarily to the church for the purpose of confirming the written Word and building up the entire body. The message is usually one of edification, exhortation, or consolation, although it can declare God's will in a particular circumstance and, in rare cases, predict future events.

Speaking in Tongues: This is a supernatural utterance in an unlearned language that is interpreted so that the entire body will be edified. Tongues may also be a sign to unbelievers. Learn more about speaking in tongues.

Interpretation of Tongues: This is a supernatural interpretation of a message in tongues, translated into the known language so that the hearers (the entire body) will be edified.

Power Gifts

Faith: *This is not the faith that is measured to every believer, nor is it "saving faith." This is special, supernatural faith given by the Spirit to receive miracles or to believe God for miracles.*

Healing: This is supernatural healing, beyond natural means, given by the Spirit.

Miracles: This is the supernatural suspension of the natural laws or an intervention by the Holy Spirit into the laws of nature.

Revelation Gifts

Word of Wisdom: This is supernatural knowledge applied in a godly or correct way. One commentary describes it as "insight into doctrinal truth."

Word of Knowledge: This is supernatural knowledge of facts and information that can only be revealed by God for the purpose of applying doctrinal truth.

Discerning of Spirits: This is the supernatural ability to distinguish between spirits such as good and evil, truthful or deceiving, prophetic versus satanic.

Motivation Gifts

Besides ministry and manifestations gifts, the Bible also identifies motivational gifts.

Romans 12:6–8

1 Corinthians 12:4–11, 28–31

Ephesians 4:7–13

1 Peter 4:10

My last chapter is an in-depth study of the motivational gifts in operation in the church. Understanding your strongest motivation gifts is probably the most important discovery you'll ever make to fulfill your ultimate destiny in Christ.

It's my gift to you.

"And they overcame him by the Blood of the Lamb and the word of their testimony."
Revelation 12:11 (NKJV)

CHAPTER FIFTY-THREE

Identifying Your Strongest Motivation Gifts to Operate in the Body of Christ

Every Christian has unique and important roles to serve in church through recognizing and embracing the specific motivational gifts as explained in scripture.

> *For by the grace given me I say to every one of you: Do not think of yourself more highly than you ought, but rather think of yourself with sober judgment, in accordance with the faith God has distributed to each of you. For just as each of us has one body with many members, and these members do not all have the same function, so in Christ we, though many, form one body, and each member belongs to all the others. We have different gifts, according to the grace given to each of us. If your gift is prophesying, then prophesy in accordance with your faith; if it is serving, then serve; if it is teaching, then teach; if it is to encourage, then give encouragement; if it is giving, then give generously; if it is to lead, do it diligently; if it is to show mercy, do it cheerfully.*

Romans 12:3–8 (NIV)

It's important to identify our God-given gifts because comparison is the root of insecurity and the frequent cause of jealousy. Understanding how gifts function and operate in unity will help us to remain humble and joyful through our divine purpose for kingdom living.

I love the way writer Mary Fairchild "pictures" these motivational gifts in operation within the body of Christ:

- Prophecy becomes the **eyes** in the body of Christ.
- Service becomes the **hands** in the body of Christ.
- Teaching becomes the **mind** in the body of Christ.
- Giving becomes the **arms** in the body of Christ.
- Exhortation becomes the **mouth** in the body of Christ.
- Administration becomes the **head** in the body of Christ.
- Mercy becomes the **heart** in the body of Christ.

The motivational gifts serve to reveal the personality of God. Let's look at them in detail as you try to pick out your gift(s).

Prophecy: Believers with the motivational gift of prophecy are the "seers" or "eyes" of the body. They have insight, foresight and act like watchdogs in the church. They warn of sin or reveal sin. They are usually very verbal and may come across as judgmental and impersonal; they are serious, dedicated, and loyal to truth, even over friendship.

Ministering/Serving/Help: Those with the motivational gift of serving are the "hands" of the body. They are concerned with meeting needs; they are highly motivated doers. They may tend to over-commit but find joy in serving and meeting short-term goals.

Teaching: Those with the motivational gift of teaching are the "mind" of the body. They realize their gift is foundational; they emphasize accuracy of words and love to study; they delight in research to validate truth.

Giving: Those with the motivational gift of giving are the "arms" of the body. They truly enjoy reaching out in giving. They are excited by the prospect of blessing others; they desire to give quietly, in secret, but will also motivate others to give. They are alert to people's needs; they give cheerfully and always give the best that they can.

Exhortation/Encouragement: Those with the motivational gift of encouragement are the "mouth" of the body. Like cheer-leaders, they encourage other believers and are motivated by a de-sire to see people grow and mature in the Lord. They are practical and positive, and they seek positive responses.

Administration/Leadership: Those with the motivational gift of leadership are the "head" of the body. They have the ability to see the overall picture and set long-term goals; they are good organizers and find efficient ways of getting work done. Although they may not seek leadership, they will assume it when no leader is available. They receive fulfillment when others come together to complete a task.

Mercy: Those with the motivational gift of mercy are the "heart" of the body. They easily sense the joy or distress in other people and are sensitive to feelings and needs. They are attracted to and patient with people in need, motivated by a desire to see people healed of hurts. They are truly meek in nature and avoid firmness.

There is in-depth research available on motivational gifts in print by various authors as well as various tests to accurately identify your strongest attributes.

The Institute in Basic Life Principles offers a motivation-gift survey that is worth considering now. Check off each trait that applies to your personality. You may have a few checks in *every* category, but the majority-check of certain traits indicates an accurate result. Usually, there are *three* motivation gifts that ring truest per test score.

Person Number One

- Making sure that statements are totally accurate and true is important to you.

- You really love to learn and want to gain as much knowledge as you can.

- You react negatively to people who make unfounded statements.

- You tend to check the credentials of your instructors and teachers.

- When made aware of a debated issue, you tend to react by mentally analyzing the facts and drawing conclusions of your own based on hard facts.

- Doing research is enjoyable to you.

- When asked to explain something, you tend to give more explanation than is necessary.

- You are attentive to details.

- You tend to be silent about matters until you have searched diligently for pertinent information and gathered the facts.

- You have good study habits and research skills.

- You prefer to solve a problem by studying it thoroughly rather than brainstorming about possible solutions or "jumping in" to fix the problem.

- You take particular delight in uncovering facts or details that have been overlooked by others.

- Others would describe you as a sincere and steadfast person.

- You would rather learn how to do something than actually do it.

- Most of your close acquaintances would say you tend not to be enthusiastic about most *things.*

Person Number Two

- You can confidently visualize a final, completed task before even the initial steps have been taken.

- You enjoy coordinating the efforts of a team to reach a common goal.

- You find it a simple task to break down a significant assignment into achievable goals and responsibilities.

- You are able to delegate assignments to others well.

- You see people as resources that can be used to get a job done efficiently.

- You are quite willing to endure resistance or criticism in order to accomplish a task.

- As a leader, you expect and require loyalty from those under your supervision.

- You tend to "rise above" petty issues to focus on reaching the final goal.

- You are good at encouraging your team members and inspiring them to action.

- Once a project is completed, you don't waste any time moving on to a new project. In fact, before the initial project is completed, you often are visualizing the next mountain that needs to be conquered.

- When made aware of a need, you tend to analyze it rather than jumping right in and starting to work on it.

- You tend to evaluate accomplishment on the basis of doing the best job with the fewest resources in the shortest amount of time.

- Although not opposed to expressing emotion, you tend to regard emotional expressions—positive or negative—as a waste of time.

- You usually make decisions based on what is best for the sake of a project, not on what is most convenient or enjoyable for the laborers.

- Because of your focus on the tasks at hand, sometimes others think you are uninterested or aloof.

Person Number Three

- You judge most actions as being either right or wrong—black or white, not gray.

- You tend to react strongly to people who are not what they appear to be.

- You especially enjoy people who are willing to be completely honest with you—even if the truth hurts.

- Before you sell an item in your garage sale, you would like to explain to the potential buyer exactly what is wrong with that item or why you don't want to keep it.

- When you observe someone doing wrong, you feel it's your responsibility to correct that person or bring it to the attention of his authority.

- You can quickly discern the true character of an individual, even when he tries hard to conceal his poor character or the wicked motives of his heart.

- You separate yourself from those who refuse to repent of evil.

- You are not hesitant to share your opinion, especially if you think obvious wickedness has been overlooked or ignored.

- When you fail, you are quick to judge yourself.

- Your employees who have bad attitudes are sources of irritation to you.

- In your opinion, compromise is *never* the best solution.

- When you observe or discern sin, to say nothing about it is, of itself, sinful.

- It is not difficult for you to accept absolutes.

- You are not easily swayed by emotions—your own or those of others—when a decision has to be made.

- You have a deep capacity to trust God.

- Sometimes others tell you to "cheer up and look on the bright side" because you tend to look on the not-so-bright side of things.

- You are committed to doing what is right and true, even if it means that you must suffer for it.

Person Number Four

- When you observe insensitivity or harshness in others, you tend to respond with anger toward the harsh or insensitive person.

- You are sensitive to the hurts of others, even when they do not express that hurt verbally or directly.

- When others express genuine love, your heart responds with joy and gratitude.

- If given a choice, you would prefer to have a few close friendships rather than a great number of shallow relationships.

- People who have problems seem to seek you out so that they can tell you about their woes.

- Being firm with individuals who need to be corrected or exhorted is something you tend to avoid.

- It is difficult for you to be decisive in some circumstances.

- You need quality time to explain how you feel about things.

- When you see someone who is hurting—physically or emotionally—you want to offer help and remove the source of the pain.

- You want to remove people who inflict hurt on others.

- You often wonder why God allows people to suffer.

- If a close friend or family member is offended, you find yourself being tempted to take up that offense too.

- You tend to cry easily when you see or hear something sad or touching.

- You sincerely and enthusiastically rejoice with those who rejoice!

- You enjoy being needed by others.

- You do not judge sin lightly—your own or anyone else's.

- You desire to pray faithfully and fervently.

- Sometimes the people you're with don't understand why you seem to be drawn to "down-and-outers," individuals whom others usually try to avoid altogether.

Person Number Five

- When you meet someone, you tend to visualize his or her potential.

- You like to give counsel to others.

- You can usually discern a believer's level of spiritual maturity pretty easily.

- Because you enjoy helping people grow spiritually, you like to encourage them by proposing projects for them to carry out, which you hope will result in spiritual growth.

- You motivate people to become what you "see" they could become.

- Sometimes you unintentionally make others think they will see results a lot faster than they actually will see those results, especially in relation to spiritual growth.

- You don't see much use for teaching that doesn't give practical instruction.

- When you counsel others, you prefer to observe their facial responses rather than correspond with them remotely, such as with a letter.

- If someone comes to you with a need for counsel, you quickly make yourself available to him or her, even if it means sacrificing family time or other activities you had planned to do.

- It gives you special delight to relate examples of success or to use illustrations of failure as effective teaching tools.

- Finishing a project is not nearly as exciting as starting a project.

- You tend to identify with people "where they are" in order to counsel them effectively.

- Enthusiasm is something that you tend to exhibit regularly.

- Your confidence in the loving sovereignty of God tends to make you a hopeful, positive person.

- You see trials as opportunities to grow spiritually rather than as reasons to despair.

- As you study God's Word, you often discern principles and patterns that should be followed.

- When someone is facing a hard situation, you are eager to support and encourage him, to come alongside him as needed.

- In your eagerness to bless someone with encouragement, sometimes you find yourself oversimplifying a solution in order to help the needy person get over his or her reluctance to embrace your counsel and give it a try.

Person Number Six

- When others have practical needs, you tend to notice them before everyone else does.

- It gives you pleasure to help others, especially if your assistance with a practical need will free him or her to carry out more important responsibilities.

- You are willing to neglect your own work in order to help others.

- As a particularly diligent person, sometimes you foolishly go beyond your physical limits and suffer for it.

- You seem to have a special ability to remember what people like and dislike, and you enjoy using this knowledge to bless them.

- You wonder why other people don't respond to needs that are so obvious to you.

- To get a job done, you are willing not only to invest your time and energy but you are often willing to invest your resources as well.

- It's hard for you to say "no" when someone asks you for help.

- You enjoy putting "extra touches" on things you do for others.

- You are dependable and hardworking.

- You don't mind doing a job by yourself, but a slothful person disgusts you.

- You don't seek out public recognition for your efforts, but you do enjoy being appreciated.

- You'd rather get busy than stand around talking about it.

- Sometimes time limits frustrate you.

- You'd much rather do a job yourself than delegate it to an unreliable helper.

- When volunteers are requested, you find yourself being one of the first to raise your hand.

Person Number Seven

- When you learn about a godly ministry, you find yourself wanting to contribute to that ministry.

- You tend to stay out of the limelight.

- You are frugal, especially with your own resources.

- You have an uncanny ability to recognize opportunities to make money.

- When you give monetary gifts to others, you prefer to do so in secret rather than overtly.

- When you hear pressure appeals for money, you tend to react negatively.

- You want your gifts (time, money, resources, energy) to encourage others to give.

- You expect others, especially those in authority, to be frugal and accountable for all decisions, especially financial decisions.

- When you become aware of a need that others have overlooked or ignored, it gives you delight to help meet that need.

- You'd rather pay a little more to get excellent quality than save a small percentage and get the cheap version.

- Learning that your gift was an answer to prayer gives you particular satisfaction and joy.

- You rarely, if ever, incur debt, even in tough times.

- You tend to evaluate spirituality in terms of resources, accountability, and dependability.

- Saving money gives you almost as much pleasure as making money!

- When you give to a family, an individual, or a ministry, you frequently enjoy getting more personally involved with that family, individual, or ministry if the opportunity to do so arises.

- Sometimes others accuse you of being too focused on getting the best deal and taking too long to do that.

- Sometimes others accuse you of being stingy.

Which One Describes You Best?

Discerning which person above best describes you will help you identify your motivational gift. If you are most like:

- **Person Number One,** you probably have the motivational gift of **teaching.**

- **Person Number Two,** you probably have the motivational gift of **organizing.**

- **Person Number Three,** you probably have the motivational gift of **prophecy.**

- **Person Number Four,** you probably have the motivational gift of **mercy.**

- **Person Number Five,** you probably have the motivational gift of **exhortation.**

- **Person Number Six,** you probably have the motivational gift of **serving.**

- **Person Number Seven,** you probably have the motivational gift of **giving.**

Discovering and embracing your *prominent three* motivational gifts will help you grow in godly character to advance the Kingdom of God.

WISE WOMEN COUNCIL
Uniting HEARTS, Helping HANDS, Igniting HOPE

Thank you for being part of my journey into the supernatural spanning the past fifty years of serving the Lord. In Psalm 90, Moses prayed, "Teach us to number our days, that we may gain a heart of wisdom." At my golden age, I am determined to make the most of my time left on earth.

The *Wise Women Council* is a 501c3 charitable foundation that values your prayer support and possible financial pledges to support mission work helping the poor and disadvantaged within our sphere of influence. In society, there is such great need of volunteers and mentors to assist the lost, especially struggling single mothers, by sharing the love of Christ through charitable deeds.

In 2019, I came into a small inheritance from my parents. I used the money to purchase a homeless woman and her son (long-time family friends) an inexpensive fixer-upper with great potential. I co-own this house, so I've spent meaningful time helping restore our 1857 historic Zanesville, Ohio, home.

As an author of fiction, my heart leaped for joy when I learned that Harriett Beecher Stowe, author of *Uncle Tom's Cabin,* had spent time in Zanesville visiting family members residing there in the 1830s. Her brother, Rev. William Beecher, was the founding clergy of the Putnam Presbyterian Church in 1935. Putnam is a small town located south of downtown Zanesville, rich in anti-slavery history with great historic significance. It was reluctantly annexed into Zanesville in 1877. The first Ohio Anti-Slavery meeting was held in the Putnam Stone Academy in 1835. This building is now the *Putnam Underground Railroad Museum.* When President Lincoln greeted Harriet at the White House, he said, "So, you're the little lady whose book started this great war."

My upcoming publication, entitled, *Hidden*, is historical fiction taking place in Putnam in 1851 before the Civil War. This suspense mystery is told from the viewpoint of a biracial little girl who experiences grave danger through racial injustice vented from evil people during our dark time of slavery in American history.

The *Wise Women Council* supports non-profit Christian agencies and programs that offer assistance to victims of abuse resulting in drug and alcohol addiction, domestic violence, or homelessness.

Please visit **www.wisewomencouncil.org** to learn more about supporting this foundation. I value your diligent and fervent prayers above all else.

Sincerely,
Barbara Taylor Sanders, B.A.
Author/Advocate/Artist
www.barbarataylorsanders.com
www.WiseWomenCouncil.org
Uniting HEARTS, Helping HANDS, Igniting HOPE

BOOKS BY
BARBARA TAYLOR SANDERS

The Laborers Are Few (Non-fiction/Inspiration)
Foreword by Coach Bill McCartney, founder of Promise Keepers
Father's Press 2011
Hidden (Historical Fiction/Suspense)
Ambassador International, 2023

Bloodline Secrets (Contemporary Fiction/Suspense)
Ambassador International, 2018

Puttin' on the Dog & Getting' Bit (Non-fiction/Humor)
Express Image Publications 2012

BOOKS BY DARYL SANDERS
www.Daryl Sanders Author.com

DAVID Chosen by God: Lord Looks at the Heart
   (Historical Fiction)
Biblical Study Series:
The Father: His Role on Our Life's Journey
God the Father: Why Did God Choose This Identity?
Peter Finds Life (Three Life Phases of the Apostle Pete)
Peter Finds Power: Divine Power Available to Believers
Peter Finds Purpose: Not What You Do But Who You Are!
WhY: Questions Along Life's Journey
Finding the Power to Heal
The Man in the Middle—Isaac: God Hated Esau—But Isaac He Loved
"How Does Jesus Pray?"

About the Author

Lifetime Ministry
Achievements
Barbara Taylor Sanders

Community Leadership in Columbus, Ohio, 1976–2010
Executive committee of *The 1993 Greater Columbus Billy Graham Crusade* and the Co-Chair of Women's Committee recruiting 4,000 women from the 1000 churches in the crusade
Founding Co-Chair of the first Columbus, *Ohio National Day of Prayer*
Executive Research Writer for Pastor Rod Parsley
President of the *Columbus Christian Writers Association*
Board Member of *Teen Challenge for Women*
Brunch Bunch Broadcast Hostess on *WCVO Christian Radio*
Co-founder *of Zion Christian Fellowship*
CLASServices member, keynote speaker for AGLOW, Christian Women's Club, and church conferences
Extensive travel to Russia, Ukraine, and Nigeria with evangelistic and medical team goodwill missions
Honored Coretta Scott King on the 25th Anniversary death of Martin Luther King Jr., for race relations
Volunteer coordinator for Scioto Village Correctional Institute for incarcerated teenage girls too young for prison
Volunteer advocate for the poor and disadvantaged, especially single mothers

Community Leadership in Ft. Myers, Florida, 2010–2022
Faith Fellowship Church, Ft. Myers, FL
Teacher/Creative Writing classes, Cape Coral Arts Studio
First Place Award for oil painting in the 2014 "May Flowers"

Exhibit at Cape Coral Arts Studio
Honorary Member of the *Cape Coral Art League*
Member of the *SW Chapter of the National League of American Pen Women*
Board member of S.I.Y.A "*Supporting Independent Young Adults*," aging out of Foster Care, Ft. Myers
Contributor with *WHOA Magazine*, a national publication for Christian Women
Life Styles After 50, a Florida Publication

Contact the author via email at:
expressimagepublications@gmail.com